Africa - The Awakening Giant (Volume 3)

Bilateral and Multinational Economic Co-operation in West Africa

Self Reliance Through Putting the Resources Together

Franklin Vivekananda

Wilfred A. Ndongko

Professor Wilfred Awung Ndongko, was born at Fontem, Manyu state in Cameroon. He was studied at the Cameroon College of Arts, Science and Technology before proceeding to Bradeis University, U.S.A., where he obtained a Bachelor of Arts Degree in Economics. He later studied at the University of Alberta, where he obtained a Master of Arts Degree in Economics and Ph.D. in Economics from Carleton University in Canada. He is a member with number of Associations, among those like the Society for International Development, Association of Third World Economists and Association of Central African Economists. He taught in University of Yaounde and University of Calabar. He is currently the ***Director of Research at the Institute of Human Science***. Prof. Ndongko has published number of books and articles in economics related to Africa and Third World.

Franklin Vivekananda, had his collegiate education at the University of Mysore. He was studied in Federal Republic of Germany and at Gothenburg University, Sweden. He obtained Ph.D. from Uppsala University, Sweden. Vivekananda was at the University of Idaho. He has published number of books in social science interdisciplinary research (economics, economic history, international development, political science, rural sociology, developing economics, peace and conflict research) He also published number of collection of poems and plays. He is the ***Editor of a Social Science Journal.***---

ISBN 91-86702-07-6

Bibliographical References and Indexing: Contributions in African Trade and Literature, African Social Science, Economic Development, African Economics, African Political Science, African and Third World Countries and Economic History, Development Economics, International Development Aid, Trade and Cooperation.

Orders can be placed through **Bethany Books, Post Box 7444, 103 91 Stockholm, Sweden**.

The people of Third World countries must plan economic co-operation among themselves by pulling their resources together for attaining self reliance and economic growth instead of foreign aid and dependency.

Discussion with Nobel laureate Gunnar Myrdal 2.12.1981 by Franklin Vivekananda.

The continuous desire for regional economic cooperation between West African states, has risen from both internal and external factors. In regard to internal factors, perhaps the most predominant one has been the awareness of West African states that the relatively small size of their national economies, limited markets, and the existing disparities in resource endowments impede individual efforts towards economic and social development exclusively at the national level. Unfair trade terms, foreign debt and dominance of rich countries are perennial external factors.

Authors

Table of Contents

Table of Contents 9
Abbreviations 23
Preface and Acknowledgements 15
List of Tables 12

CHAPTER I The Foundations of Economic Cooperation...25
1. Introduction......25
2. Historical Origins...........26
   A.The Pre-Colonial Period..27
   B.The Colonial Period......28
3. Early Attempts Towards Economic Cooperation.................30
   A.The Sanniquellie States Association..30
   B.Ghana-Guinea-Mali-Union..32
   C.Africa-Malagasy Union....33
   D.Organization of the Senegal River States...34
4. The Lessons for Contemporary African Governments.................35

CHAPTER II Integrative Forces and Institutional Setting..41
1. Introduction......................................41
2. The Role of Integrative Forces......41
3. Institutional Setting for Cooperation.46
4. Recent Attempts Towards Economic Cooperation......49

CHAPTER III River and Lake Basin Commissions.............55
1. Introduction......................................55
2. Lake Chad Basin Commission (LCBC)......55
3. Organization for the Development of the Senegal River (OMVS)....59
4. The Niger Basin Commission..61
5. The Volta River Authority (VRA)..63
6. The Mano River Union........64
7. Conclusion.................77

CHAPTER IV Banking and Monetary Cooperation..187
1. Introduction..................87
2 West African Clearing House (WACH)..87
3. West African Monetary Union.........92
4. Conclusion..........................95

CHAPTER V Economic Organizations With Limited Goals..99
1. Introduction.........99
2. The Entente Council..99
3. African And Malagasy Common Organization (OCAM)..............104
4. The Liptako-Gourma Region Development Authority...........107
5. West African Rice Development Association (WARDA)...111
6. Multinational Program and Operational Center (MULPOC)...114
7. Other Bilateral Organizations.......115
8. Conclusion..........................116

CHAPTER VI Economic Orgainizations With Broad Objectives..123
1. Introduction...............123
2. West African Economic Community (CEAO)...........123
3. Economic Community of West African States (ECOWAS).......136
   Article 1: Aims of the Community..138
   Article 2: General Undertakings...138
   Article 3: Cooperation Among Member States and With Other Bodies..140
4. Conclusion............170

CHAPTER VII Problems and Prospects for the Future..203
1. Introduction..........203
2. Multiplicity and Multi-Membership...205
3. Trade Liberalization..207
4. Financial and Monetary Harmonization...216
5. Industrial Cooperation....222
6. Free Mobilility of Labor...230

7. Distribution of Costs and Benefits...235
8. Harmonization of Legal Systems.......236
9. Ideological Differences and Political Instability.......238
10. Conclusion.........238

VIII. References...249

I. Africa Economic (Cooperation and Integration)...249

II. West Africa (Economic Cooperation and Integration...260

List of Tables

3.1 LCBC: Area Distribution of the Conventional Basin.............79

3.2 LCBC: Population in the Conventional Basin, 1970..............80

3.3 Poplulation, Annual Growth Rate and Per Capita Income of Mali-Mauitania and Senegal (1972)..........................81

3.4 VRA Comparison of Planned and Actual Performance, 1960-70......82

3.5 How Customs Tariff Will Change in the Mano River Union.........83

4.1 Economic Features of UMOA Countries............................97

5.1 Economic Indicators of Entante Council States..................118

5.2 OCAM: Economic Indicators (1960-1972)........................119

5.3 Financial Assistance Received by Tropical African States of French Colonial Legacy From the EEC......................120

6.1 Economic Characteristics of CEAO Member States, 1972..........173

6.2 CEAO: Percentage Share of Intra-Regional Trade, 1960 and 1970............174

6.3 CEAO: States Exports Trade Structures, 1961-66...............175-176

6.4 CEAO States: Commodity Distribution of Imports..............177-178

6.5 CEAO Budges, 1974-1979..........179

6.6 Regional Cooperation Tax for Beer (1975).......................180

6.7 CEAO: Inter-State Trade, 1976.................................181

6.8 CEAO: Groups of Products Subject to RCT, 1978................182-183

6.9 CEAO: Companies Subject to RCT, 1979.........................184

6.10 CEAO: RCT Rates in Respect to SOAP (1979)....................185

6.11 CEAO:Community Fund for Development 1975-76...............186

6.12 Utilization of 1975 Fund for Development Projects.............187

6.13 Distribution of 1976 Fund Between Some States.................188

6.14 CEAO: Community Fund for Development, 1977-78................189

6.15 Compensation for Member States (1976-78).......................190

6.16 Distribution of Part of the 1976 and 1977 Fund Between the Less Developed States.........................191

6.17 Solidarity Fund (1977-80)....192

6.18 Allocation of Solidarity Fund Resources--July, 1980...........193

6.19 ECOWAS: Development Indicators of Member States, 1973........194

6.20 Principal Products of Some ECOWAS States......................195

6.21 ECOWAS: External Trade, 1971.................................196

6.22 ECOWAS: States: Pattern of Trade, 1971......................197-198

6.23 Customs Receipts as Percentage Share of Total Government Receipts (1973)....199

6.24 Currency of Member States of ECOWAS...........................200

6.25 Indices of Agricultural Production per Head in Selected West African Countries..........201

7.1 Central Banks and Currency Units of West African States.......246

7.2 Central Bank Discount Rates in Some Africa States...247

Fig. 1 Multilateral and Bilateral Groupings in the West African Sub Region...248

Preface and Acknowledgements

Since the end of World War II, the problems of economic development has to preoccupied all the nations of the world; but countries of the Third or less developed World more so than the developed or industrialized nations of the West. This preoccupation with economic development has come to override other social and political considerations, perhaps rightly so, in many African countries. Indeed, economic development has come to be regarded as a universal panacea for national or regional survival.

Consequently, many studies have been devoted to and large sums of money spent on the development of concepts, theories, models, and strategies, with a view to helping the less developed nations or regions achieve economic development. Unfortunately, however, so far no universal theory or themes of economic development have been formulated to respond to the needs of the poor and rich nations alike. There may never be one because of geographical, political, national and cultural differences.

In Africa, like in many Third World countries and particularly in West Africa, the problems of economic development have been compounded by a legacy of European imperialism, ethnic diversity, linguistic differences and a low level of technological advancement. Though these problems can be attributed to some extent to West Africa's past history as a region which has gone through colonial influence, the various nations of the region have had their own unique experience of economic development.

Thus, it would be fair to say that since independence, the leaders have endeavored very hard to tackle these challenging problems with great determination and purposefulness. However, individual efforts mainly at the national level by the West African leaders have not produced the desired sustained economic development.

Consequently, the need for regional economic cooperation, particularly in the vital areas of agriculture, industry, finance, etc., so as to ensure collective self-sustained economic development has become more and more evident. Although cooperation, both as an ideology and in practice, is not completely new to West African leaders, there has been since independence, a more and more recurrent discussion of the scope and necessity for the formation of regional economic groupings, the potential advantages and costs, the nature of the institutional machinery, the attendant problems and the prospects for their long-run viability and stability.

The continuous desire for regional economic cooperation between West African states, has arisen from internal as well as external factors and their economic situation and relations. In regard to internal factors, perhaps the most predominant one has been the awareness by West African States that the relatively small size of their national economies, limited markets and the existing disparities in resource endowments impede individual efforts towards economic and social development exclusively at the national level.

For this reason, it has been contented by many African scholars and policy makers that if West Africa is to achieve self sustained development, and raise their standards of living in the long run, cooperation in the production an distribution of the basic necessities and strategic goods and services, on at least a regional level, must be regarded, by all African governments as a necessary condition for the successful attainment of this social and economic objective.

Secondly, the level of industrial activity in most West African States in extremely low, and the export manufactured goods is negligible, despite the existence of excess capacity in many national industries. More disturbing is the fact that there are few or no linkages between the manufacturing and other sectors of the national economy such as agriculture, so that intermediate, capital and even some primary goods used in the manufacturing are imported.

Thus, it has been argued that economic cooperation at the regional level in West Africa will lead to the efficient allocation of industrial activity, production capacity, encourage the effective use of local raw materials and it will reduce dependence on foreign intermediate, capital and even consumption goods.

Thirdly, the strategies that many West African States have adopted in solving their socio-economic problems since independence have been potential sources of conflict and friction in the sub region. Some of them like Mali, Ghana, Burkina Paso, etc., have relied on financial and technical assistance from China, Nigeria, etc., have leaned more to Western countries like France and the United States for the same type of help.

Unfortunately, this existing situation has set the states for ideological confrontation, mutual mistrust and disharmony among the West African leaders. Under the circumstances, it has been argued that regional economic cooperation between West African States, will enable the identification of those areas which require concerted common action; particularly in the planning and financing of industrial development projects.

Fourthly, the long standing vexing problem of little or no intra-West African trade which has been aggravated over the years by the inconvertibility of some national currencies, the absence of an adequate intra-West African payment system, the rapid decrease of the foreign exchange obtained from the sale of the regions' major primary products, the high cost of both imported capital and consumption goods from the advanced countries and differences in the fiscal systems have hastened the movement towards the creation of regional economic groupings in West Africa. The overriding objective of such groupings is to alter the heavy metropolitan-colonial orientation in these areas and in the management of their national economies; especially as this undesirable situation has continued to prevail even after independence.

Furthermore, one of the most important considerations, particularly during the early years of independence, has been the necessity to increase and stabilize the bargaining strength of West African States in various international financial and economic organizations, in the negotiations for the different commodity agreements and most recently, in the efforts to establish a just new international economic order.

All these considerations have reinforced the interest of West African leaders in regional economic cooperation with a view to presenting a collective African front in these various issues affecting the economic and political destiny of the sub region.

To be sure, at the continental level the establishment of the Organization of African Unity (OAU) was intended partly to increase the bargaining power of African States in the important areas which is mentioned earlier. This has been given considerable weight by the rapid growth of national consciousness within many African States and subregions and the continuing determination of African leaders to reshape some of the colonial economic and political arrangements through the bargaining process within the framework of their contemporary economic and social problems, aspirations and needs.

Secondly, the coming into being of the United Nations Development Decade: 1960-1970 and the substantial steps initiated by the Economic Commission for Africa, and especially the creation of the African Development Bank, encouraged and sustained the efforts of the various African States towards economic cooperation, with a view to pulling both national and external resources together for the collective and harmonious development of their national and subregional economies.

Finally, the creation of the European Economic Community, other regional groupings like Latin American Free Trade Area, the Adean Group, the defunct East Africa Economic Community, the Central African Custom and Economic Union, etc., demonstrated both the necessity and possibility of regional cooperation in West Africa. Although some people may maintain that the experience of the groupings may have little or no relevance for the West African States, there is no doubt that the European and Latin American approach as well as the institutional framework, has appealed to the developing West African nations, especially with respect to the nature of the objectives and the obvious problems which could arise from economic cooperation between politically autonomous states.

In view of the above reasons, the objective of this study is to critically examine the efforts of the independent West African States in this direction and the attendant economic problems. However, consciously or unconsciously, the entire region of West Africa is dotted with a multiplicity of regional economic groupings and institutions which have been created to promote economic cooperation between the various African States. Consequently, the challenge which faces the West African governments, national financial and economic institutions and the people of West Africa in general, is to ensure that the protocol agreements and the treaties establishing the groupings do not remain on the shelves of government ministries and the headquarters of the various organizations.

To prevent this undesirable outcome, it is essential that the policy instruments and measures adopted are capable of making an effective and lasting contribution to the attainment of the many interrelated and often conflicting objectives of the different regional economic organizations. However, to the extent that the multiplicity of regional economic groupings tends to divide the West African subregion into micro-groupings with varying memberships, there are bound to be real and potential economic problems arising from the obligations which individual West African States generally assume under the different treaties and protocol agreements setting up the regional economic organizations.

To be sure, the multiplicity of regional economic organizations does have far reaching economic implications for the member states and for the collectivities as a whole. The reasons are not far to come by. Firstly, the signatories to the treaties and trade conventions of West African regional economic groupings, individually and profess to expand their national markets through the immediate or progressive elimination of tariff barriers to inter-state trade. Secondly, they also profess to ensure the gradual complementarity and integration of their national economies through initial cooperation and eventual harmonization of monetary, fiscal financial policies; industrial and taxation policies, free mobility of factors pf production, etc., on the basis of effective reciprocity of benefits and costs. For these reasons, it seems to me that it is of vital importance for the point of effective policy making and implementation to analyze the various economic implications arising from multi-membership in regional groupings by some African States, within the framework of the most important objectives of those regional groupings.

An additional significance of this study, is that it will attempt to shed light on some of the important socio-economic issues which many West African States rarely consider and ponder upon before signing multiple protocol agreements which very often have conflicting objectives with respect to the treatment of third countries and the obligations which they collectively have to assume. So far, no study attempts to expose, with a view to indicating the relevant policy measures that can be initiated to solve them even on a short-term basis.

Although it is recognized that there are other regional groupings, like OCAM in which political, social and cultural objectives dominate the provisions of their treaties and protocol agreements; whose constituent treaties do not provide for concrete economic cooperation machinery such as the Council of the Entente States and the Maghreb.

We wish to state from the outset that this study is focused on River and Lake Basin Commissions, Banking and Monetary institutions, economic organizations with limited goals such as the Entente Council, West African Rice Association, the Liptako-Gourma Region Development Authority, etc., and economic organizations with broad objectives such as the West African Economic Community (CEAO) and the Economic Community of West African States (ECOWAS). The reason for this selection is that ECOWAS and the CEAO cut across existing traditional, cultural, political, administrative and economic barriers, which have separated them for a long time because of their different colonial influence and experiences.

Against this setting, the study will attempt to critically analyze the issues and economic problems of these regional groupings in the light of the provisions, of the various treaties and agreements, which deal with the objectives of trade liberalization, financial fiscal and monetary harmonization, and the free mobility of persons and citizens, etc., as the case may be. There is no doubt that these are objectives, which usually dominate the provisions of most Treaties and Protocol Agreements, and which always give rise to conflict of interest between member states, when it comes to their eventual implementation even in the letter and spirit of the accords.

This study consists of seven chapters. Chapter one is devoted to the foundation of economic cooperation in West Africa with particular emphasis on the historical origins and the early attempts towards economic cooperation. In Chapter two, an analysis of the role of external and internal integrative forces and institutional setting for cooperation is undertaken. Chapter three addresses itself to the functioning of the River and Lake Basin Commissions. In Chapter four, cooperation in the areas of banking and monetary policies is examined. Here emphasis is placed on the West African Clearing House and the West African Monetary Union. Chapter five takes up economic organizations with limited goals such as the Entente Council, OCAM, LIPTAKO-GUARMA Region Development Authority, West African Rice Development Association, Multi-National and Operational Programming Centres (MULPOCS) and other Bilateral organizations of subregional character.

An analysis of economic organizations with broad objectives is taken up in Chapter six. Here special emphasis is on the African Economic Community (CEAO) and the Economic Community of West African States (ECOWAS); the former being a micro-grouping and the latter being a macro-organization. Finally, in Chapter seven, the problems and prospects of regional economic cooperation in West Africa are critically examined.

It is hoped that the other African subregions will draw on the experiences of West Africa in its attempts to form viable regional economic organizations with realistic goals and objectives.

Many people assisted us during the preparation of this book. We are unable to acknowledge by name all the staff of the governments of West Africa whose painstaking labour provided first hand material analysed in this work. University of Calabar Senate Research Grant Committee, provided some grant at the beginning of the project. Gratitude is also expressed to Professor S.M. Essang, former Head of the Department of Economics, University of Calabar, providing stimulating atmosphere for research.

A special thanks to Professor Paul Gowens, Dean, School of Business and Professor Celia Morgan, Chair, Department of Economics and Finance, who encouraged me to complete this research during my stay at Southwest Texas State University, San Marcos, Texas, U.S.A.

We wish to thank the following persons in preparing, compiling the statistics, typing and editing the book; Nkenganji Oliver, David Mfonyam, Emmanuel Moh, Dr. Linda Fischer A & M University, Marjorie Holden M.S.E. read the entire manuscript and made comments to improve the book. We are also grateful to the anonymous readers whose constructive criticisms and suggestions helped us in revising the original version of this study.

We are also indebted to the Editors of Cultures et Developpement, (Vol. VII, 1975), Presence Africaine (No. 3, 1976), Internationales : AFRIKA FORUM (No. 1, 1977) and CERES: FAO Review on Development (Vol. 10 No. 1, 1977), African Studies Review (Vol. XVI, No 2, September, 1973), Intereconomics, (No. 3, March 1973, Afrika Spectrum (No. 3, 1976): Quarterly Review of Information, Economic and Financial Studies (No. 5 1976, Nigerian Journal of Economic and Social Studies (Vol. 19, Mo. 3, 1977), for permission to use material from previous articles published on different aspects of this study.

Franklin Vivekananda
Department of Finance and Economics
Southwest Texas State University, San Marcos, Texas, U.S.A

Wildfred A. Ndongko
Institute of Human Sciences
Yaounde - Cameroon
15th December 1990

Abbreviations

ASEAN Association of South East Asian Nations
BCEAO Vanque Centrale des Etats de l' Afrique de l'
CEAO West African Economic Community
EEC European Economic Community
ECOWAS Economic Community of West African States
ECA Economic Commission for Africa
OERS Organization of the Senegal River States
FAO Food and Agricultural Organization
GATT General Agreement of Tariffs and Trade
LCBCLake Chad Basin Commission
MULPOC Multinational Program and Operational Center
OMVS Organization for the Development of the Senegal River, i.e., Organization pour la Misi en Valeur de Flueve Senegal
OCAM African and Malagasy Common Organization
OAU Organization of African Unity
RCT Regional Cooperation Tax
USAID United States Agency for International Development
UAM Africa-Malagasy Union
UNCTAD United Nations Commission for Trade and Development
UNDP United Nations Development Program
UMOA West African Monetary Union,i.e., Union Monetaire Ouest Africaine
UDEAC Union Douaniere Economique d' Afrique Centrale (Central African Customs and Economic Union) Central African Customs Union
VRA Volta River Authority
WARDA West Africa Rice Development Association
WAUA West African Unit of Account
WACH West African Clearing House

CHAPTER I

The Foundations of Economic Cooperation

1 Introduction

There have been recurrent discussions on the scope and necessity of forming regional economic groupings among African countries who have achieved independence. The potential advantages and costs, the nature of the institutional machinery, the attendant problems of cooperation, and the prospects for long-run viability and stability have all been examined. Today the African continent in general and West Africa, in particular, contain many regional economic organizations and institutions designed to promote economic cooperation between African states.

Ensuring that the treaties and protocol agreements creating the economic organizations remain functional has been the challenge that faces African governments, international financial and economic institutions, and people. It is essential that policy instruments and institutions make effective and lasting contributions to the many interrelated, and often conflicting objectives of the regional economic organizations. The purpose of this study is to analyze the economic cooperation in the West African sub-region.

Our study is divided into seven chapters. Chapters I, II, III and IV are devoted to the foundations of economic cooperation, integrative forces and institutional settings, river and lake basin commissions, and banking and monetary cooperation. Chapters V, VI and VII deal with economic organizations with limited goals and those with broader objectives, and with the problems and prospects for the future.

It is hoped that this study will clarify pertinent issues to policy-makers and leaders in Africa and West Africa as they enter into multiple accords and treaties. It is also hoped that other African sub-regions will consider the experience of West Africa in their regional economic strategies.

2 Historical Origins

Before attaining independence, several African states attempted to foster regional cooperation and integration. To understand the rationale for the rapid growth of many regional groups in post-independence Africa, the history of the collectives must be examined, especially during the pre-independence era when many of them were, according to Levine,

> designed to provide collaboration of several distinct sovereign states for common political, economic, social and cultural tasks on the one hand, and on the other, the super-state political unifications such as had produced short-lived political associations like the Mali Federation between 1959 and 1960. [1]

Despite the fact that "the road had been hard and long and many were pioneers who labored to build it,"[2] the ancestors of contemporary African regional economic organizations included those operations and institutions established, particularly during European colonial rule, with the dominant objective of achieving regional cooperation and integration.

The success record of these organizations was much more remarkable in French West African colonies, where the organic conception of government constituted the basis for extreme centralization of administration and which later helped in the course of cooperation and integration between the French African colonies and with the assimilation between them and metropolitan France.[3] French West Africa was integrated not only in terms of a centralized administration but also in the economic, cultural, and political spheres. Because of a common monetary zone and currency, there was complete and uniform assimilation of the French language and culture by their West African colonies. This enabled them to continuously exist together as a distinct political, administrative, cultural, and even economic zone in the West African subregion.

The British approach to administration in their African colonies revolved around the decentralization of responsibility and authority. There were efforts towards interstate cooperation and integration including the establishment of a common West African Court of Appeal, common currency and market boards, and a

West African Conference of Governors of British Colonies. These and other institutions provided a common ground and venue bringing together the various British African colonies formerly ruled as separate entities.[4]

The series of inter-colonial state relationships fostered between the British and French colonies were relevant to African regional cooperation and integration efforts. (Many of these ex-colonies now constitute the majority of the present day States on the African Continent and are also the leading members of contemporary regional economic groups like ECOWAS and CEAO.) These interstate relationships were formalized.

There were also informal exchanges of views between countries, often in the form of official reciprocal visits between French and British colonial administrators. Such visits usually involved governors and provincial and district officers on both sides of colonial borders. A brief examination of the earlier attempts towards regional cooperation and integration in pre-colonial and colonial Africa will elucidate the necessity for such endeavors in post-colonial Africa, and the challenges and frustrations that they have subsequently generated.

(A) The Pre-Colonial Period

The efforts toward regional economic cooperation and integration by many African states took place at different levels and in various forms before the European partition of the African continent. Africa, from a socio-economic viewpoint, has historically formed a complex whole. The phenomenon of long-distance trade can be traced back to antiquity. This is particularly true of the history of trans- Saharan trade which covered both the Savannah and forest belts of West Africa.[5] The phenomenon of migration is also ancient and has facilitated and fostered the tradition of familial relationships among many West African groups.[6]

The extensive long-distance migration of people and movement of goods within West Africa during the pre-colonial era confirms the argument that the subregion has been a natural common market zone. Many parts of the West African subregion, despite the fact that they were separate political entities, made efforts to encourage and sustain the harmonization of socio-economic activities including common market systems and techniques over many centuries.[7] As shown by early European explorers' records, trade was the dominant means of contact between the West African peoples, particularly in fostering socio-economic cooperation among themselves and other regions of Africa, most notably North Africa.[8]

2 (B) The Colonial Period

The European partition of Africa increased the need for socio-economic cooperation and integration especially in the West African subregion. The main objective of partitioning was commerce. Economic interests brought the Europeans to West Africa and have continued to keep them there.[9] Apparently, the partitioning has hampered economic efforts because it led to political division and the vitiation of an essentially indivisible economy. The new political boundaries cut across existing trade routes impeding the free movement of goods. Eventually, a clause permitting the free movement of goods and services to all European nationals in any colonial territory was inserted in diplomatic agreements and protocols.[10]

France and Britain were forced by the realities of the West African situation to abandon self-interest and isolation and cooperate with each other to cope with their many common economic and political problems which they, individually and collectively, were facing in the colonies. For example, there were implications for Anglo-French and other inter-colonial state relations of the strong historic, ethnological, and cultural connections between African peoples on both sides of the inter-colonial state boundaries. This was particularly true of the case of the Yoruba who, until 1918, were divided into British Nigeria, French Dahomey, and German Togo. In addition, there were political and administrative problems such as political agitation, armed revolts, and protest migrations.

Another factor necessitating mutual cooperation between the British and French colonial administrators in West Africa was smuggling.[11] The evolution of inter-colonial frontiers led to the development of two distinct markets on both sides of inter-colonial state boundaries with price differentials between the goods sold in the two markets.[12] As a result, the smuggling across the frontiers began as an endeavor by local West African businessmen to evade custom duties and increase their profit margin. This illegal practice [13] has continued to preoccupy contemporary African governments and decision-makers, [14] especially in view of the multiplicity of regional economic groups.

Coupled with these internal forces, were external factors like the German threat to European peace during the First and Second World Wars (1914-1918 and 1939-1945). It was to the advantage of the British and the French to work together to defeat a common enemy.[15] The colonial administrators set up formal channels of communication to cope with this and other problems. For example, during the 1930's and 1940's regular consultations and meetings between administrators, particularly those responsible for frontier districts, were encouraged. The importance placed on this exchange of views at the local level was reflected in a standing order issued by a Provincial Commissioner in the Gold Coast (now Ghana) regarding the need for close cooperation between French and British political officers in the frontier districts.[16]

The similarity between this standing order and the opening speeches of the Nigerian and Togolese heads of state at the inauguration of ECOWAS in May,1975, is a fitting example of the link that must be recognized between the European colonial administration and the post-colonial West African governments` efforts towards regional cooperation and integration in the subregion. [17]

Several of the states in West Africa were united into federations through the efforts of colonial governments prior to independence. This contributed to an easy and effective administration. This was the case with the former French West Africa (AOF). In the mid-fifties, pressure was brought to bear on the French colonialists by the constituent territories for disintegration and de-colonization. Their collective action resulted in the passage of the "**Loi Cadre**" by France. Each territory of French West Africa was to be granted semi-autonomy along one of two plans.

The first plan advocated the implementation of a federal executive with the existing functional structures of AOP intact. The second argued for entire disintegration (abolition) of the existing structures. Another area of dissension was whether there should be complete independence from France or whether there should be retention of some ties. Finally, all the states accepted the terms of the constitution of the Fifth French Republic with the exception of Guinea which later pulled out of the French colonial union and proclaimed independence. Accepting the terms of the constitution made it possible for those states to retain both their ties and economic dependence on France.

3 Early Attempts Towards Economic Cooperation

Despite the limited success of political integration in Africa since the collapse of the French West African Federations during the 1950's, a number of encouraging Pan-African attempts were made to link both contiguous and distant states economically. In the West Africa subregion, the major attempts were the formation of the Sanniquellie States Association (1958), the Ghana-Guinea-Mali Union (1958), the Africa-Malagasy Union (1961), and the Organization of the Senegal River States.

(A) The Sanniquellie States Association

Before the creation of the Sanniquellie States Association in 1958, there had been no Pan-African attempts made towards genuine economic cooperation in West Africa. One reason for this was that the newly emerging independent nations struggled for dominance of the region. The individual nations feared that any form of regional economic cooperation would jeopardize their positions in the quest for area leadership.

The Sanniquellie Declaration, based on the concept of establishing a federation while preserving each nation's "national identity" and constitutional structures, was a partial answer to the call for an economic and political union. It was plagued with the problems of nations vying for leadership, and the newly independent West African states did not adequately achieve economic integration.

President Tubman of Liberia, in his welcome address to the Monrovia powers, dealt with the leadership problem this way:

> "It should be crystal clear to every leader that Africans cannot live in isolation if they expect to allay suspicion, fear and tension. The idea of *Primus inter pares*, first among equals, is destructive of African Unity and Peace. . .The sense of oneness should be

> deeply rooted in the breast of every African. But the whirls of circumstances and ambition can make it difficult for us to fit ourselves into the picture of a unified Africa, the foundation for which we hope will be heard before this Conference closes. I come now to the question of leadership of. . . . In this connection, I have observed that there seem to be three schools of thought on this subject. There are those who feel that Liberia should assume leadership based on the fact that she is the oldest African Republic and is more ripe in political experience; but it will require more than age and political experience to assume leadership of Africa. There are others who assume that Ghana should assume that role because she is physically more developed and embraces larger territories. It will require more than development and larger territory to assume leadership of Africa. And there are yet those who opine that Egypt, with its rich traditions dating back to the remotest antiquity, should do so. It will require more than rich traditions of antiquity. It will require, in my opinion, the aggregate of the best that is in all compounded in such a manner as to represent the divisibility of Africa indivisible." [17a]

Against this background, a summit of independent African states was held in Addis Ababa in May 1963. It was attended by 30 of the 32 then independent African countries with Morocco sending an observer. State officials were unwilling to recognize the credentials of the next Togolese government which had recently seized power after the assassination of President Olympio. The main conference of the heads of state was preceded by a meeting of foreign ministers.

Although that meeting produced little or no results, the heads of state were able to draft a Charter of the Organization of African Unity out of the Casablanca and Monrovia Declarations, the proposal of Ghana for a new Union of Africa States, and some new proposals submitted to the meeting by Ethiopia. The heads of state signed the Charter of the Organization of African Unity on May 25,1963.

One of the provisions of the charter was to coordinate and intensify cooperation and efforts to improve the lifestyle of the peoples of Africa. To this end, the member states were required to harmonize their general policies, particularly in the fields of economic cooperation, transport and communication, and industry. Through Article XX, the Charter created a number of specialized commissions. One of them was the Economic and Social Commission charged with the responsibility of encouraging various forms of economic cooperation among African states.

(B) Ghana-Guinea-Mali-Union

The Ghana-Guinea-Mali Union, formed in 1958, called on the member countries to coordinate their defense, finance, and external affairs policies. The three countries pledged to write a constitution that would create the United States of West Africa. However, it was agreed that neither the relations between Ghana and the Commonwealth, nor those between Guinea and Mali, nor any connection with the Francophone community would be affected. Because of a strong commitment to political integration by the leadership, the Ghana-Guinea-Mali Union was able to secure ten million Ghanaian pounds for Guinea during the difficult early years of its independence.

Different sources of external dependence, the nature of Ghana's and Mali-Guineas's respective links to the Anglophone and Francophone communities, and the separation from each other by the Ivory Coast, hampered the functioning of the Union. Ghana, Guinea and Liberia formed an association of states based on a "**Friendship Convention**" in navigation and trade in 1959 at Sanniquelliq (Liberia). The organization rejected any idea of political unification.

Ghana and Mali became partners in the "**progressive**" Casablanca group in 1961. It included such states as the United Arab Republic, the provisional government of Algeria, Morocco, and Libya. This group was more adamant than its counter part, the Monrovia Powers, in combating economic neo-colonialism and imperialism and in demanding the removal of foreign military bases from their territories.

The Casablanca group supported the leadership of the late Patrick Lumumba, Prime Minister of the Belgian Congo (now

Zaire), and the Monrovia group supported President Kasavubu. On October 1, 1961, the Casablanca group formed a common market that was scheduled to come into being over a four year period. However, after the formation of the OAU, the Ghana-Guinea-Mali Union and the Casablanca group were dissolved.

(C) Africa-Malagasy Union

The Africa-Malagasy Union (UAM) included all the French-speaking states in the West Africa sub-region except Guinea and Mali. The UAM was created in 1961 to coordinate currency transport and foreign technical assistance among member states and between member states and France. It had other objectives including:

1. to work to preserve peace;
2. to foster mutual aid among members;
3. to support non-interference in the international affairs of other members;
4. to develop economic and cultural cooperation based on equality;
5. to promote concerted diplomacy in international affairs.[18]

The Algerian War and the Congolese crisis were major events that affected the creation of the UAM. The importance of these events was stated by Albert Tevoedjre, former Secretary-General of the UAM:

The formation of the UAM had to do with the position of France in 1960. The worst hour of the Algerian War was at hand. Negotiations were bogged down. Several Afro-Asian, Socialist and even Western States seriously contemplated a United Nations intervention. The DeGaule government was resolutely hostile to such a solution. . .Whether or not the idea was entirely their own, Houphouet Boigny, Senghor and their friends wanted to avoid the UN. . .The UAM to some extent owed its existence and development to the Congo Crises, over which African States were and still remain sharply divided. It was above all at the Brazzaville Conference of December 19, 1960, that the UAM became a reality.[19]

Trevoedjre acknowledged that Pan-Africanism was a glorious myth--centrifugal forces among African states of a French colonial legacy had resulted in balkanization and "***Vassalization***". He stated that:

The greatest shortcomings of the UAM in diplomacy was the impression it sometimes gave of an excessive dependence on France. The ties between each of the UAM States and France were in effect so close as to give the impression that the organization itself drew its entire aspiration from the former metropole.[20]

Tevoedjre thought he was acting with some detachment from French authority and without interference of his Dahomeyan Constituency. His assessment was that the UAM was the most effective and important organization of solidarity on the continent of Africa during the early 1960's.[21]

As a result of the settlement of the Franco-Algerian War in 1962, the formation of the OAU in 1963, and the reluctance of many UAM members to recognize the Togolese regime involved in the coup in which President Sylvanus Olympio was murdered, the UAM was dismantled in 1965. In the words of Tevoedjre, the UAM died because some of its members were trying to stop the union from being a "**satellite nation**" against the will of those member states that were too closely tied to France.[22]

(D) Organization of the Senegal River States

The Organization of the Senegal River States (OERS) came into existence following a meeting held in Dakar in 1968. Guinea, Mali, Mauritania, and Senegal formed the OERS with the major objective of economically developing the Senegal River Basin. This was to be accomplished by regulating the flow of the Senegal River to a minimum of three hundred cubic meters per second and constructing a dam on the Senegal or one of its tributaries to provide controlled irrigation, thus enhancing grain cultivation and agricultural self-reliance.

The OERS envisioned an integrated industrial development, better trade arrangements and an eventual political union. In the meantime, the states were to encourage trade and to support the creation of a common market. At the time of its inception, OERS member states belonged to different monetary zones. This posed a problem in converting their respective national currencies. For the OERS to have succeeded, states issuing currency would have had to comply with the requirement that the bulk of exchange transactions be handled in the Franc Zone, unless inter-state payments were created. [23] Although the OERS provided a great deal of hope for the people of Guinea, Mali, Mauritania, and Senegal, it was dissolved in December, 1971.

It is clear from this brief examination of the earlier attempts towards economic and political cooperation in the West African sub-region that by deciding to embark on the socio-economic cooperation and integration of their national economies, the African states were operating within a certain economic, political, social, and historical awareness and continuity. Although these attempts failed, they nevertheless laid the foundation for more concrete and effective economic cooperation in the West African sub-region in the 1970's and later.

4 The Lessons from Contemporary African Governments

In retrospect, efforts of colonial governments both hampered and aided regional economic cooperation and integration between West African states. On the negative side, the colonial governments could not effectively transform their efforts at interstate cooperation into an instrument of regional economic cooperation because of traditional Anglo-French rivalry. They failed to agree on such complex and difficult issues as protest migrations, smuggling, currency, and marketing boards. In Anglo-French African relations, there were wide gaps in attitude, culture, institutions, value systems and inherited prejudice. All these problems have continuously prevented full regional economic cooperation and integration between contemporary French-speaking and English-speaking African states, even after independence. ECOWAS and LCBC are the real test cases.

Colonial rule did leave a semblance of the presence of interstate cooperation from which present African leaders may learn.[24] The colonial period helped to foster unity as several African peoples adopted the English and French languages. It was for this reason that ECOWAS adopted English and French as the official languages of the community. The CFA Franc has proved to be much more popular and widely accepted of the two colonial currencies and it is being considered as one of the most logical currencies for the ECOWAS.[25]

The African states are operating within a certain historical context by deciding to embark on socio-economic cooperation and integration of their national economies. The independent African states, like many other developing countries, have been striving for more rapid economic growth and the attainment of a higher standard of living for the masses of their people. Because the size of the national economies and markets of these states is too limited and resources are too scarce to allow for the rapid transformation of their small economic structures and the achievement of economies of scale individually, economic cooperation among the African states has offered the only practical means for building viable national economies.[26]

Footnotes

1. Victor T. Levine, "The Politics of Partition in Africa: The Cameroons and the Myth of Unification," Journal of International Affairs, XVIII, 2,1964, p. 199.

2. Sunday Renaissance, June 1, 1975, p. 3.

3. For more details on the organization of administration in French Africa, see Michael Growder, West Africa Under Colonial Rule, Hutchinson, London, 1968;and R. L. Buells, The Problem of Native Administration in West Africa, Vol. 1, 1965 (pp.160-206 in particular).

4. See Crowder, West Africa Under Colonial Rule op. cit.; and Lord Nailey, An African Survey, 1956 edition.

5. See A. C. Hopkins, An Economic History of West Africa (Longman Group Ltd., London, 1973) particularly Chapter 3.

6. There are many examples of myth and legends which tend to explain the relationship between various African peoples in terms of common ancestral origin. For example, the Kisraa migration story is generally used to explain the relationship between the Bariba and the Yoruba.

7. The concept and practice of "silent trade" was, for example, widely known, and when the use of money was introduced, certain currencies, notably the cowry, gold, pieces of durable cloth, etc., gained wide acceptance in many African regions.

8. H. Clapperton, Journal of a Second Expedition Into the Interior of Africa, London, 1829; and Lander, Richard and John, Journal of an Expedition to Explore the Course and Termination of the Niger, Vol. 1, London, 1832.

9. Among many other studies that stress the economic objective of European imperialism and colonialism in Africa, see Hobson, Imperialism A Study; i Surret-Canale, Afrique Noire a l'Ere Coloniale, Paris; Samir Amin, "Underdevelopment and Dependence in Black Africa: Origins and Contemporary Forms," Journal of Modern African Studies, Vol. 10, No. 4, December, 1972.

10. Article IV, section 2, of the Anglo-French Agreement of August 10, 1889, which defined the boundaries between French and British African Colonies, guaranteed freedom of trade everywhere for all European nationals. Section 3 of the same Article IV legitimated the trans-frontier movement of people, like the Ketonou in the Southern extremity of the Nigeria-Dahomey boundary, who were arbitrarily split into two colonial spheres.

11, 1963-1964, pp. 17-59.

12. This was the case in British Southern Cameroons and French Cameroon. See W. A. Ndongko, "The Origins of Price and Wages Difference Between West and East Cameroon," (Mimeo), Yaounde, 1974.

13. It did not only lead to the loss of much needed revenue by the colonial administrators, but it also precipitated the illegal flow of alcoholic beverages from the French territories to the British colonies.

14. The persistence of smuggling today in Africa can be explained by the fact that the local people have an intimate knowledge of the terrain and of the countless footpaths crossing the frontiers between the African states. In addition, the low salaries in the

customs service have continued to expose officials to the temptation of bribes by the African businessmen operating across inter state boundaries.

14a.the African Research Buelletin op.cit, page. 12

15. See Jide Osuntokun, Nigeria During the First World War (unpublished Ph.D. thesis, Dalhouse University, 1970).

16. "In these days when the interests of Great Britain (and France) in West Africa are more or less bound together in the common desire to further the development and prosperity of the peoples, and when many of the problems of administration and development are common to both governments, the need for cooperation, I think, is sufficiently apparent..." Quoted from Standing Order No. 3/1933 Ref. No. 1201/56/1925 date 25 April 1933 at Sekondi by W. Duncas, British Commissioner from Western Province of Gold Coast to the District Commissioner of Aim--copy in Dossier V-16-150-3487: Archives Nationales de la Cote d'Ivories, Abidjan.

17. See Sunday Renaissance, June 1, 1975, pp. 8-9, the complete speeches of the two heads of state.

17a. Quoted from President Tubman's speech December 15th 1972.

18. Afrique Nouvelle, December 21, 1960.

19. Tevoedjre (1965, p. 11).

20. Ibid., p. 19.

21. Ibid., p. 13.

22. Ibid, pp. 17-20.

23. Yasane, (1971) pp. 64-76, 113-131, 133-156, 187-197.

24. For a further discussion of integrating and disintegrating effects of colonial rule in Africa, see Michale Crowder, "Colonial

Rule in West Africa: Factor for Unity or Disunity," in Civilization, (Vol. II. No. 3), 1964.

25. The Nigerian Naira is the other currency under consideration.

26. W. A. Ndongko, "Regional Trade and Economic Arrange ments: Alternatives to African Association With the EEC," Internationales Africa Forum, Munich, No. 1, 1977.

CHAPTER II

Integrative Forces and the Institutional Setting

1 Introduction

The desire for regional economic cooperation and integration among African states has been brought about by internal as well as external factors. The purpose of this chapter is to examine the nature of these factors, to analyze the institutional setting for economic cooperation, and to provide a brief review of the recent attempts towards economic cooperation in the West African subregion.

2 The Role of Integrative Forces

Perhaps the most predominant internal factor contributing to economic cooperation has been the awareness of West African states that their small national economies, limited markets, and disparities in resource endowments impede individual efforts towards rapid economic and social development. Many scholars and policy-makers have contended that if West Africa is to achieve self-sustained development and raise its people's standard of living, cooperation in the production and distribution of basic necessities and strategic goods and services (on at least a regional level) must be regarded by all African states as a necessary condition for the successful attainment of social and economic objectives.

The level of industrial activity in most African states is extremely low, and the export of manufactured goods is negligible despite the existence of excess capacity in many national industries. There are few ties between manufacturing and the other sectors of the national economies such as agriculture. As a result, intermediate, capital, and even some primary goods used in manufacturing are imported. It has been argued that economic integration at the regional level in West Africa will lead to the efficient allocation of industrial activity and production capacity, encourage the effective use of local raw materials, and reduce dependence on foreign capital as well as consumption goods. [1a]

The problem of little or no intra-African trade has been aggravated over the years by the inconvertibility of some national currencies, the absence of an adequate intra-African payment system, the rapid decrease of the foreign exchange earnings obtained from the sale of the region's major primary products, the high cost of both imported capital and consumption goods from the developed countries, and differences in fiscal systems. These factors have encouraged the creation of regional economic groups in West Africa, with the overriding objective of altering the heavy metropolitan-colonial orientation in the sub-region.

One of the most important considerations since the early years of independence was the need to increase and stabilize the bargaining strength of West African states in various international financial and economic organizations, in the negotiations for different commodity agreements, and in the effort to establish a fair and effective new international economy. All these factors have reinforced the interest of West African leaders in regional and even continental economic integration, in order to present a collective African front in various issues effecting the economic and political destiny of the sub-region and the continent.

At the continental level, the establishment of the Organization of African Unity (OAU) was intended to increase the bargaining power of West African states in vital economic, financial and commercial areas. The OAU has benefited from the rapid growth of national consciousness within many African states and by the continuing determination of African leaders to reshape colonial arrangements through a bargaining process.

The coming of the United Nations Development Decade (1960-1970), the substantial steps initiated by the United Nations' Economic Commission for Africa, and the creation of the African Development Bank sustained the efforts of the various African states towards regional economic cooperation and integration by pulling both domestic and external resources together for the collective and self-reliant development of the countries.

The creation of the European Economic Community and regional groups like the Latin American Free Trade Area and the Adean Group demonstrated that regional economic cooperation in West Africa was possible. Although some may argue that these regional groups have had little or no relevance to the West African states, there is no doubt that the European and Latin American approaches, as well as the institutional frameworks, have appealed to the West African leaders.

In the case of French-speaking African states, there was a close monetary, economic, and commercial association between the colonies and France. All the French-speaking countries belonged to the Franc Zone, a monetary area using a common currency. The local French Franc that circulated in both French West Africa and Equatorial French Africa was issued by the French African Bank and backed by France.

Equatorial French Africa opted for independence from France in 1941, during World War II. Its monetary links with France and French West Africa were broken, leading to the creation of a new bank-issued currency (the CFA franc) for French Equatorial Africa and Cameroon. The maintenance of an "**Operation Account**" in the French Treasury by each French African colony was obligatory. All colonies were required to deposit into this account all of the foreign currencies that accrued from the sale of each country's exports. The use of the reserves was to be made with the permission of the French Central Bank.

The French colonial monetary, economic, commercial system, and other forms of financial arrangements operated with relative ease. This was due to it's guaranteed convertibility of local currencies into metropolitan ones. This arrangement facilitated inter-state trade, payments, and movement of capital and labor between the Francophone countries by maintaining the stability of the exchange rates between the CFA Franc and other currencies. These advantages accounted for the creation of several organizations of the French-speaking West African countries. The attainment of independence in the early 1960's by many of these countries also led to the renegotiation of the Cooperation Agreements between France and her ex-colonies and to the relaxation of the rigid rules that had governed the functioning of the monetary, economic, and commercial relationships.

The West African sub-region is comprised of countries with both British and French traditions. Gjana, Nigeria, Gambia, and Sierra Leone were once included in the British-ruled territories. The Ivory Coast, Senegal, Guinea, Togo, the People's Republic of Benin, Upper Volta, Mali, Niger and Mauritania were associated with France. The territories of Guinea-Bissau and Liberia had strong economic ties with Portugal and the United States.

Under the leadership of Kwame Nkrumah, Ghana contributed immensely to the awakening of an African consciousness concerning the need for freedom and African unity in economic planning, a military and defense strategy, and a unified foreign policy. Although Nkrumah was the driving force behind the notion of continent unity, he did not live to see it through. He was deposed in 1966, partly for supposedly having failed with his experiment of state farms, and partly because little international attention was paid to the cocoa industry. The general experience was that government revenue fluctuated widely along with fluctuations in the value of cocoa exports (the largest source of revenue) and imports of essential commodities. It was ironic that after the reversal of Nkrumah's policies by his successors, the economy of the state did not improve.

Perhaps the Nigerian economy has undergone more far-reaching structural changes than any other West African country since the mid-1960's when the production and export of petroleum became important. Nigeria, the most populous country in Africa, has had abundant agricultural products and mineral resources. There has been several problems besetting the economy of the country. Among these was a low production in the agricultural sector partly due to the rapid rate of expansion of non-agricultural sector, i.e., the mining sector. Manufacturing is at the import-substitution stage, while problems associated with balance of payments have developed into a national issue.

There has been little structural change in the Gambian economy since independence. Agriculture, dominated by groundnut production and related activities, accounts for a large proportion of the GDP. Fluctuations in the value of exports also lead to shifts in government revenue. Also, Gambia has had a very liberal import policy.

Sierra Leone, like other West African countries, depends heavily on diamonds and iron ore for most of its foreign exchange earnings. Although, agriculture has engaged a large percentage of the work force.

The economy of the Ivory Coast has maintained a growth rate of about 8 percent annually. This is partly because it has been dominated by a private enterprise system coupled with a liberal policy of profit and wage repatriation thereby attracting many overseas investors. In addition, most of the investments went into diversifying agriculture and manufacturing. To the extent that growth has been generated and maintained by considerable outside investment, yet not accompanied by the creation of firm socio-economic structures, the economy has often been described as one of "growth without development."

Senegal, unlike most other countries in the sub-region of West Africa, benefited from a wide range of development infra-structures during the colonial era. It has also enjoyed the many advantages of being the federal headquarters of the defunct French West Africa. Senegal has been experiencing difficult times, however, since the disintegration of French West Africa and the more relatively restricted market coupled with deteriorating world prices for groundnuts.

Guinea, known for its policy of non-alignment, has embarked on several development projects based on hydro-power schemes since independence. Both bauxite and iron ore are found in Guinea, and bauxite production is estimated to soon reach a record high. At present, the economic situation is difficult, but with expansion in agriculture and in bauxite production, a surplus foreign exchange is expected to improve the economy from its present state. With a centrally planned economy, Guinea's economic goals have appeared possible.

Except for Togo, which experienced economic growth during the 1960's while suffering large trade deficits in the early 1970's, most other French West African countries have experienced seriously deteriorating growth rates since independence. The economy of the Republic of Benin, for instance, has been unstable since independence. It has experienced trade deficits due to increasing import costs. Similarly, Upper Volta, Mali, and Niger have had to depend on subsidies to compensate for the lack of trade balance because drought and unfavorable prices in the world market have seriously affected livestock, groundnut, and cotton prices.

In Mauritania the predominantly rural economy is stabilized not only by iron and copper earnings but also by Arab petro-dollars. The Mauritania economy is heavily dependent on iron ore and rubber cultivation which is dominated by large-scale foreign-owned plantations. This has been made possible by its open door policy which has called for little or no state interference.

In summary, the varying levels and problems of economic development in the West Africa sub-region, plus external factors, have created a momentum towards the creation of regional economic organizations.

3 Institutional Setting for Economic Cooperation

An important step in the regional economic cooperation in Africa was the signing of the Agreement of Cooperation between the Organization of African Unity and the United Nations Economic Commission for Africa on November 15, 1965, in New York. The Economic Commission for Africa (ECA), however, was created bu the Economic and Social Council of the United Nations in 1958. The Commission, by 1965, had fully established itself, and had decentralized its presence beyond its headquarters in Addis Ababa. It had opened two regional offices in Niamey (Niger) and in Tangier (Morocco) by 1973. It also had an administrative outpost in Lusaka (Zambia).

The Commission's operation by 1973 had expanded into a number of fields necessitating such institutions as the Land Policies Development Centre for East and Central Africa (1960) and the Agricultural Credit Centre (1962). In its report for the fifth year of its operation (1963), the Commission declared its readiness to embark on regional economic development schemes. Emphasis was placed on the establishment of an African Common Market, the creation of an African Payments Union, and the coordination of national development plans.

Two major projects of the Commission have been the African Development Bank in Abijan and the African Institute for Economic Development and Planning in Dakar. In their respective spheres of activity, these projects are intended to contribute to a closer regional economic cooperation in Africa.[1]

The Charter of the African Development Bank has had definite intentions regarding regional economic cooperation. Article 2 of the Bank's Charter states that the bank's functions, inter alia, are:

A. To use the resources at its disposal for the financing of investment projects and programs relating to the economic and social development of its members, giving special priority to those which, by their nature or scope, concern several members and to those designed to make the economies of its members increasingly complementary and to bring about an orderly expansion of their foreign trade.

B. To undertake, or participate in, the selection, study and preparation of projects, enterprises and activities contributing to such development.

C. To mobilize and increase, both inside and outside of Africa, resources for the financing of such investment projects and programs.

An agreement establishing the Bank occurred in September 1964, and its doors were opened in 1966. Mahomoun Beheiry of the Sudan, its first president, made it clear that the policy of the Bank was to consider multinational projects, thus setting a foundation for regional economic cooperation in Africa.

Complimenting the Bank's activities towards promoting closer cooperation among African nations in their economic pursuits has been part of the work conducted by the second projects of the Commission. The African Institute for Economic Development and Planning in Dakar has functioned mainly as a post-graduate research organization, and has provided bilingual training to about 34 students each year (19 Francophonic and 15 Anglophonic), of whom 31 receive U.N. Fellowships. The training provided to these students has reflected the policies generated by the ECA. To this extent, the African Development Bank, created in 1964, and the Dakar Institute, established in 1963, have complemented each other. However, they both function as separate special projects of the ECA.[2]

Through a resolution passed in the Economic and Social Council on April 29, 1958,[3] the terms [4] of the United Nations

Economic Commission for Africa were adopted. The Commission, inter alia, was empowered to: (a) Initiate and participate in measures for facilitating concerted action for the economic development of Africa, including its social aspects. . .,[5] (b) assist in the formulation and development of coordinated policies as a basis for practical action in promoting economic and technological development in the region,[6] (c) in carrying out the above functions, to deal appropriately with the social aspects of economic development and the inter-relationships of economic and social factors,[7] and (d) the Commission may, after discussion with any specialized agency concerned and with the approval of the Economic and Social Council, establish such subsidiary bodies as it deems appropriate for facilitating its responsibilities.[8]

These four powers of the Commission were considered separate from the rest of its powers by suggesting a number of avenues for the economic development of Africa. First, the Commission could become engaged in organizing an integrated strategy for economic development. Under this heading, the promotion of regional customs unions,[9] and adjusting and regulating tariffs over goods produced within the Union became a concern for the Commission.

Customs unions aren't always perceived as beneficial to each member state of the Union. If the Union resulted in "trade creating", or influencing the replacement of a high cost commodity produced by one member of the Union, this is considered beneficial to the Union as a whole. On the other hand, if the effect of the customs union was to replace a low cost commodity produced external to the Union with a "high-cost" commodity produced by a member of the Union, then the arrangement is believed to be a "trade diversion," and therefore harmful to the Union.[10]

The second role that the Commission could play in fostering regional economic cooperation of Africa was promoting shared technological knowledge that could advance these goals. An additional dimension to this role was seen in the Commission's relationship with the organization of African Unity. By an agreement signed in New York on November 15, 1965, the two bodies formulated a basis for cooperation within an agreed framework and in defined areas of interest.[11]

The formation of regional economic organizations and customs unions in Africa, and in the West Africa sub-region, has been encouraged and sustained since independence due to the activities of the institutions that have been briefly examined in this section of the chapter.

4 Recent Attempts Towards Economic Cooperation

African and West African states, since independence, have made substantial efforts towards more rapid economic growth and development and the attainment of a higher standard of living for the masses of their people. The size of the national economies and markets and the scarce resources of these states are too limiting to allow for a rapid transformation of their stagnant economic structures and the achievement of economies of scale.

As a consequence, economic cooperation among these states, especially in the areas of river and lake basin development, banking, and monetary affairs (including the establishment of more sub-regional economic organizations with wide ranging economic, commercial, financial, industrial, agricultural, transportation, and telecommunications objectives), has offered the only practical means for building viable national economies.[12]

Footnotes

1a. For a thorough discussion on the questioin of dependency see Amalendu Guha and Franklin Vivekananda, Development Alternatives, 1985 and See also Premises and Process of Maldevelopment, Franklin Vivekananda (edt) 1986.

1. See a chapter written on the work of The Economic Commission for Africa by a member of the Commission, published in Africa: A Handbook to the Continent, Ed. Legum, (C), Praeger, New York, 1968, p. 502.

2. Ibid, p. 503.

3. See resolution 671A (XXX) of the Economic and Social Council of April 29, 1958. This resolution was subsequently amended by resolution 974D (XXVI) of July 5, 1963, and by 1343 (XLV) of July 18, 1968.

4. Terms of Reference of the United Nations Economic Commission for Africa:

(i) The Economic Commission for Africa, acting within the framework of the policies of the United Nations and subject to the general supervision of the Economic and Social Council shall, provided that the Commission takes no action with respect to any country without the agreement of the Government of that country:

(a) Initiate and participate in measures for facilitating concerted action for the economic development of Africa, including its social aspects, with a view to raising the level of economic activity and levels of living in Africa and for maintaining and strengthening the economic relations of countries and territories of Africa, both among themselves and with other countries of the world;

(b) Make or sponsor such investigations and studies of economic and technological problems and developments within the territories of Africa as the Commission deems appropriate, and disseminate the results of such investigations and studies;

(c) Undertake or sponsor the collection, evaluation and dissemination of such economic, technological and statistical information as the Commission deems appropriate;

(d) Perform, within the available resources of its secretariat, such advisory services as the countries and territories of the region may desire, provided that such services do not overlap with those rendered by other bodies of the United Nations or by the specialized agencies;

(e) Assist the Council as requests in discharging its functions within the region in connection with any economic problems, including problems in the field of technical assistance;

(f) Assist in the formulation and development of coordinated policies as a basis for practical action in promoting economic and technological development in the region; and

(g) In carrying out the above functions, deal as appropriate with the social aspects of economic development and the interrelationship of economic and social factors.

(ii) The commission is empowered to make recommendations on any matter within its competence directly to the Governments of the members or associate members concerned, to Governments admitted in a consultative capacity, and to the specialized agencies. The Commission shall submit for prior consideration by the Economic and Social Council any of its proposals for activities that would have important effects on the economy of the world as a whole.

(iii) The Commission may, after discussion with any specialized agency concerned and with the approval of the Economic and Social Council, established such subsidiary bodies as it deems appropriate for facilitating the carrying out of its responsibilities.

(iv) The geographical scope of the Commission's work shall be the whole continent of Africa, Madagascar and other African islands.

(v) Membership of the Commission shall be open to Algeria, Botswana, Burundi, Cameroon, the Central African Republic, Chad, Congo (Democratic Republic of), Dahomey, Equatorial Guinea, Ethiopia, Gabon, Gambia, Ghana, Guinea, the Ivory Coast, Kenya, Lesotho, Liberia, Libya, Madagascar, Malawi, Mali, Mauritania, Mauritius, Morocco, Niger, Nigeria, the People's Republic of the Congo, the Republic of South Africa, Rwanda, Senegal, Sierra Leone, Somalia, Sudan, Swaziland, Togo, Tunisia, Uganda, the United Arab Republic, the United Republic of Tanzania, Upper Volta, Zambia and to any other State in the area which may hereafter become a member of the United Nations, provided that States which shall cease to have any territorial responsibilities in Africa shall cease to be members of the Commission.

(vi) The following shall be associate members of the Commission: (a) The Non-Self-Governing Territories situated within the geographical area defined in paragraph iv above, and (b) Powers other than Portugal responsible for international relations of those Territories.

(vii) Representatives of associate members shall be entitled to participate without vote in all meetings of the Commission, whether sitting as Commission or as Committee of the whole.

(viii) Representatives of associate members shall be eligible to be appointed as members of any committee or any other subordinate body which may be set up by the Commission, and to hold office in such bodies.

(ix) The Commission shall invite any member of the United Nations not a member of the Commission to participate, in a consultative capacity, in its consideration of any matter of particular concern to that non-member, following the practices of the Economic and Social Council.

(x) The Commission shall invite representatives of specialized agencies to attend its meetings and to participate, without vote, in its deliberations with respect to items on its agenda relating to matters within the scope of their activities; and it may invite as it may consider desirable, in accordance with the practices of the Economic and Social Council.

(xi) The Commission shall take measures to ensure that the necessary liaison shall be maintained with other organs of the United Nations and with the specialized agencies, with special attention to the avoidance of a duplication of effort. The Commission shall establish appropriate liaison and cooperation with other regional economic commissions in accordance with the resolutions and directives of the Economic and Social Council and the General Assembly.

(xii) The Commission may establish such liaison as it deems appropriate with inter-governmental organizations in Africa operating in the same field.

(xiii) The Commission shall make arrangements for consultation with non-governmental organizations which have been granted consultative status by the Economic and Social Council, in accordance with the principles approved by the Council for this purpose.

(xv) The administrative budget of the Commission shall be financed from the funds of the United Nations.

(xvi) The Secretary-General of the United Nations shall appoint the Executive Secretary of the Commission. the staff of the Commission shall form part of the Secretariat of the United Nations.

(xvii) The Commission shall submit to the Economic and Social Council once a year a full report on its activities and plans, including those of any subsidiary bodies; for those years in which the Commission does not hold a session, the Executive Secretary shall submit to the Economic and Social Council a full report of its activities and plans, including those of any subsidiary bodies after approval by the Chairman of the session in question and circulation to Governments of member States for their comments and any necessary modifications.

(xviii) The headquarters of the Commission and its secretariat shall be located in Africa. The site of the headquarters shall be decided by the Economic and Social Council in consultation with the Secretary-General of the United Nations. The Commission may, in due course, also establish such sub-regional offices as it may find necessary.

(xix) The first session of the Commission shall be called by the Secretary-General of the United Nations as soon as practical, but not later than the end of 1958. The Commission shall at each session decide upon the locality of the meeting of its next session, due consideration being given to the principle that the Commission should meet at its headquarters or in the different countries of Africa.

(xx) The Economic and Social Council shall, from time to time, make special reviews of the work of the Commission.

5. F.N. 24, Resolution 1(a).

6. F.N. 24, Resolution 1(f).

7. F.N. 24, Resolution 1(g).

8. F.N. 24, Resolution 3.

9. Egs., the Treaty Establishing the Customs and Economic Union of Central Africa (UDEAC), signed in Brazzaville (Congo) on December 8, 1964, and The East African Common Market, established under Part II of The Treaty for East African Cooperation, signed in Kampala, Uganda, on June 6, 1967.

10. A. Nazlewood (ed.),African Integration and Disintegration, A. Oxford University Press, London, 1967, pp. 5-6.

11. The text of the Agreement can be found in U.N. Document A/6174 (16 December 1965). This agreement resulted from OAU resolution, ECOS/RES.17 (II) (Cairo, January 1965), and ECA resolution, E/CN 14/RES/132 (VII) (Nairobi, February 1965).

12. W. A. Ndongko, "Regional Trade and Economic Arrangements to African Association with EEC," Internationale Afrika Forum, Munich, No. 1, 1977.

Chapter III

River and Lake Basin Organizations and Commissions

1. Introduction

The need for the development of river and lake basins has been given considerable attention in the West African sub-region since the 1970's. Intergovernmental organizations and commissions have been created for the development of the Lake Chad and Niger Basins and the Senegal, Gambia and Volta Rivers. The following sections will examine these development organizations.

2. Lake Chad Basin Commission (LCBC)

The Lake Chad Basin Commission was established in 1964 as a non-political regional organization that works to develop the water resources of the area. Its long-term goal has been to promote the economic development of the area and its four member countries while encouraging fair trade practices in agriculture and livestock products. A medium-term goal has been the development of drought-resistant projects.

The main branch of the Lake Chad Basin Commission has been the Commission with two commissioners from each of the four member states who meet biannually. The Executive Secretariat is located in Ndjamena, formerly Fort-Lamy. The five permanent technical divisions are concerned with the following fields:

(a) hydraulics and civil engineering;
(b) agriculture;
(c) animal husbandry;
(d) fisheries and forestry; and
(e) general economic affairs.

Parts of Nigeria, Niger, Chad and Cameroon are included in LCBC's well defined geographical area around the basin of Lake Chad which covers an area of 400,000 square km. Two of its members, Nigeria and Cameroon, have been the major economic powers in West Africa and Central Africa, respectively. [1a] Niger and Chad, the other two members, are unfortunately landlocked states.

These four member countries have represented a diversity of population, population density, gross national product, per capita income, and level of development. LCBC has had a population of about 5.5 million people. Of this, Cameroon and Chad individually accounted for a little over a million, Niger 200,000, and Nigeria approximately 3 million people. (Tables 3.1 and 3.2).

Nigeria with the largest population of 85 million people had an approximate growth rate of 2.5 percent based on a mid-1972 analysis. It had a GNP of $12,000 million (U.S.), and a per capita income of $200. The GNP per capita growth rate between 1960-1972 and 1965-1972 was estimated to be 2.0 and 5.4 percent, respectively.

Cameroon had a population of over 10 million with a GNP at market prices of $2,000 million (U.S.), and a per capita income estimated to be $260. The population growth rate between the period 1960-1972 and 1965-1972 was estimated to be 4.0 and 3.8 percent.

Niger and Chad had populations of 5 million and 4 million. Their GNP at 1972 market prices were $400 million (U.S.) and $320 million, and their per capita incomes were estimated to be $90 and $80. The population growth rates in these two countries between 1960-1972 and 1965-1972 were 2.9 and 1.8 percent for the first period and 2.8 and 1.8 percent for the second period. Niger had GNP per capita growth rates of -0.4 percent between 1965-72. Chad had 0.5 percent. During this period Niger had -5.1 percent while Chad had 1.6 percent growth rates.[1]

The last census and related maps of population density data were available for Cameroon (1969), Chad (1963), Nigeria (1963), and Niger (1960). (Table 3.2.) Population densities have varied enormously within the Basin area. In the Cameroon sector,for example, the population density was 28 inhabitants per km^2 in the mountainous region of Guider, Mokolo and Mora, but only six inhabitants per km^2 in the Foureau area.

The population density in some parts of the Kenem Province of Chad was 1.4 inhabitants per km^2. The Niger area had 4 inhabitants per Km^2 and in the Nigeria sector the population distribution appeared to be homogeneous.[2]

Urbanization in the basin area has been generally low. Although the Chadian capitol of Ndjamena is located in this sector, 91 percent of the working population is engaged in agriculture, animal husbandry, and fishing. In the other sectors, 94 percent of the labor force of Cameroon and of Niger and 85 percent of the Nigerian labor force are employed in agriculture or fishing.

Within the Basin Area, three geographical and agricultural zones can be distinguished:

(a) a zone of extensive semi-nomadic livestock rearing covering that part of the sector belonging to Nigeria and Chad;

(b) an agricultural zone dominated by non-irrigated crops (coarse cereals and pulses) stretching over most of the Nigerian and Chadian sectors and over an area of the Cameroon sectors; the major economic centers of this zone being Maiduguri and Ndjamena; and

(c) a zone located in the sector belonging to Cameroon which receives considerable rainfall; it has had a diversification of economic activities (for example, sorghum and paddy rice are the main crops in the northern part and cotton and groundnuts in the southern part).

Projects for the economic development of this diverse area have been a major concern of the Lake Chad Basin Commission. Particularly noteworthy in this program were the development of animal husbandry in Assale-Serbewel and fisheries in each of the four LCBC member states.

In the Cameroon-Chad districts of Assale-Serbewel on both sides of the Chari River, a model cattle farm is being built on an area of over 2,000 square miles (5,120 square km). In addition, agricultural development centers are being established in Diffa (Niger), N'Gala (Nigeria), Fort Foureau (Cameroon) and Koundow (Chad). These centers are expected to concentrate quite clearly on an intensification of soil use by irrigation, both in cultivation and in cattle raising. The provision of fishing centers in Gortogol

(Niger), Baga (Nigeria), Dole (Cameroon) and Heykoalou (Chad) has been another program to improve fishing methods.[3]

The development budget of the LCBC has consisted of contributions from the United States, France, Great Britain and, above all, the United Nations Development Program. These contributions amounted to $3 million (U.S.) in 1973 with member nations contributing $500,000 to the administrative budget. Presently, the main source of revenue for the development fund has been contributions from the member states. Each has contributed one thousandth of its national budget. The Commission has also received financial assistance from Canada and other countries for various projects.

A project to appraise the potential of the natural resources of the Lake Chad Basin has been financed by the United Nations Development Program (UNDP) and initiated by the Food and Agricultural Organization (FAO). The tse-tse fly eradication project was financed by French aid for 200 million CFA Francs. Other projects included the development of roads and telecommunication links between member countries and the preparation of an accurate map of the Lake Chad Basin and its environs in order to facilitate proper lake and river navigation. The Commission received credit for the completion of the new 128 million CFA Secretariat. Additionally, a British assisted aerial survey of the mineral wealth of the Basin and the Lake areas was planned.

Agreements have been reached between the Commission and UNDP, USAID and the French Aid Agency to jointly finance an Animal Husbandry Project for approximately $3 million. It would cover half a million hectares in the area of Assale in Chad and Serbewel in Cameroon to provide livestock with watering points and grazing areas. The $400,000 in French aid, in addition to the Cameroon and Chad contributions, has completed the financing.

With the proclamation of the LCBC territory as a disaster area in December 1973, a medium-term program to combat drought was jointly drawn up by the Commission and the UNDP.

Other programs established with the aid and material support of the United States, France and Great Britain and the UNDP have included:

i) establishment of a Chari Delta Fodder Belt;

ii) agro-Pastoral use of artesian water in Kadzell Plain;

iii) creation of an irrigation belt at Bosso;

iv) creation of four fishing development centers;

v) creation of four afforestation centers; and

vi) examination and supervision of the underground water at the edges of Lake Chad.

Financial concerns have continued to present problems for the Commission. Three road construction projects (Fort Lamy to Maiduguri, Kalle to Bongor, and Bama to Maroua) were discontinued due to a lack of funds. Member states were unable to agree on methods to generate additional financial support or on the feasibility of the project.[4]

It is imperative for member states to pay particular attention to the overall importance of the Commission, especially given the declining productivity in the agricultural sectors of these states. The various agricultural projects embarked upon, especially the fisheries and animal husbandry projects, is expected to increase protein intake of the people in the Basin area.

3. Organization for the Development of the Senegal River (OMVS)

In an attempt to compensate for the failed development programs planned by the Organization of the Senegal River States, the Senegalese authorities established the 'Organization pour la Mise en Valeur de Fleuve Senegal' (OMVS), which was reminiscent of an earlier interstate organization (OERS).[5] The other members of the OMVS included Mali, and Mauritania.

The member states have represented differences in land area, population sizes, growth rates, and per capita income. Mali had three times Mauritania's population, and a GNP of $400 million, at market prices of 1972, twice that of Mauritania. (Table 3.3) Senegal's population of 3,990,000 was 75 percent of Mali's while Senegal at the same time had a GNP of $1,050 million. Out of the three states, Mauritania had the smallest GNP per capita. However, it had the highest rates of GNP per capita growth of 5.2 percent and 2.0 percent between 1960-1965 and 1965-1972.

The OMVS's main goal has been to implement the major interstate development projects initiated by the defunct Organization of the Senegal River States (OERS) in order to revive the long proposed West African Economic Community. [6] The Council of the Heads of States and other committees have been responsible for initiating and implementing the programs of the organization. [7]

Plans to provide water for a land area of over 430,000 hectares included the construction of dams at Manantali (Mali) and at Diama (Senagal); the construction of ten modern ports between St. Louis and Kayes (Senegal); and aspirations for the development of the Senegal River delta area. [8]

Another concern was the protection of farm areas from the effects of cyclical droughts such as the one in 1977. The OMVS introduced the use of improved fertilizers, new pumping methods for irrigation, and a maintenance system for these pumps. Successful rice experiments allocated land to farmers, although certain lots were no more than 0.2 hectares.

Intensive research has also been conducted with goals for the prevention and eventual eradication of diseases such as sleeping sickness and malaria.

The land reclamation program, which envisaged the reclamation of about 10,000 hectares annually, has fallen behind schedule. Mauritania, which hoped to reclaim 160,000 hectares of irrigated land, was diverted by its iron production problem which was disrupted by the Polisario Front guerillas. At the same time, Mali's priority has not been immediately agricultural. Mali, which is rain fed, has not had the same urgency for the development of the 50,000 hectares which could be reclaimed through the Manantali project.

The resources of the
OMVS are generated from foreign countries and international bodies such as the World Bank, the African Development Bank, France, West Germany, Canada, Iran, Saudi Arabia, Kuwait, USAID, and others. The Nouakchost meeting of international organization held on January 20, 1974, resolved to provide financial resources for OMVS development projects. By July 24, 1974, approximately 34 billion CFA Franc (U.S. $151 million) had been contributed by the international organizations, although the projects were estimated to cost 87 billion CFA Francs (U.S. $390 million).

OMVS has benefited from a high level of cooperation from its member states. Senegal and Mali who both belong to other sub-regional organizations, have been in a position to contribute to the successful functioning of the OMVS. The implementation of numerous viable projects and the ability to attain international financial support have underscored its achievements.

The OMVS, however, has experienced the same financial problems as other similar organizations. After 30 years of existence, inadequate funds have continued to prevent the effective development of the Senegal River.

4. The Niger Basin Commission

The Niger Basin Commission was formed in November 1980, with nine member countries: Guinea, Mali, the Ivory Coast, Niger, Upper Volta, the Republic of Benin, Cameroon, and Chad. The zone of influence included five other countries: Sierra Leone, Togo, Ghana, Liberia, and the Central African Republic.

The main objectives of the Commission have been to regulate the flow of the Niger River and to identify additional beneficial uses of the water as only 3 percent of it is currently utilized. In attempting to formulate its developmental strategy, the Commission has defined priority projects as:

(a) those that interest at least two member states:

(b) those of sufficiently wide scale to have an impact, even indirectly, on the Niger Basin; and
(c) those which concern known priority sectors as well as those minor important projects that could allow two member states to form a cooperation.

The developmental strategy of the Commission has been to:

(a) concentrate development efforts on the Middle Niger;
(b) give priority to projects of multiple objectives, particularly irrigation for agricultural purposes; and
(c) focus attention on the continuous fight against the degradation of the area within the entire Sahel - Soudanese Zone of the Basin, (a short-term priority).

The 1981/82 biennial development program of the Niger Basin outlined a definite development program. The cost of this program was estimated at $29,737,000 (about $15 million per year) with four integrated projects costing nearly one half of the total estimated expenditure - about $14,037,000. Interstate projects were estimated to be about one quarter of the total expenditure with $8 million for project identification.

The development program included the study of the electrical inter-connection of Cameroon-Nigeria-Chad (The Delta Region), the studies of the construction of dams on the Bani River and its tributaries in the Middle Niger area, and the hydro-electric dam on the Upper Niger and its principal tributaries. Studies for the improvement of the navigability of the Niger River and the expansion of the river transport systems in the Basin are planned. Another project was the extension of the down-stream as far as Nigeria (Cameroon included), and upstream as far as Guinea. The institutional development for the construction of the headquarters of the Niger Basin Authority and the interstate center for hydrological forecasting are planned.

The Niger River Basin Commission has made a number of achievements. First, each region of the Basin has established a pre-project development scheme of the Niger Basin. The development of the Upper Basin has been of interest to Guinea, Mali, and the Ivory Coast. The Guinea - Mali project with dams on the Upper Niger and its tributaries, and the Ivorian-Mali projects with dams on the Basin River and its tributaries has qualified for consideration under the "priority project" definition.

Another viable project has been the development of the Middle Niger as far as the Nigerian border. The first stage of the project was in connection with the Kandji project which would allow for the irrigation of all areas recognized as irrigatable to that side of the Niger River downstream in Mali. Five other projects to supply hydro-electric power and water for use in agriculture have been identified as possible choices according to the order of priority.

Analysis of the activities of the Niger Basin Commission have indicated that the economies of the member countries along the Basin area have been provided the opportunity to be transformed if adequate funding can be obtained.

5. The Volta River Authority (VRA)

The Volta River Authority was set up in 1960 as part of the Volta River project with the task of supervising the transmission of hydro-electric power, developing fishing and transportation on the Volta Lake, and developing the lake side area. The dam and associated works were estimated to cost a total of $142 million. Financial sources for this project included an equity investment by the Ghanaian Government for $59 million, loans from the World Bank for $48 million, and loans from the United States and the United Kingdom for $35 million. The Authority was to be a public corporation similar to other state enterprises except that it was to be responsible directly to the president of Ghana.

The VRA, in terms of its main objectives, has been a success story. This success came despite the fact that attempts to resettle the former residents of inundated areas ran into serious difficulties, especially in the improvement of the agricultural sector. This resettlement problem has been attributed to the fact that the dam was finished ahead of schedule and well below the original estimated costs. Since the turbines began generating, the VRA has generally out-performed the initial World Bank projections (Table 3.4).

One question which has repeatedly surfaced is to what extent exceptional conditions have caused the superior records of the VRA. Unlike many other state investments, the VRA project was exhaustively prepared and evaluated before it was implemented and the establishment of a preparatory commission which presented a favorable report in 1956.

The objectives of the VRA were unambiguous. The principal duties were economic in character enjoining it to conduct its affairs on sound commercial lines, and to fix its power rates in order to earn profits. A third related factor was that the VRA was not plagued with the 'political interference' that impeded so many other state ventures.

Due to the success of the VRA, the Electricity Authority of Benin-Ghana-Togo has been established. Its main function has been to ensure the continuous and adequate supply of electricity generated from the Volta River Dam to Benin and Togo. Ghana has also supplied electricity to Upper Volta which is not a member of the organization. Needless to say, the success story of the VRA was a positive example to other similar endeavors in the West African sub-region.

6. The Mano River Union

The heads of states of Liberia and Sierra Leone signed a declaration in 1973, to establish a customs union to become known as the Mano River Union after the river which forms the boundary between the two countries. The Mano River Union has evolved rapidly into an organization of considerable complexity. Thus, the Union Ministerial Council, the Union Standing Committee, and the Union Secretariat have been formed.

There was a development from the early ad hoc meetings of the heads of state towards a more formal institution with characteristics of an assembly of the heads of state. The efficient instituting of the principal objectives of the declaration, namely the ongoing integration of Liberia and Sierra Leone, also necessitated action in peripheral areas. Among the bodies consequently created were the Training and Research Board, the Postal Affairs Committee, and the Transport Commission and Fund.

The approach to integration adopted by the framers of the Union was original in the respect that no comprehensive treaty was drawn up. The Declaration was quite brief and, in essence, contained nothing more than a pronouncement of policy. The Declaration, however, granted the authority to expand its meaning and purpose. The adoption of protocols, i.e. normative statements on the issues the Union in each instance wished to regulate, was envisaged.

Approximately 18 protocols have been added to the declaration covering subjects ranging from training and research establishment within the Union to industrial investment and trade policies. Each protocol was signed by the heads of state and ratified in accordance with the internal procedures of the member states. Thus, each individual protocol is an international treaty which confers upon the states rights and obligations under international law. [9]

The Union Declaration did not make separate provisions for any Union organs other than the Union Secretariat and the Customs and Training School. It did, however, establish an assumption in respect to the existence of the most vital of the Union organs, namely, the meeting of the Union presidents. With time the original ad hoc meeting of the presidents for the purposes of signing the declaration and additional protocols has developed into an orderly procedure. The two heads of state, in fact, have constituted an assembly of heads of state thereby forming a regular body of the Union.

The Sixth Article of the Declaration designated the Joint Ministerial Committee as the principal body of the Union. Subsequently, this body was renamed the Union Ministerial Council, and was so designated in the Third Article of the Second Protocol to the Declaration. In the Sixth and Eighth Articles of the Declaration, the functions of the council were illustrated in general terms. It was a feature of the Union that within these general powers, the Ministerial Council assumed quite specific functions for designated activities. The various protocol relating to the specific concerns of investments, customs, training and research, and transportation, to name the four main ones, further specified the council's function in relation to each sector separately.

The Sixth Article called for the establishment of a Union Secretariat to be located in Freetown. Although never the subject of a protocol, a sub-office was established in Monrovia through a council resolution. The latter facility was, therefore, also a part of the Secretariat. The Secretariat itself was conceptually a service and coordinating organization to the Ministerial Council and to the Assembly of the Heads of State; these two bodies were established through the same instrument as the Secretariat. Subsequently, the Secretariat is subordinated to the Council and the Assembly.

The Secretariat is allowed to serve other Union bodies in so far as it is so authorized either through a Council Resolution or Directive or through a Protocol. To facilitate the work of the Secretariat, it has been possible for the Secretariat to establish working groups provided that the necessary authority to that effect is obtained from the Ministerial Council. As distinct from the Council appointed working groups, the Secretariat's working groups have been responsible to the Secretariat. The findings of such groups are incorporated in the Secretariat's recommendations.

It is an accepted practice that all recommendations and proposals brought to the attention of the Ministerial Council by the Secretariat, must be submitted to the standing committee for discussion and approval. Article 10 of the Second Protocol made it apparent that, in as much as the standing committee was a preparatory body for the Council, the Secretariat is allowed to serve the Standing Committee in much the same manner as it does the Council. In fact, part of the task of servicing the Council has been the servicing of the Standing Committee. In the protocols dealing with trade, investments, and transport, certain specific functions were given to the Secretariat which would not, in view of the aforementioned features of the secretariat's legal position, otherwise have fallen within the Secretariat's duties.

The Secretariat was given authority on behalf of, and under the direction of, the Commission on Industry and Trade to perform quite specific functions. One important function in this context was to coordinate the implementation and entry into forced change in the classification of goods for customs and statistical purposes and in the valuation of goods for customs purposes. This is an example of duties entrusted to the Secretariat which do not flow from its original function as a service body to the Assembly and to the Council and their sub-bodies. The

Secretariat has also had important responsibilities in respect to the union investment application procedure.

The Secretariat is headed by a Secretary General who is assisted by a Deputy Secretary General. The Secretary General was granted powers and functions distinct from those of the Secretariat, and this office is regarded as a branch of the Union. This branch is designed to ensure that the interests of the Union as a whole are taken into account in decisions made on the affairs involving the Union. He has been virtually the only independent member of the union, whereas all other branches are composed of national representatives with national view points.

Although there were no expressed provisions detailing the powers and functions of the Secretary General in the declaration and its protocols, the language in the Sixteenth Article of the Second Protocol gave a clear indication of, and foundation for, the independence of the position of the Secretary General. It expressly provided that neither he nor his deputy would be in any way influenced by the national governments. In fact, the position of the Secretary General was further safeguarded in the protocol dealing with the privileges and immunities of the Union.

While the functions of the Secretary General were designed to be independent, he is designated to serve on the key bodies of the Union, although normally without a vote. His duties have encompassed presenting the viewpoints of the Union as a whole to the national representatives and to insisting upon the implementation of Union policies. In this regard, he is prevented from taking instructions from national governments. The Secretary General is instructed to take the initiative to instigate new measures for the Union as is the Council. Therefore, the Secretary General has had a substantial role in the implementation of Union policies.

Among the Secretary General's functions in the Union structure, the most crucial one has been presenting a Union point of view to decision making bodies. His views are appended to the minutes of any subordinate body whenever a decision by such a body has appeared not to conform with either the legal structure or the overall policies and interests (as defined by the Ministerial

Council) of the Union. By registering his dissent in this form the action on that issue is suspended until the matter is resolved.

At the heart of the Mano River Declaration was the free movement of goods, services and persons across the borders between Liberia and Sierra Leone. The Second Article of the Mano River Declaration contained a statement that the aims and objectives of the Union were to expand trade by the elimination of all barriers to mutual trade, "...in spite of the fact that such trade liberalization during the first phase, in accordance with the Fourth Article, should be in `goods of local origin'."[10]

Border crossing procedures, likewise, are being coordinated. An additional feature that the Declaration expressly provided for was the establishment of a Customs Training School in Liberia.

The secretariat is engaged in formulating common rules and regulations for both customs and excise duties. To achieve this objective, the criteria for what constituted goods of local origin have been specified as a guideline to the Commission on Industry and Trade, which makes the final determination. Traders and businessmen are permitted to apply to the Commission for recognition of a particular product as being within the group of products qualifying for local origin treatment. The commission's decisions are published in the Local Origin List. This list is considered significant because it identifies duty free goods allowed to be transported across the borders of member states. Such goods are not exempt from applicable excise duties in the country of consumption nor in the country of manufacture or origin. However, this measure has not been fully implemented.

The Rules of Origin have produced additional paperwork and cost to the manufacturers and to the Customs Administrations. Manufacturers are required to maintain different records of local content for both ACP (Lome Convention) and Union purposes. Different customs certificates must also be employed.

To some extent, the Manor River Union has already coordinated the Common External Tariff. In addition, the Union must have the responsibility of harmonizing the protection it contributes to industries through protective tariffs, as well as to the trade policies of the two countries, since tariffs are one of the major instruments of trade policy. In brief, harmonization of trade policies, i.e. tariffs and import licensing, harmonization of investment incentives, and control of Union industries, should suffice as a means of dealing with the problems of encouraging the use of local raw materials in the production process.

Duty free access to both markets is also allowed for such goods and products which licensed Union Industries produce and trade. In this case, the problem of record keeping for the local content is made easier. Few such industries are planned to be established in the near future, and those who have enjoyed this status can be regulated rather easily. The regulatory process is designed to use a selective process in the granting of Union licenses, and to provide the right of access to books and records by government auditors. The limited number of such enterprises would place the task of regulating them within the available resources of the governments.

Not only should policies regarding protective tariffs be closely coordinated, but these policies should also be involved with aligning the import and export license policies. Incidental fees for landing goods, such as harbor fees, consular fees, transit fees, warehouse charges, etc., must not be allowed to differ appreciably in the two countries.

Furthermore, the economic policies and, in particular, direct and indirect taxation must be coordinated within the two countries, since this has an effect on the domestic price level. If a basic industrial commodity, such as fuel, were to be priced much higher (through taxation or otherwise), in one of the member states, distortions of the industrialization patterns would follow, since industry would tend to establish itself where costs are the lowest. A certain undercutting of local industry has appeared possible if price and cost levels differ. Industries producing at cheaper costs in one country could, with only transport costs added, sell the product in another country. Thus, the industry would have taken advantage of its lower cost of production to undercut local entrepreneurs in the other market who were unable to lower their prices because of higher production costs and thus, would not be able to respond to the challenge.

In addition to free trade, the other major tool to be used for achieving the objectives of the Mano River Declaration has been industrial cooperation. Apart from the establishment of joint public ventures, which is discussed in detail below, the problem of industrial cooperation can be categorized into two distinct concerns. On the one hand, existing domestic industries must be encouraged to expand, when feasible, into both markets; and on the other hand, has been the possibility of attracting larger industries that need the relative advantage of the economies of scale made possible by the Union. Such industry is termed "**Union industry**".

There have been several problems in this connection. First, industries must be induced to take advantage of the Union market. Second, through a conscious effort to distribute industries evenly between the two countries, the development of economic imbalance must be prevented. An effective utilization of the domestic markets for industry ideally has required free movement of goods, a common external tariff and a currency union. Even though these conditions can be realized in the long term, more modest goals are necessitated in the short term.

The foundation of the Twelfth Protocol, which sets out the policies for Union industries, is based upon the precept that the national legislation of its members must remain essentially independent with regard to the subject, except for references to the Union law in the form of specific provisions in the protocol. Taking the investment legislation of the Union as the fundamentally higher law currently effecting the inflow of investment into the two countries and, therefore, centrally important in the present respect, the Liberian and Sierra Leonean national laws on the subject are to be legislated to encompass the concept of Union industry.

In order to distinguish the different situations involved, the following three groups of industries should be noted:

(a) non-incentive domestic industries,
(b) incentive industries (domestic and Union), and
(c) joint public ventures.

In the last group are found, for the most part, small scale businesses. In some instances, however, industries that have had "development" status under either Liberian or Sierra Leonean investment laws are allowed to operate in non-incentive conditions since their incentive privileges have expired.

Normally only the latter type of enterprise has been large enough to expand into a combined market. As long as the possibility exists, the same procedure would be applicable for incentive industries described below. In this context perhaps it would be useful to consider making a special effort to assist indigenous entrepreneurs, not only by giving them access to investment incentives, but also by actively assisting in the export of their products within the Union.

Existing industries who have already enjoyed investment incentives under the domestic incentive codes should be encouraged to expand Union-wide. Additional incentives may be required for this purpose. Some measures which can be viewed as incentives would also be effective in eliminating locational imbalances. For example, an external protective tariff must be harmonized. If not, the whole purpose of protection would be negated if the tariffs were not coordinated in both countries. Similarly, import and export licensing procedures should be coordinated.

The granting of privileges to existing industries should be carefully done (i.e., to Group 2(a) industries). To prevent the overprotection of these industries, it may be considered necessary to give different protection to Group 2(b) industries. Some of the investment incentives granted to purely domestic industries may not be needed by the larger type of industries that are a present concern. In the long run it would be desirable to consider the harmonization of domestic incentive codes in the two countries in order to prevent possible distortion of industrial establishment through the availability of more favorable incentives in one country than in the other.

Over a period of time industrial interchange between Liberia and Sierra Leone may be anticipated to fully meet ambitions. Nevertheless, methods should be developed whereby institutions designed to accelerate the process might be formed. Thus, it would seem desirable to have a measure of cooperation between already existing industries and, in particular, with the large, raw material extracting industry, which would otherwise be left totally out of the Union industrial development.

Raw material concessions have partly constituted self-sufficient entities and have not required anything other than overseas markets. Their contributions to present Union objectives would be augmented by considering:

(a) providing purchasing power;
(b) providing training facilities; and
(c) constituting a favorable influence on other prospective investments.

At present, the national investment legislation has been the fundamentally important law effecting the inflow of investment into the two countries and has therefore also been centrally important in the present respect. The Liberian and Sierra Leone national laws on this subject must be supplemented by legislation covering the concept of Union industry.

Short term objectives of defining the investment incentives specifically applicable to Union industries may be required. Separating domestic incentives from Union incentives may be considered a problem in those instances where Group 2(a) industries would be upgraded into Group 2(b) category industries. Such 2(a) industries would perhaps still enjoy the benefits of investment incentives granted under a domestic system and, at the same time, have to be granted the specific Union incentives when upgraded to category 2(b) industry. This problem could be resolved by requiring such industries to specify the investment required for its expansion into the second market and by applying to these investments only the added specific Union investment incentives.

The danger of imbalance occurring through the concentration of investments in one part of the Union can only be alleviated through the assurance that both markets appear approximately and equally attractive to investors. It would not seem feasible, in the light of experiences elsewhere, to attempt to compel investors to move into a location regarded as unsuitable by the investor, whether he holds his opinion on economic or psychological grounds. It may be deemed necessary, for this reason, to grant, at least marginally, more liberal incentives to industries locating themselves in specific locations.

The use of financing, and, in some instances, even the use of subsidies (especially in the form of construction of essential infrastructure), as a means of attracting the investor to an alternate location might be considered in order to equitably balance the location of industries in the two countries. Having not only one government participating in a venture, but, for psychological reasons, two participating governments may be observed to be enticing to investors. For purposes of funding Union industries, a Union Industries Fund is being established.

With the development of free trade, the Sierra Leone exchange control must be considered. The Liberian situation is characterized by a total absence of restraints on the movement of currency (the currency being the United States dollar), with the only coinage being Liberian. The Sierra Leone currency has had strict exchange controls. The problem has been largely Sierra Leone's in as much as it has hardly appeared practical to suggest similar exchange control restrictions on the part of Liberia as those currently intact in Sierra Leone.

The core of the problem has been to ease the Sierra Leone restrictions in respect to Union trade, without, at the same time, negating the effect of Sierra Leone exchange control entirely. In the event of Union industries being established, one feature of such an industry would be the operation in two markets. Already, the mechanics of everyday management require that capital be moved from one location to another in response to actual business needs.

A secondary problem has entailed employees who will have to commute carrying cash with them and, for convenience, retain foreign exchange. Could establishing industry be discouraged because each time such a transaction takes place, an application has to be made to the Sierra Leone National Bank? Obviously, if the major part of all earnings were in dollars, no problem of exchange arises, since dollars can be used freely to pay expenses in Sierra Leone. However, Leones cannot be used for expenses in

Liberia unless, under present law, special permission is obtained for each case. In the short term, and given the Sierra Leone assurances to businesses that foreign exchange will be made available in accordance with their needs, no real problem other than that of inconvenience should is expected to arise.

The essence of the Exchange Control Regulations has been to control all movement of capital into or out of Sierra Leone. Accordingly, it has not been possible for a Sierra Leone resident to engage in any capital transactions with Liberian interests, except with the permission of the Bank of Sierra Leone. Furthermore, it has been necessary to obtain specific authorization for both import and export transaction in respect of exchange required in payment.

Non-residents, to which group Liberian nationals belong, are not allowed to hold resident accounts in Sierra Leone banks and therefore can only be credited with funds cleared by the Bank of Sierra Leone, (or in some minor instances authorized by an authorized dealer). This means that a Liberian national is prevented from building up funds in Sierra Leone, even if his transactions were made through a branch office, since the headquarter state has been the determining factor for whether or not the enterprise is considered a "resident".

All travel for business purposes must be approved by the Bank of Sierra Leone. Even though such approval has been normally given, it has represented an additional encumbrance upon the free movement of goods to Liberia. It has often been necessary to promote the sale of one's products in person. Furthermore, a Sierra Leone resident is not allowed in any circumstances to hold balances in dollar currency except for some older accounts. Thus, it has not been possible for a resident of Sierra Leone to hold even small amounts of dollar currency for convenience between business trips to Liberia, nor, of course, has it been possible for him to hold current balances in Liberian Banks.

Attention should also be drawn to the fact that the import procedures relating to currency control formalities appear to be cumbersome. These and other rules must be liberalized or modified not only to permit travel and free trade, but also in order to permit Sierra Leone participation in Liberian owned business and Union industry, unless one is to restrict the concept of Union industry to exclude mutual shareholding. This would mean adoption of the concept that a Union industry is either a strictly Liberian, or strictly Sierra Leone, owned business. The companies would merely have the right to market products in the other country (which can be done already in any event). Only when restricted in this manner, would the concept of Union Industry be permitted to operated under present national banking laws and exchange rules. This situation would then merely be viewed as an inconvenience; but this is hardly the intent. The choice has also depended upon the attitude of the larger question of Union industry.

Public utilities, as well as the development of the Mano River Basin, are seen requiring lose cooperation between the governments. It would be useful to establish joint corporate bodies for each project, as required. A Basin Authority which will be the instrument for developing not only power, but the Manor River Basin as a whole would be useful. Presently, the desired action in these areas has concentrated on the generation of power; what is required is, therefore, a framework for the joint production of power.

At the heart of the Mano River Union has been trade and industrial cooperation, but at the heart of both trade and industrial cooperation - aside from the political climate - has been the exchange of goods, services and persons.[9] This, in turn, has ideally required removal of internal tariffs and duties, a common external tariff, free capital movement, and removal of restrictions and formalities for free and unrestricted travel (including the right to work), inside Union borders.

This, then, is considered to be the start of a common market, which is seen by many as a precondition for maximizing the combined utilization of scarce resources. Even though at this stage of the Mano River Union development, emphasis must be placed on trade and industrial cooperation, there have been broader perspectives involved. The Mano River Union has succeeded, among other things, in making significant progress in establishing a closer economic, social, and cultural integration between the peoples of the Republic of Liberia and those of the Republic of Sierra Leone.

The Union has taken steps towards the liberalization of mutual trade in goods of local origin through the elimination of tariff and non-tariff barriers and through other fiscal measures for developing cooperation in the production of agricultural and manufactured products. Arrangements have been made towards harmonization of all customs duties and for the protection of the Sierra Leone and Liberia economies by a common external tariff. Neither country has agreed to a detailed list of customs duty adjustments.

Both countries had to make major compromises in achieving harmony. On some items, customs duties were slashed by as much as 50 percent; on others, the increase was equally great. While negotiations were being conducted, there was always the fear that Sierra Leone, in particular, might loose a sizeable chunk of desperately needed customs revenue; while on the Liberian side the existing fear was that the changes wrought by increasing duties would inflate prices, and thus annoy the Liberian public. The only disagreement concerned motor cars and tomato paste. (Table 3.5).

With the completion of the first phase of the Custom Union on May 1, 1981, trade arrangements and tariff barriers have been eliminated, and the joint market of Liberia and Sierra Leone has become available to the producers within the two countries. Thus, they have been provided a substantially larger and protected domestic market. All manufactured goods and goods wholly produced in member states can be traded from Sierra Leone to Liberia and from Liberia to Sierra Leone without any customs import duties or equivalent charges. It must be remarked here that this Union Common Tariff has been only the first step in the complete economic integration of Sierra Leone and Liberia.

Another achievement of the Union has been the Freetown/Monnrovia highway. The current cost is estimated at $97 million. Out of this, about $40 million has been committed by the government of the Federal Republic of Germany, and the African Development Bank. The Basin Development Project (Manor River Development Project) has been another achievement. Feasibility studies were completed by the consulting firm SOFRELEC (a French agricultural and forestry consulting firm), and is being funded by the EEC. This is expected to boost agricultural development and tourism within the area. Presently, adaptive research studies are being undertaken in order to increase the degree of self-sufficiency in animal protein intake in member states. Improved fermentation methods and better storage facilities for crops are also being developed.

Economic development must be sustained by parallel social development. In five years, the Manor River Union has established some mid-level manpower training institutions: a telecommunications and postal training institute; a customs excise and trade statistics program; a forestry training institute; and a marine training program. Other projects have included the Union scholarship and fellowship program to provide opportunities for students in member states to obtain middle level and high level training. There has also been the Union Curriculum Planning and the Institutional Materials Production and Book Development (CIB).

However, the rate of development of the Mano River hydro-electric scheme has not progressed as expected. The power station which is likely to have a generating capacity between 104 MW and 182 MW is estimated to cost between $250 million and $300 million. The union hopes this project, which is the biggest of all, will become operational this year.

7. Conclusion

Our analysis has revealed that the existing river and lake basin commissions in the West African sub-region have made considerable achievements. Although a number of problems have been confronted, the prospects are considered favorable.

Footnotes

1a. See Chapter 8 for more analysis of the Lake Chad Basin Commission in Economic Development of Cameroon, Wilfred A. Ndongko and Franklin Vivekananda.

1. Africa Report, April, 1975,p. 13.

2. F.A.D. Lake Chad Basin Commission: Economic Aspects of the Agricultural Sector, Rome 1974, p.4.

3. West Africa, Vol, 3, p.1210, 1975.

4. West Africa, February 18, 1972.

5. West Africa, December 10, 1971, p.1439.

6. Ibid

7. African Research Bulletin, May 25, 1974 and July 13, 1974.p.7.

8. Sundstrom, in Material Area-Ratt, Tidskrift utgiven av Juvisdiska Foreiningen if Finland 1964. p. 336ff, suggested that international treaties within cohesive areas of law should be read in conjunction with each other.

9. African Research Bulletin op. cit, p.12.

10. Sundstrom, The Public International Utility Corporation, Helsinki, 1971,p.106.

TABLE 3.1. LCBC: AREA DISTRIBUTION OF THE CONVENTIONAL BASIN

COUNTRY	TOTAL AREA Km2	LAKE AREA Km2	% OF CONVEN- tional Basin	% OF NATION- al Territory
Cameroon	37,000	1,600	8.5	8.0
Chad	178,300	10,000	41.5	14.0
Niger	121,000	3,400	29.0	9.5
Nigeria	90,000	5,000	21.0	9.7

TABLE 3.2. LCBC: POPULATION IN THE CONVENTIONAL BASIN 1970

COUNTRY	POPULATION IN CONVENTIONAL BASIN	% IN CON-VENTIONAL	% OF NATIONAL	POPULATION DENSITY
Cameroon	1,050 000	19 19	18.1	28.0
Chad	1,150,000	21	32.0	6.5
Niger	200,000	4	5.0	2.0
Nigeria	3,050,000	56	4.5	34.0

Source: FAO. LCBC, Cameroon, Chad, Niger and Nigeria: Economic Aspects of Agricultural Sector. Rome 1974, p.4.

TABLE 3.3. POPULATION, ANNUAL GROWTH RATE AND PER CAPITA INCOME OF MALI- MAURITANIA AND SENEGAL (1972)

COUNTRY	POPULATION (000)	GNP US ($) MILLION	GNP PER CAPITA US ($)	GNP PER CAPITA GROWTH RATE 1960-72	GNP PER CAPITA GROWTH RATE 1965-72
Mali	5,260	400	80	2.1	1.3
Mauritania	1,210	210	180	5.2	2.0
Senegal	3,990	1,050	260	-0.8	-0.7

Source: World Bank - based on - Population (Mid-1972) GNP at Market Prices (1972) GNP per capita (1972).

TABLE 3.4. VRA COMPARISON OF PLANNED WITH ACTUAL PERFORMANCE
1960-1970

1. POWER SALES (GWH)					
(a) Projected	384	884	1,753	2,257	2,402
(b) Actual	450	1,455	2,478	2,674	2,806
2. NET EARNINGS (cmn)					
(a) Projected	2.29[a]	-3.06	-8.83	0.78	1.84
(b) Actual	1.33	-2.08	0.35	1.55	1.82
3. NET EARNINGS (as % of Ghana Investment)					
(a) Projected	-	-	-	0.97	2.29
(b) Actual	1.8	-5.2	0.60	2.60	2.10

Source: World Bank: <u>Appraisal of Volta River Hydro-electric Project</u>, Annex 6.
VRA Annual Reports (Various issues).

Note [a] = there was no provision for depreciation in 1966.

TABLE 3.5. <u>HOW CUSTOMS TARIFF WILL CHANGE IN THE MANOR RIVER UNION</u>

	OLD LIBERIAN DUTY	OLD SIERRA LEONEAN DUTY	NEW UCT DUTY
Sugar	4 cents 16	Le 60.0 ton	$96 ton
Sardines	11%	15%	15%
Jam	40%	15%	30%
Coffee (Processed)	50%	15%	50%
Ice Cream	50%	15%	50%
Beer	$2.57 gal.	Le 3.02 gal.	$1.25 Litre
Wine	$25 or 70%*	Le 11.75	$3.50 Litre* Or70%
Tobacco (Virginia)	40c 16	Le 50c 16	$1.45 kg
Wheat	50c per 100 lb	Free	10%
Rice	50c per 100 lb	Free	0.10kg
Palm Oil	20c gal.	Free	Free
Palm Kernel Oil	40c gal.	Free	Free
Tinned Fish	$1.20 or 40%	15%	15%
Chocolate	Free	60%	60%
Children's food	30c lb	15%	10%
Biscuits/Cakes	50%	60%	60%
Animal Food (Vitaminised)	11%	Free	Free
(cereal based)	11%	40%	10%
Petrol (refined)	14c gal.	36c gal.	0.10 Litre
Crude oil	11%	40%	Free
Most chemicals	11%	40%	15%

continued on next page

continued

Most pharmacauticals	Free	40%	15%
Most Fertilizers	Free	5%	Free
Soap (toilet)	20c lb or 40%*	40%	40%
Soap (Washing)	15c lb	22 1/2%	40%
Tyres (Cars)	40%	16%	40%
Grey Cotton	20 sq. yd. or 20%*	100 c sq. yd. or le 5.00*	0.08 sq. m. or 29%*
Most clothes	40%	45%	20%
Glasses (drinking)	11%	40%	20%
Other glass	11%	40%	40%
Most metal bldg. materials	11%	40%	15%
Pumps (Machine)	11%	40%	20%

Rates of duty are generally increased on items where goods could be made locally from local raw materials, Building materials are adjusted to encourage house building with local materials. Other rates to protect local Industries raised.

* Where two rates exist the higher rate is chosen.

CHAPTER IV

BANKING AND MONETARY COOPERATION

1. Introduction

This chapter examines the nature of economic cooperation, banking, and monetary policies in the West African sub-region. The two major organizations to be analyzed are the West African Clearing House and the West African Monetary Union that have a majority of the member states who all have a common central bank - the Central Bank of the West African states. The Central Bank issues a common currency, the CFA Franc, which is related to the French Franc.

2. The West African Clearing House (WACH)

The WACH was established following the signing and ratification of the Articles of Agreement June 25, 1975. The members of the WACH have comprised the Central Banks of 12 countries, including : Benin Gambia, Ghana, the Ivory Coast, LIberia, Mali, Niger, Nigeria, Senegal, Sierra Leone, Togo, and Upper Volta. The WACH is the first major experiment in multi-lateral monetary cooperation in West Africa and is the result of detailed consultations under the auspices of the African Central Banks.

The approach of the Association of African Central Banks was first introduced on May 25, 1963, following the meeting of the African heads of state and government in their first summit conference in Addis Ababa. The February 15-22, 1966, meeting of the governors of the African Central Banks resolved unanimously to organize a preparatory economic committee in collaboration with the governments and in consultation with the ECA. The essential purpose of the 1966 meeting was essentially to consider the mechanism for monetary cooperation and the type of necessary institutional arrangements.

The WACH principally serves the West African sub-region that has included 12 countries and the following Central Banks: the Central Bank of West African States (BCEAO) that has served the members of the West African French Zone and has embraced Benin, the Ivory Coast, Niger, Senegal, Togo and Upper Volta; the Central Bank of Gambia; the Bank of Ghana; the National Bank of

Liberia; the Central Bank of Mali; the Central Bank of Nigeria; and the Bank of Sierra Leone.

The main objective of WACH has been to provide a facility through which the participants can utilize national currencies for imports from the West African sub-region, thereby economizing in the use of foreign exchange reserves and transfer costs. Other objectives of WACH listed in the Article of Agreement were:

(a) to promote the use of currencies of the members of the clearing house for sub-regional trade and other transactions;
(b) to bring about economies by the use of foreign reserves of the members of the clearing house;
(c) to encourage the members of the clearing house to liberalize trade among their respective countries; and
(d) to promote monetary cooperation and consultation among members of the clearing house.

Among the institutions of WACH have been the Association of African Central Banks with the governors of the African Central Banks and the heads of monetary institutions serving as members. Their principal objective has been to seek to promote cooperation in the monetary, banking and financial spheres and to assist the formulation of guidelines for the member countries.

The eligible instruments by which payments can be made through the Clearing House facility have been telegraphic transfers, mail transfers, bank drafts, bills of exchange and other approved instruments. The Clearing House has provided a medium for all payments relating to current account transactions within the sub-region between the countries of member banks. Inter-governmental grants and inter-governmental loans and payments that are not current international transactions as defined by the International Monetary Fund are included by a mutual agreement between the contracting parties.

In view of currency differences and different exchange rates, there has existed a West African Unit of Account which has been equivalent to one Special Drawing Right of the International Monetary Fund. It should be stressed that the Unit Account has not only been useful for statistical and accounting purposes, but it has been, in practice, the only effective guarantee of maintenance of the value of the creditor's claims.

Regarding the exchange rate, the daily rates of each member country are stated in the amount of their particular currency per one West African Unit of Account (equivalent to one Special Drawing Right). WACH subsequently has managed the rate for each country's currency from the daily information received from the member banks and the International Monetary Fund. The currencies that are currently involved include: the CFA Franc (for Benin, the Ivory Coast, Niger, Senegal, Togo and Upper Volta), the Gambia Dalasi, the Ghanian Cedi, the Liberian Dollar, the Malian Franc, the Nigerian Naira, and the Sierra Leone Leone.

The financial sources of WACH are generated from the budget contributions of member nations and other investment ventures that have included Sierra Leone government treasury bills, time deposit with the Sierra Leone Commercial Bank, and interest on staff loans. Other sources of finance have been contributions from the UNDP (United Nations Development Programme).

The WACH commenced its operations on July 1, 1976. The establishment of the WACH was impeded primarily due to the existence of bilateral agreements, although other reasons also contributed to the hindrance of the WACH's development. However, in its transactions between July 1, 1976 to August 31, 1977, the volume of payment orders received amounted to 51,267,428 West African Unit of Account. Payments effected, for which the Clearing House was informed, accounted for 50,721,786 WAUA. Outstanding transactions amounted to 554,642 WAUA. The above figures included capital transfers of WAUA 19,409,480. Settlements during the period amounted to 38,014,095 WAUA, which represented 74.96 percent of the total transactions.

These settlements were made in the following currencies: U.S. Dollars, Pound Sterling, French Franc, Deutsch Mark, and Swiss Franc.[1] Settlements that did not necessitate the transfer of funds from one country to another is clearing. The volume of cleared transactions amounted to 12,698,692 WAUA, which is 25.04 percent of the total transactions.

It must be emphasized that, although a high percentage of clearing was recorded for some months, the net average was comparatively low. A suitable example was the total transactions for May 1977 which was 2,134,889 WAUA, of which 1,272,438 WAUA was cleared. This gave a percentage clearing of 59.6 percent in comparison to the net average of 25.04 percent.[2] For the year 1977-78, transactions channelled through the Clearing House for the 12 months ending in August 1978, totaled 43,791,797 WAUA, compared to 50,921,786 WAUA for the foundation for a month period ending August 31, 1977. Monthly transactions ranged between a high of 5,843,177 WAUA, and a low of 2,318,875 WAUA. Clearing figures should indicate the extent to which member's transactions offset one another thus alleviating the need to transfer funds form one country to another. Despite fluctuations in total transactions, the trend has been generally upward. Where the percentage clearing above the total transactions for the first 14 months of operation was 25.04, the average for the year 1977-78 was 32.43.[3]

Other activities of the WACH were study tours of other clearing systems in Asia, Central America, and South America. In the 1977-78 operations period, an attempt was made to seek assistance for WACH from the UNDP. The WACH also participated in the following meetings:

(a) The second meeting of experts of the West African Intergovernmental Organization held in Cotonou in the Republic of Benin; and
(b) the first meeting of the Coordination Committee on Multilateral Payment Arrangement and Monetary Cooperation among Developing Countries held in Bangkok, Thailand from July 11-14, 1978. WACH also hosted the first seminar on Commercial Banks in Africa held in Monrovia, Liberia in May 1977.

During the period under review, the level of African trade is estimated to be between five and ten percent of the total external trade of the continents. In West Africa most of the external trade was with countries outside the sub-region. A disquieting trend has been that while within the past few years external commercial exchanges of African countries have increased slightly, intra-regional trade has declined. The design of an active intra-regional trade as a first priority has become imperative, especially when considering the rapid promotion of intra-regional trade alone as a development factor.

The lack of sanctions between the economies of West African countries has been the result of intense competition. A common occurrence has been the existence of the same factories and some industrial development programs on both sides of a common border. The sub-region has suffered from transport inadequacies that have impeded development of trade and, hence, the activities of the WACH.

The West African sub-region has remained divided into different monetary zones which maintained close relations with the former colonial powers. This has been the case with both the Franc Zone and the Sterling Zone. Obviously, the plurality of this type of system has represented a negative element in the growth of external trade. In practice, trade settlements are carried out in the major reserve currencies, which are the U.S. Dollar, the French Franc and the Pound Sterling, while payment orders for bills are processed by foreign banks situated in the United States, Paris and London. The disadvantages of such a practice have been numerous and have caused delays in settling payments, the high cost of services performed by intermediaries, and the imprudent use of foreign exchange reserves for non-priority items.

The existence of exchange controls in the different countries within the sub-region has introduced a certain amount of rigidity in transactions. This has resulted in an excessively long and costly administrative procedure in monetary transfer operations.

Although the present banking arrangements has not presented the primary obstacle to trade expansion in the subregion, banking relations between the English and French speaking countries have been rather weak and the payment system is unsatisfactory. There are delays under the system whereby transactions are carried out under a commercial banking arrangement where there are no direct correspondent relationships. At the same time, this situation is aggravated by a lack of confidence by some traders and in the reliability of the banking system.

Given the above problems, it is therefore difficult to obtain correct statistics of trade within the sub-region since a representative proportion of such trade is unrecorded. Letters of credit must be approved and confirmed through English or French first class banks, and this, no doubt, has lead to extensive delays. The situation is worsened by the inexperience of traders who often submit incomplete or incorrect documentation and as a result are not usually paid at the time of the submission of the documents. This fact has made the system costly. However, the expense of operating such a system has not been so much from the bank charges, and the need for confirmation through London and Paris, but from the interest charges and other expenses incurred by traders as a result of the delays.

It should be noted that since the commencement of WACH's operations on July 1, 1976, there has been a steady increase in the volume of transactions. The operation within the first few months was not consistent due to difficulties in understanding the rules and regulations, operating forms, serial numbering, and questions of procedures.

The establishment of ECOWAS gave evidence to a steady increase in political and economic consciousness in the sub-region. The growth of the ECOWAS will be enhanced by the expansion of the activities of WACH. This growth will help to facilitate trade transactions among member states. In addition to this growth, the international transactions in which WACH is involved are also a credit to the Clearing House.

3. West African Monetary Union (UMOA)

Until 1962, the West African currency was regulated by the West African Currency Union which was a pre-independence Union established in 1959. On May 12, 1962, the West African Currency Union was replaced by the Union Monetaire Ouest Africaine - UMOA, (the West African Monetary Union). A treaty establishing UMOA was signed in Paris by Dahomey, the Ivory Coast, Mali, Mauritania, Niger, Senegal and Upper Volta. Mali withdrew from the Union in July 1962, without ratifying the agreement, but Togo joined the Union on November 27, 1963.

UMOA is situated within the sub-region of West Africa. The Union has operated principally within the French Monetary Zone. Existing differences in the countries forming the Union have been similar to other organizations in West Africa. These dissimilarities have ranged from variations in GNP at market prices, population sizes, GNP per capita to GNP growth rates.

Table 4.1 presents the essential economic features of the member states of UMOA. It can be observed that national population figures have ranged from 5,613,000 for Upper Volta to 1,210,000 for Mauritania. In terms of GNP at market prices, the highest figure has been $1,840 million U.S. for the Ivory Coast, and $210 million U.S. for Mauritania.

Before the creation of UMOA, the position of the Francophone African countries was quite similar to that of the Anglophone countries (which operated the West African Currency Board), aside from the fact that monetary arrangements which were perfected in the colonial period were perpetuated after independence in the former French colonies. In the former French colonies, the Banque Centrale des Etats de l'Afrique de l'Ouest - BCEAO, (the treaty for its establishment which was signed on May 12, 1966) is the bank of issue for the former French colonies of West Africa except for the colonies of Guinea, Mali and, since 1973, Mauritania.

Countries in which the BCEAO operates have not had individual Central Banks, and they maintain no independent foreign exchange reserves. This is due to the fact that their foreign currency earnings are generally channelled to the French Monetary Zone foreign exchange pool in Paris in exchange for credit to their operations accounts maintained with the French Treasury. Additionally, foreign exchange needs are met first by converting CFA Franc into French Francs, which are eventually converted in the Paris exchange market into the required foreign currency. The CFA Franc is linked to the French Franc. As a result, the CFA Franc was automatically devalued along with the French Franc in 1969, and by April 1974, the CFA Franc was floating with the French Franc.

The establishment of a regime of fixed exchange rates between the colonies and metropolitan currencies suggested that the metropolis and the colony constituted an optimum currency area. As an adjunct to the treaty, France was to provide economic, financial, and monetary assistance to the signatories. It was to support the volume of a common currency, the Commuaute Financiere Africaine - CFA Franc.

The Banque Centrale des Etats de l'Afrique de l'Ouest - BCEAO (the Central Bank of West African States) was organized as the main institution of UMOA. The BCEAO was designed as the bank of issue for all former French colonies in West Africa with the exception of Guinea, Mali, and since 1973, Mauritania, as earlier mentioned. This design included an Administrative Council with two representatives from each member state. The French government representation has been one-third of the African representation. The president of the bank has acted as an ex-officio member of the Administrative Council, who presides over its deliberations.

The policy instrument of UMOA is associated with the functioning of the BCEAO, which operates according to a law annexed to the trade or commercial agreements. This notwithstanding, the main objective of UMOA has been to control credit in the sub region. France, from all indications, has been the major source of finance for the UMOA. With the signing of the Second Accord on May 12, 1966, the BCEAO replaced a similar institution created by the 1959 decree, thus receiving about 500 million francs from its predecessor.

UMOA member states are guaranteed the convertibility of their currencies into other metropolitan currencies and are virtually protected from balance of payment problems. However, these benefits have been achieved at the expense of the development of interstate trade and capital movements between UMOA states and foreign non-metropolitan countries. Additionally, a disproportionate part of the UMOA states trade has been channeled to the metropolitan country of France. Furthermore, the monetary system has encouraged the subordination of West African countries to the former metropolitan power. In particular, budget deficits have been largely financed by subventions from the former colonial power since there were no national central banks to finance such deficits through the purchase of treasury securities. In recent years, there has been a change in the operation of the system since the amount of budget subvention from France is now determined by an annual bilateral negotiation between France and each of the BCEAO countries. The BCEAO currently has been able to extend limited short term credits to member countries in the form of either direct advances or rediscounts of treasury bills presented by the Commercial Banks.

4. Conclusion

It should be noted that one of the problems facing the UMAO and WACH has been the fluctuation of currency. Specifically, the currency in the Francophone region has tended to fluctuate with the former metropolitan currency in times of international monetary crisis. In contrast, the EEC, with its various national currencies closely linked to national sovereignty and myth has been in the initial stages of a process that may eventually lead to a uniform monetary system.

Another problem challenging UMOA and WACH has been the exchange rate quotations between currencies which have been largely fixed. There have been normally modest margins between buying and selling rates periodically announced by the central banks before the monetary crises and uncertainties in the international economy occur.

The foregoing problems notwithstanding, it can be argued that the future of UMOA and the WACH has appeared bright considering the possibility of a formation of a West African monetary system or union that will transverse language barriers. The past experiences of UMOA and WACH would be very useful in such an endeavor. However, it must be made clear to the proponents of such a sub-regional monetary union that the first step towards a meaningful and successful monetary integration in West Africa can be assured only if the political differences between the UMOA states and the remaining states are not manifested. There is no doubt that monetary unions would be beneficial to the members as a result of intra-West African trade, increased regional monetary autonomy, increased risk apportionment in international transactions, free exchange markets, and increased efficiency in the management of foreign exchange reserves.

Footnotes

1. West African Clearing House, Annual Report 1976-1977, Freetown, September 1977,p. 10.

2. Ibid., p.15.

3. Ibid., p.16.

TABLE 4.1. ECONOMIC FEATURES OF UMOA COUNTRIES

COUNTRY	POPULATION (000)	GNP US ($) MILLIONS (MARKET PRICES)	GNP GROWTH RATES	
			1960-72	1965-72
Dahomey	2,860	300	0.9	1.7
Ivory Coast	5,400	1,840	4.2	4.1
Togo	2,052	330	4.9	3.3
Mauritania	1,210	210	5.2	2.0
Niger	4,250	400	-0.4	-5.1
Senegal	3,990	1,050	-0.8	-0.7
Upper Volta	5,613	400	0.9	0.6

Source: World Bank (based on 1972 estimates)

Chapter V

Economic Organizations With Limited Objectives

1. Introduction

In addition to the Lake and River Basin Commissions and the WACH and UMOA (Chapters III and IV), there are also many sub-regional economic organizations and unions with more limited objectives. This chapter will focus on the Entente Council, the Liptako-Gourma Region Development Authority, the Africa and Malagasy Common Organization (OCAM), the West African Rice Development Association, Multinational Programming and Operational Centers (MULPOCS), and other bilateral bodies.

2. The Entente Council

Historically, regional economic organizations in the Francophone West African states can be traced to the French Colonial Decree of October 18, 1904. By that decree, the French government established a Counseil de l'Entente (the Entente Council) embracing first, in 1904, Dahomey, Guinea, the Ivory Coast, Senegal, and what was then called Upper Senegal-Niger; in 1920, this council was enlarged to eight by including Mauritania, French Sudan (Mali), and Upper Volta.

It must be remarked here that until the Loi-Cadre was enacted in 1956, along with the legislation on which it was based, the administration of French West Africa and French Equatorial Africa was part of the centralized administration of France. Unlike the East African administrative capital of Nairobi, there was never so much as a rudimentary form of federal administration in these regions competent to handle the affairs of the colonies at the time.

Presidents Senghor (of Senegal) and Keita (of French Sudan, later Mali) attempted to form a new regional structure at a meeting held at Dakar in 1958. This new structure, the l'Assemble Constituaute Federale, was formed at a Dakar meeting in 1959. This regional structure, however, was short lived. It was followed by several attempts to establish a regional economic organization in Francophone West Africa.

Eventually, in 1959 the leaders of Niger, Dahomey, Upper Volta, and the Ivory Coast agreed to link their countries together through attempts initiated by President Houpho et-Boigny (Ivory Coast) by creating the Counseil de l'Entente.

The Counseil de l'Entente has existed largely within the sub-region of West Africa. There is a marked difference between its member states in terms of population, population growth rates, GNP at market prices, and per capita incomes, (Table 5.1). The GNP at market prices of Niger, Dahomey, Upper Volta, and Togo fall almost within the same range, i.e. $300 - 400 million U.S. The Ivory Coast had $1,840 million U.S. between 1960 and 1972. In fact, the combined GNP at market prices of the other four members was about 77.7 percent of that of the Ivory Coast. The Ivory Coast also had the highest rates of population growth (4.2 percent and 4.1 percent between 1960-1965 and 1965-1972).

The Entente Council's main objective was to coordinate the economic and foreign policies of the member states by coordinating taxation systems, and by creating a customs union, public administration, public works, and communications networks. These activities have expanded to cover virtually all areas of regional economic development such as the promotion of rapid economic development and the integration of the region. It has worked to assist member states in preparing specific economic projects and to obtain financial and technical assistance from donor international financial organizations.

The Secretariat is an institution of the Entente Council. It was set up in Cotonou (Dahomey) in 1960. There are additional meetings held regularly by the heads of state of the member nations. A characteristic feature of the council and its bodies has been the fact that each of the member states has had the right to veto any resolution or policy which is not in its best interest.

An important instrument for implementing the programs of the Entente Council has been the Mutual Aid and Guarantee Fund founded on the assumption that there is a relatively high risk of insolvency among African investors because of the shortage of capital in almost all developing countries. The fund, therefore, has acted as a buffer or protective device against any lack of confidence. Feasibility studies are generally sponsored by the fund with a view to expanding fruit and vegetable production for both the African market and out-of-season exports to Europe.

Other strategies have included measures for evolving a common statistical system and a common regional industrial development policy. There has also been the effort made towards improving transport and telecommunications and solving payment problems among member states and Ghana and Nigeria.

The resources of the Entente Council have been mainly the contributions of member states. The remainder of the resources are generated from non-African (mainly French) and other Western European and American sources. The contributions of member states now has currently been 650 million CFA ($2.7 million U.S.). The Ivory Coast has contributed, by far, the largest amount. The allocation of the funds' resources to projects in the five member countries is inversely related to their individual contributions. As a consequence, the projects in Niger, Upper Volta, Dahomey, and Togo are financed mainly with Ivorian capital. The Ivory Coast, which is the most developed member of the council, has made an important contribution towards the economic development of its economically weaker partners.

Loans for financing the Entente Council's projects have also been obtained from international financial institutions such as USAID totalling $13.5 million U.S., French Aid and Cooperation Fund (FAC) amounting to $3.5 million U.S., the EEC's European Development Fund in the amount of $1 million U.S., and $5 million U.S. from the Canadian International Development Agency. In addition, these loans have provided a guarantee fund established to encourage investments among the member states and to expand interstate trade. Other resources of the Entente Council have included subsidies and grants and profits on investments and commissions on its guaranteed operations.

The Entente Council has so far operated on the basis of a balanced development of the member states. By early 1974, the Entente Council established a Common Court of Appeal; coordinated development efforts in the fields of transport, communication, public administration, labor relations and public works; abolished double taxation among the member states (the Ouagadougou agreement of October 30,1961); and established a development fund to which each member state is required to contribute 10 percent of its national revenues.

The Entente Council has also combatted substantial meat deficiencies in the coastal regions, established the meat and livestock organization, and supported a program of annual health care for livestock, cattle trails and slaughter houses. In the area of international trade, the settlement of payment problems to ensure a trade equilibrium has been a worthy example of the achievements of the Entente Council.

In spite of the remarkable success of the Entente Council in the areas of industrial cooperation and of labor laws, there has been little achievement in the area of political cooperation. Indeed, shortly after becoming independent in the early 1960s, the heads of states of the member countries of the Conseil de l'Entente agreed to coordinate their foreign policies by making regular consultations, holding conferences on major international issues affecting the states, and establishing uniform internal political and administrative structures.

In the area of political cooperation, it should be pointed out that the member states pursued a policy of close cooperation with the western world and had only sporadic contact with the communist states. The position has changed, however, with regard to internal African political problems. Unanimity only truly prevailed for as long as Kwame Nkrumah's government was in control in Ghana. The common opposition against the former Ghanaian president gave rise to strong solidarity on foreign policy issues between the members of the Conseil de l'Entente. The member states were afraid of subversive interference from Accra, especially after the assassination of the Togolese president, Sylvanus Olympio in 1963. They resolved to form a common army to repel any attempted interference or intervention from outside; however, the resolution was not actually enforced.

Solidarity on matters which affected their common interest quieted in subsequent years. It need only be recalled that Togo, Dahomey, Niger, and Upper Volta did not follow the Ivorian government's policy regarding the recognition of the erstwhile state of Biafra. The same countries also disagreed with the Ivory Coast regarding its demand for a dialogue between the black Africans and the white minorities in South Africa.

The endeavors to unify the internal political and administrative structures has not been successful. This failure can largely be explained by the fact that, unlike the Ivory Coast and Niger, the army in Upper Volta, Dahomey, and Togo has, at least occasionally, played an important part in the political destiny of these countries. This trend of affairs has been all the more unfortunate since the homogeneity of these structures has been absolutely essential for the dynamic and problem-free future development of the Entente Council.

The problems of the Entente Council are mainly political and financial. It is of great importance to observe the political differences between the member states, since these differences may likely disintegrate the Entente Council. Perhaps financial problems can be alleviated by intensifying the efforts of member states towards generating more resources for implementing the projects of the Entente Council.

The fact that the Entente Council has achieved more success than many other African attempts at economic cooperation has implied that the organization has overcome a number of serious crises such as the de facto exclusion of Dahomey. Any optimism for the future, however, must be cautious. It is extremely important for the Entente Council to make rapid progress in the area of political cooperation. Indeed, the Entente Council must follow the example set by Western Europe and other countries of the world. It likewise must embark on a course of economic and political integration. It seems to be in the Entente Council's best interest not to allow a reverse tendency to set in, especially at a time when economic integration is yielding considerable results, i.e., industrialized countries of Western Europe.

If the leaders of the Conseil de l'Entente succeed in moving beyond the present stage of rather loose economic cooperation, and the leaders provide the needed political will and support, it eventually may well serve as a prototype for the entire West African sub-region-- a prototype which Africa urgently needs. The nature of future economic cooperation between the Entente Council members and the neighboring country of Ghana will have a great bearing on the future of the organization.

Perhaps by its linking with Ghana, the Conseil de l'Entente can one day prove that linguistic barriers are only artificial. This seems possible, given the present relations between Ghana and these countries such as the Ivory Coast, the undisputed leader of the Conseil de l'Entente.

3. African and Malagasy Common Organization (OCAM)

The Union Africaine et Malgache de Cooperation Economique (formerly the UAM) became the Organization Commune Africaine et Malgache (OCAM) in 1965, after the admission of Rwanda and Zaire (former Congo Kinshasa). The present membership of OCAM is comprised of Benin, Gabon, the Ivory Coast, Togo, Senegal, the Upper Volta, Niger, the Central African Republic, Rwanda and Mauritius. It should be remembered that Mauritius has replaced Madagascar. Cameroon, Chad, Madagascar, Mauritania, and Zaire have withdrawn.

Members of OCAM are all countries with marked differences in gross national products, per capita incomes, and rates of growth of population. The member states are located within the sub-region of West Africa, and the Central African Zone with the exception of Mauritius and Rwanda. The salient economic features and indicators of OCAM member states are presented in Table 5.2.

On the whole, Upper Volta had the largest population with 5,613,000 in contrast with Benin, which had only 300,000 in 1972. Regarding GNP at market price, the Ivory Coast had $1,840 million U.S., while Benine had only $110 million U.S. in 1972. The population growth rates range from 7.0 percent to 10 percent for Gabon to -0.8 to 0.7 percent for Senegal between 1960-1972 and 1965-1972, respectively. It should be noted that all members of OCAM are French speaking and most are still linked to France by bilateral treaties and protocol agreements of an account, cultural, and military nature.

The objectives of OCAM have included the harmonization of the activities of member states in the economic, social, technical, and cultural areas. Member states have also agreed to coordinate their development programs and respect the sovereignty and fundamental options of each other. In addition, a provision is also made for facilitating consultation in foreign policy matters among member states.[1]

The Secretariat General is designated the main operational institution of OCAM. Other sub-committees have been responsible for the various aspects of interest to the organization. In pursuance of the objectives of the organization, attempts are usually made to protect the overall interest of member countries by the Secretariat General. OCAM has been known for its aggressive lobbying strategies for higher prices for its tropical produce in keeping with the high prices of industrial equipments that its members are obliged to buy.[2] Another aim of the organizations is to make the group completely non-political and to become a true instrument of cultural and social solidarity, and economic development.[3]

OCAM's resources have been principally made up of loans and grants from the EEC, and direct bilateral aid from countries such as France, West Germany, Italy, Belgium, Luxemburg, and others. A break down of OCAM resources shows that EEC contributions (grants and loans) to the 18 associated states of the organization was $800 million U.S. between 1964 and 1969, and $1 billion U.S. during 1970 - 1975. The financial contributions from individual countries mentioned above are presented in Table 5.3.. It can be observed from Table 5.3 that France and West Germany have been the major contributors, giving over 74 percent during 1964 - 1969, and over 72 percent between 1970-1975. The two major contributors are followed by Italy, Belgium and Luxemburg, in that order.

The OCAM at one time guaranteed the market of its former members - Congo/Brazzaville and Madagascar. These two sugar exporters had a guaranteed market of 70-80 percent of the total sugar imports by OCAM member states.[4] Also, OCAM has always aggressively lobbied for higher prices for its tropical produce in line with the high prices of industrial equipment.[5]

At OCAM's Ministerial Council Meeting held in Kigali (Rwanda) between December 12-16, 1975, an agreement was reached on the creation of three new joint enterprises. There were: (a) the African and Mauritanian Institute of Bilingualism (Mauritius); (b) the Interstate School of Architecture and Town Planning (Togo); and (c) the Institute for the Training of Statisticians (Rwanda). The initial budget for the three enterprises was fixed at 387.4 million CFA Francs (about $2 million U.S.).

OCAM has failed in some very important areas. These were: (a) disagreement on how the remaining areas of French-speaking Africa was to share OCAM's facilities that had been built during the decade of its existence; (b) deferment of the project to set up an OCAM Guarantee and Cooperation Fund; and (c) Air Afrique, the showcase achievement of OCAM, but which had problems because of the failure of member states to honor their debts and because of the recent conflict between Senegal and the Ivory Coast over OCAM's leadership.

The problems of OCAM have ranged from inadequate finances to the tussle for leadership. Due to financial problems, the organization has depended upon France, and this,as a result, has ultimately impeded rapid economic integration. An example of the competing for leadership can be seen in the case of Air Afrique. Again, the leadership problem has led to the defection of countries such as Cameroon, Chad, Madagascar, Mauritania and Zaire.

Other reasons have been advanced for the defections by these countries. First, OCAM is stereotyped by African nationalists as a moderate organization which, in their context, means that its membership remains closely linked to the neo-colonist and imperialist centers of the world. In addition, the suggestion by the president of the Ivory Coast for dialogue with South Africa has increased dissatisfaction with OCAM. This is consistent with the fact that any political references which might suggest foreign policy coordination among members have been eliminated. It has appeared that the Ivory Coast, as a leading member of OCAM, was justifiably dissatisfied with the lack of support from other member states for her initiative regarding the policy of dialogue with South Africa. This initiative was opposed by an overwhelming majority of African states.

Taking into consideration the objectives and operational areas, it has appeared that OCAM's future seems promising with the exception of a few sensitive issues that might possibly cause more defections from the organization. The desire of the few more economically developed states to look for 'rapprochement' and dialogue with South Africa has been the issue at stake. For example, the Ivory Coast invited other African states to examine ways in which a dialogue might be established with South Africa some time ago.

A similar approach was suggested at the 1969 OAU Conference in Lusaka ("The Lusaka Manifesto)"), with the provision that such contacts should only be established if South Africa indicated that it was, in principle, prepared to move towards the eventual abandonment of its apartheid policies. It is possible that President Houphouet-Boigny attempted to introduce a note of moderation into this issue. On the other hand, his move indirectly caused a major split in OCAM and in the OAU. In fact, Cameroon, the then Congo Brazzaville, Mali, Nigeria, Senegal, and Zambia followed the presidents of Guinea and Tanzania in denouncing that move. Other countries, including the Central African Republic, Gabon, Ghana, Lesotho, Malawi, Sierra Leone, Madagascar, and Zaire, have concluded major economic agreements with South Africa. Other states of the Entente Council might be expected to follow the example of their affluent leading partner - the Ivory Coast.

OCAM's rate of economic cooperation has been limited by a number of factors, such as economic inequalities among member nations, differences in their political systems and ideologies, and the divergences in the lessons they have drawn from their previous development strategies. Because of the overwhelming sensitive and moral nature of certain political issues, disagreements could affect the economic and social progress that economic cooperation among OCAM member states might engender. It is important, therefore, for OCAM states to place the need for rapid economic and social development of the organization above their political differences.

4. The Liptako-Gourma Development Authority

The Liptako-Gourma Region Development Authority was established by the neighboring countries of Mali, Upper Volta, and Niger. The Liptako-Gourma Region Development Authority's headquarters are located at Quagadaugou in Upper Volta. It was created by the Protocol Agreement signed on December 3, 1970, by heads of member states and by the convention on its status on

June 3, 1971. It is comprised of the Council of Ministers, the policy making branch, and the General Secretariat, the branch of policy implementation.

The geographical area of the Liptaku-Gourma Development Authority can be approximately delimited by the following outermost points: Po to the South of Upper Volta's capital of Ouagadougou, Gaya in the South Western area of Niger, and Kidal and Timbuktu, both in the South Eastern of Mali. The region's population of 5,000,000 inhabitants are unequally distributed over an area of 470,500 sq. km.

Regarding the salient economic indicators of member states, Mali has had a population of 5,260,000, a GNP at market prices of $400 million U.S., and a per capita of $80 U.S. Its population growth rate between 1960 to 1972 has been estimated at 2.1 percent while its GNP per capita growth rate was 2.1 percent between 1960-1972 and 1.3 percent between 1965-1972. On the other hand, Niger has had a population of 4,250,000, a GNP of $400 million, and a per capita income of $90. The growth rate of its population was approximately 2.9 percent and 2.8 percent between 1960-1972 and 1965-1972, respectively. The growth rate of its GNP per capita was -0.4 percent during 1960-1972 and -5.1 percent between 1965-1972.

Upper Volta has had a population of 5,613,000, a GNP of $400 million, and a per capita income of $70. The population growth rate was 2.1 percent and 3.0 percent for the period 1960-1972 and 1965-1972. Its GNP per capita growth rate during the same period was 0.9 percent and 0.6 percent.

Article 4 of the Convention signed in Bamkako, Mali, on June 3, 1971, defined the status of the Development Authority of the Lipatko-Gourma Region, and stated the objectives of the Liptako-Gourma Region Authority as follows: ... is empowered to jointly promote, within the regional framework, the development of mining, energy, water, agricultural, pastoral and fishing resources within the Liptako-Gourma area.

Article 5 of the Convention stipulates that the Authority will develop and distribute the resources of Liptako-Gourma through economic and pre-investment studies and project appraisals; by seeking financial support for projects concerning the infrastructure, water supplies, energy, mines, stock-breeding, agriculture, and fishing by establishing companies to participate in implementing the projects which have been examined and approved in all of the areas indicated earlier.

The construction of an infrastructure system was the sine qua non for an even only partial development of the resources of the Liptako-Gourma region. Considerable importance, was, therefore, given to extending the railway line (Regie de Chemin de Fer Abidjan (Ivory Coast)) to as far as Ouagadougou (Central Upper Volta), directly through to Mali and Niger.

As an additional effort towards building an adequate and modern infrastructure, a railway linking Ouagadougou - Kaya-Dori-Tamboa Ansongo (Mali) was envisaged with a branch line from Dori Via Tera to Niamey (Niger). Not only have technical feasibility studies already been completed for this project, but financial negotiations have been made between the Liptako-Gourma Development Authority and representatives of the World Bank, the French government, the Japanese government, and the European Development Fund which has been extremely active in the development of this region for many years.

The Program of Priority Action provided inter alia for studies on the economic and effective use of the River Niger by building a canal along the 848 km. stretch from Timbuktu to Niamey. Dams to be built in Tossaye (Mali) and Kandaji (Niger) are envisaged to improve electrical power, agriculture, and fish production for the benefit of the three member states.

The question of whether these distinctly projects, as well as a wide variety of similar projects, can eventually be implemented depends on two things. First and foremost, implementation has depended upon the mineral resources discovered in the area and other deposits that are expected to be developed. Second, it has depended upon whether such resources are feasible and worthwhile despite the high subsidiary cost involved.

Substantial funds are expected to be generated from the mineral resources of the region and from financial aid from international organization such as French Aid and Cooperation

Funds, and the United Nations Development Program (UNDP). The member nations of the Authority have planned to contribute a percentage of their GNP.

Other projects which the Authority has considered are the exploration of the Manganese deposits in Tambao (northern Upper Volta) and Ansongo (Southeast Mali), the phosphates in Bourem (Tilemsi valley, Southeast Mali) and lime deposits in Tin-Hrassam (Northern Upper Volta). The exploitation of the Manganese deposits in Tambao have been undertaken by the French Aid and Cooperation Fund (FAC) and the United Nations Development Program (UNDP). The surveys of the Azongo Manganese deposits have been made by various French companies over a period of twenty years.

The major problems of the Liptako-Gourma Authority have been finances and manpower. The Authority was unable to promptly execute all its envisaged projects under its 'Program of Priority Action'. Manpower problems have manifested themselves in the area of feasibility studies of Senegal projects such as the exploitation of phosphate that was undertaken solely by a West German firm using only foreign technical personnel with no indigenous participation.

The future of the fundamental objective of the Liptako-Gourma Authority, which essentially has been to develop the mineral, energy, water, agricultural, pastoral, and fisheries resources of the region has been perceived as bright. Establishing a regional body responsible for the development of all resources is considered essential for integrated regional development. The simultaneous participation of several indigenous experts would be advised in order to achieve this fundamental objective..

The Lipatko-Gourma Authority should be reminded that for a smooth process of economic and social development of the region, the strategy should be carried out on a short, medium, and long term basis. This is important because the effects on the region of the exploration of the mineral resources in Liptako-Gourma, an intensification of agricultural production, and an improvement of the transport system would be feasible only if the projects are properly planned with the concerted efforts of all the member states.

It is gratifying to observe that those responsible for decision-making in the member countries have taken the projects which were initiated by the Authority for the integrated development of the Liptako-Gourma Region very seriously. It is hoped that the member states will take appropriate steps to assist the Authority in overcoming the financial difficulties and labor problems which have, no doubt, slowed the pace of implementing the various projects. The prevailing low development indicators reinforce the reasons for cooperation and mobilization of resources for greater long-term individual and collective benefits.

5. West Africa Rice Development Association (WARDA)

WARDA was developed as an inter-governmental regional organization made up the Republic of Benin, Gambia, Ghana, Guinea, Guinea Bissua, the Ivory Coast, Liberia, Mali, Mauritania, Niger Republic, Niger, Senegal, Sierra Leone, Togo, and Upper Volta. With its headquarters in Monrovia (Liberia), WARDA started operation on December 1, 1971. The 140 million people of the 15 member states have resided mainly in the rural areas as subsistence farmers with rice as their most important staple food.

The member states have continued to be net importers of food because of the stagnant output level and the increasing level of consumption. WARDA was formed to improve the living standards of the people of the sub- region and to contribute to their overall development. In 1976, 1.6 million metric tons of milled rice was produced by the region's subsistence farmers, and this was supplemented by 394,000 metric tons imported at the cost of $131 million U.S. It was estimated that $345 million U.S. and $500 million U.S. was spent on rice imports in 1977 and 1978. WARDA was created to help end to this excessive spending.

The main objectives of WARDA have been to: (a) promote and increase the quantity and quality of rice produced in West Africa; (b) encourage the production and use of varieties suited for the conditions of member states and for the existing and predicted demand; (c) explore, introduce and contribute to the extension of national production methods adapted to the conditions prevailing in the region; (d) promote and implement measures for effective phytosanitary controls in relation to rice, and (e) promote storage, processing, and marketing of rice within the region and with external rice trade.

The activities of WARDA are carried out by three major institutions. The Executive Secretariat is charged with the managerial control of the association.

The research department has been given the responsibility of establishing coordinated agronomic, varietal, plant introduction, protection trials, phytosanitary services, and integrated special research projects for dry-land irrigated rice, mangrove rice, deep flooded and floating rice, and rain-fed rice. In addition, it has undertaken the reinforcement of the existing network of research stations to facilitate their efforts. It has arranged conferences, seminars and workshops on topics relating to research; sponsored high and low level training; coordinated regional research from the headquarters and from a net-work of sub regional coordination offices.

The Development Department has been responsible for adding expertise to national rice development programs. It has focused attention on developing new methods of rice production, reducing post-production losses, and finding the most economical ways of achieving any desired objectives. This department has provided experts in various fields who assist WARDA in investigating the problems within the rice industry. The Development Department has cooperated with the financial institutions in project identification, formulation, appraisal and supervision. It has maintained a catalog of rice projects both in operation and in the pipe line within each member country, and it has mediated between member countries and financial institutions. It's statistics and data processing division disseminates information on different rice projects to member countries.

WARDA has depended upon the contributions of member states for its administrative budgets and upon a number of countries and organizations from outside the region to finance its technical projects. The Consultative Group on International Agricultural Research (OGIAR) has financed a greater part of research and research administrative costs.

There have been number of successes in some areas. Since its creation, it has conducted research review meetings annually. The research report incorporating the results obtained from the coordinated trials and special research projects have been presented, discussed, and published. It has summarized and published research activities on rice. These publications have become valuable documents for research and extension workers in West Africa and elsewhere. WARDA has annually organized seminars, workshops, or monitoring tours in order to provide opportunities to exchange ideas and improve knowledge.

WARDA and a national staff have succeeded in sub-regionalizing the region into five zones in order to allow for an efficient ecological network and supervision of trials and closer supervision of trials. This has served to bridge the gap between member countries and WARDA, to provide a better idea of national research problems and the support that it can give, to promote its participation in farm trials, and to provide more rapid feedback to the international research centers. The output of rice has increased in the region since its inception, from 156,820 tons in 1960-1964 to 2,764,600 tons in 1976-1978.

There have been serious problems in the execution of its programs. The problem of manpower has often hindered the successful implementation of some of WARDA's projects. As a result, WARDA has had to engage in training programs for its personnel. With an estimated population of 140 million people in the West African region, WARDA has had to invest a large amount of capital into research,and capacity development, etc., in order to produce the required quantity of rice. A shortage of finances has resulted in poor research equipment in several institutes. National boundaries and languages have posed a problem in communication and dissemination of experimental results. Economic and political instability within member countries have effected the commitment to the needs and aspirations of WARDA. The expected cooperation has not been achieved in many instances.

Whatever the problems facing WARDA, its endeavors have been promising. All well conceived efforts towards the development of the food industry, especially the rice industry, in the low income countries of the world a have good chance of success. Rice, as rightly pointed out by Nyle C. Brady, "rivals wheat and for the low income peoples of the world has no rival." Among the low income peoples of the world, 90 percent have rice as their primary or secondary food.

WARDA has investigated numerous areas in an attempt to increase rice production in West Africa and has been winning the support of many governments. More countries are realizing their potentials for rice production, given the research results published by this association. These countries have been ready to contribute to the success of WARDA with the expectation of benefits. The training programs undertaken by WARDA have been a positive step towards overcoming the problem of manpower. With better financial resources, improved training programs would benefit this effort.

On the whole, WARDA has succeeded in proving to the world, and especially to the low income countries in Africa, that science has had a role in helping subsistence rice farmers to increase their output. With the introduction of scientific methods in subsistence agriculture, many problems have been eliminated and output has increased with the positive effect of increasing the moral of farmers. Moreover, through WARDA, Africa has focused attention, not only on the technological problems, but also on the rice production problems of farmers.

6. Multinational Program and Operational Center (MULPOC)

The Multinational Program and Operational Center (MULPOC) was organized under the auspices of the Economic Commission for Africa (ECA) and is based in Niamey. The inaugural meeting of MULPOC took place on May 29-31, 1978. The meeting occurred at three levels: the meeting of officials, the meeting of senior intergovernmental organizations, and the meeting of ministers. The membership comprised all ECOWAS member states; and financial support is to be received from donor countries and the United Nations Development Program (UNDP). The latter has committed itself to a $200,000 U.S. annual contribution up to 1981. MULPOC's major objective is to "promote inter-country cooperation through identification and implementation of multi-sectoral and operational projects."

The work program of MULPOC commenced with the commissioning of research projects. Research is contemplated in the following areas: the promotion of trade among countries of

West Africa, for which detailed import and export profiles of each country were to be provided; the feasibility of a multinational coastal shipping line and the creation of a West African Multinational Shipping Company; the promotion of African owned multinational road transport companies. In the area of industry, research is planned with respect to the promotion of industrial development with specific reference to basic industries, such as multinational fertilizer plants, and to industrial development with specific reference to basic industries, such as multinational iron and steel complex.

It has not been difficult for those who are familiar with the details of the ECOWAS research projects on trade, customs and tariffs, transportation and communication, and general economic survey to recognize that the MULPOC research areas are a sub-set of the entire ECOWAS research endeavor. There have been a number of other similarities. Trade, customs and tariff, and the transport and communications research projects of ECOWAS were commissioned to ECA. In fact, some of the results of these projects have been made available. Also, ECOWAS has received financial and technical support from the UNDP - from the same source as the ECA.

In view of the very important role which the ECA played in the founding of ECOWAS, why has MULPOC's program competed so strongly with ECOWAS' and why has ECA appeared to be engaging in a supplication of ECOWAS efforts. There has existed an urgent need for both ECOWAS and ECA to cooperate in their efforts to raise the standard of living in the West African sub-region. Any apparent conflicts and duplication of the efforts of the two regional organizations in the areas of trade, customs and tariffs, transportation, and communication should be resolved.

7. Other Bilateral Organizations

Apart from the intergovernmental organizations briefly examined above, West- African states at the bilateral and multilateral levels, have made attempts to coordinate their efforts and policies to implement certain economic ventures. Examples of such attempts abound in the sub-region.

The Ghana Volta River Authority (mentioned earlier), has concluded arrangements within Benin and Togo by which Benin would procure hydro-electric power from the Ghana Volta River Authority.6 Nigeria and Guinea have all agreed to develop bauxite mining in Guinea. Along the same vein, Nigeria and Benin have implemented a sugar project that will cost about N80 million with a production capacity of over 300,000 metric tons of sugar a year.[7]

There were similar undertakings in the areas of transportation and communication. The goals of the Dakar-Ndjamena Highway Coordinating Committee, with headquarters in Addis Ababa have been planning, building, and maintaining the Dakar-Ndjamena Road. Also, the Port Management of West and Central Africa has had a large membership of 14 states who are concerned with improving and standardizing harbor operations in the two Africa sub-regions. For purposes of building and maintaining a telecommunications network in Africa, the PanAfrican Telecommunication (PANAFTEL) inaugurated in 1981, has been the Senegalese link with Mali, Niger, Upper Volta and Benin and has covered 1,600,000 miles and 60 relay stations.[8]

It should be noted that there are other attempts, both regional and sub-regional, at cooperation in the areas of insurance, commerce, education and banking. There have been similar attempts among African producers of export crops. For example, exporting states have combined efforts either within the framework of UNCTAD or through such limited producers' associations as the African Groundnut Council, Cocoa Producers' Alliance, or Inter-African Coffee Organization to seek and insure higher and more stable prices in the international markets.

8. Conclusion

It has been apparent that African states at both bilateral and multilateral levels have exhibited reluctance in some areas of economic cooperation in order to minimizes conflicts and, at the same time, preserves the economic sovereignty of participating member states. Unfortunately, the exercise of such sovereign rights has not precluded the heavy dependence of the African states upon foreign capital, technical experts, and technology for the implementation of many of the programs initiated by the organizations.

Footnotes

1. Secretariat Generale de l'OCAM, Annual Report, 1966, p.6.

2. Africa Research Bulletin, August 15, 1974, p.60

3. West Africa, August 13-19, 1974 and Le Moniteur Africaine August 15, 1974, p.51

4. Marches Tropicaux et Mediterranean, December 19, 1975,p.35

5. Ibid, p.37

6. West Africa, No. 3346, September 14, 1981, p. 215.

7. African Research Bulletin, July 15-14, August, 1976, p. 3962.

8. West Africa, No.3361, January 4, 1982, p.56.

TABLE 5.1. ECONOMIC INDICATORS OF ENTENTE COUNCIL STATES

COUNTRY	POPULATION (000)	GNP US $ (M)	POPULATION GROWTH RATES 1960-72	1965-72
Niger	4,250	4,004	-0.4	-5.1
Dahomey	2,860	300	0.9	1.7
Upper Volta	5,613	400	0.9	0.6
Ivory Coast	5,400	1,840	4.2	4.1
Togo	2,050	330	4.9	3.3

Source: World Bank Reports.

TABLE 5.2. OCAM: ECONOMIC INDICATORS (1960-1972)

COUNTRY	POPULATION (000)	GNP US ($) Ms.	POPULATION GROWTH RATES 1960-72	1965-72
BENIN	300	110	0.9	1.7
GABON	494	440	7.0	10.0
IVORY COAST	5,400	1,840	4.2	4.1
TOGO	2,052	330	4.9	3.3
SENEGAL	3,990	1,050	-0.8	-0.7
UPPER VOLTA	5,613	400	0.9	0.6
NIGER	4,250	400	-0.4	-5.1
CENTRAL AFRICAN REPUBLIC	1,673	260	2.2	2.3
RWANDA	3,904	250	-0.4	2.1
MAURITIUS	849	250	-0.2	0.0

Source: World Bank, 1974

TABLE 5.3. FINANCIAL ASSISTANCE RECEIVED BY TROPICAL AFRICAN STATES OF FRENCH COLONIAL LEGACY FROM THE EEC (US $ MILLIONS)

COUNTRY	1964-1969	1970-1975
FRANCE	246.5	298.5
WEST GERMANY	246.5	298.5
ITALY	100.0	140.6
BELGIUM	69.0	80.6
LUXEMBERG	2.0	2.4
OTHERS	--	--

Source: ECEAO, Rapport d'Activite 1964-1975 and Quarterly Economic Review, Former French West Africa and Togo Annual Supplement, 1969.

Chapter VI

Economic Organizations With Broad Objectives

1. Introduction

The main efforts for economic cooperation in West Africa were centered in the French speaking states. Several organizations which were formed under Equatorial and West African Francophone states provided a picture of regional integration of the economy of former French colonies. Since independence two specific attempts have been made by West African States to forge a cooperative effort to integrate the economy along somewhat broader regional lines. The West African Economic Community (CEAO), and the Economic Community of West African States (ECOWAS) have both had wide ranging economic objectives.

2. West African Economic Community (CEAO)

The West African Economic Community (Communaute Economique de l'Afrique de l'Ouest, or CEAO), the oldest economic organization existing within the Economic Community of West African States (ECOWAS), was launched in 1970 by a protocol agreement in Bamako, Mali. The Treaty setting up the regional organization was signed in June 1972 by the French-speaking West African States of Upper Volta, Senegal, Niger, Mauritania, Mali and the Ivory Coast. This organization was a by-product of many previous attempts at regional cooperation.

Prior to the creation of CEAO, there existed the Federation of French West Africa which was dissolved in 1958; the Mali Federation created in 1959, by Dahomey (now Benin), Senegal, Mali, and Upper Volta; and the Council de l'Entente, the brainchild of the Ivory Coast with Upper Volta, Niger and Benin.

There was also the more ambitious organization of the West African Customs Union (UDEAO) with Benin, the Ivory Coast, Mauritania, Niger, Togo, Senegal, and Upper Volta. It was set up in 1962, with the objective of preserving intra-regional pre-independence economic links. The Convention of UDEAO provided for a free movement of goods between the member states, and for an equitable distribution of customs revenue derived from imports originating from nonmember countries. Due to the narrow tax base of some members and the heavy reliance on customs revenues, many difficulties arose over the administration of common customs duties and the subsequent criteria for the distribution of the revenues among the states. Despite the attempts made to revise the Convention in 1966, to alleviating these problems, the situation grew worse as the member countries unilaterally imposed domestic taxes and import controls.

In the long-run, all the member states of the UDEAO came to discover that the organization did not foster the development of inter-state trade and economic cooperation. It became increasingly necessary to find a lasting and effective solution to the growing economic and social inequalities and conflicts among the member states. The reduction of interstate customs barriers only encouraged the concentration of productive activities in the economically developed states. The pre-union economic inequality was aggravated instead of eliminated.

As a result of these problems, UDEAO collapsed and was replaced by CEAO following the signing of the annexed protocols in April 1973. The newly established organization began to function on January 1, 1974. It was envisaged that CEAO would mature into a full customs union by 1986 while the 15 year preliminary period projected for ECOWAS placed its maturity into a customs union by 1990. To the extent that the primary objective of CEAO was to foster the balanced development of its member states, it appeared that its existence would enhance the common intra-regional administration, economic, political, cultural and colonial links which existed before independence.[1]

Understanding the pre-community economic setting against which the organization was formed, the features the development indicates, and the economic and social differences among the members would provide an appreciation of the basis of the fundamental objectives and goals of CEAO.

As indicated, the West African Economic Community (CEAO), was formed as a subunit within ECOWAS. Covering an area of 3,861,900 km, CEAO has a potential market size of approximately 26 million people, with a GNP of $4,252 billion (U.S.) in 1972. Upper Volta, with the largest population of 5.6 million, had a per capita GDP of only $70 while Mauritania, with the smallest population, had a per capita of $190, more than double that of Upper Volta.[2] (Table 7)

The economies of the member states have remained largely competitive with the production of:

(a) coffee in Ivory Coast and Upper Volta,
(b) cotton in Mali and Upper Volta,
(c) groundnuts in Mali, Niger, Senegal, Upper Volta,and
(d) mineral products of iron-ore, uranium, and phosphates in Mauritania, Niger, and Senegal.

Despite this competitive nature, Senegal and the Ivory Coast, the two most economically developed members, together accounted for more that 50 percent of the CEAO's GDP in 1972. Their individual GNP per capita of $270 and $360, respectively, more than tripled that of some of the poorer states like Mali, Niger, and Upper Volta. It appeared that these disparities between the per capita incomes were not reduced under the UDEAO. According to an EEC study undertaken in 1967, the per capita GNP in the monetized sector was estimated to average 19,500 francs CFA for the grouping (CEAO) as a whole, while the Ivory Coast and Senegal produced 47,000 Francs CFA and 36,000 Francs CFA, respectively.[3]

Furthermore, of the 470,000 industrial wage earners in the entire CEAO, the Ivory Coast and Senegal accounted for 304,000 or 65 percent. Abidjan (Ivory Coast) and Daker (Senegal) together accounted for approximately 44 percent of the manufacturing units established in the region, and 60 percent of the electrical power generated and consumed for industrial use in 1960. With the exception of Mauritania, where mining has been a major economic activity, the ratio of total output in the secondary sector (mining, manufacturing, construction, handicraft and power) to GDP was highest in the Ivory Coast and Senegal (16 percent).[4]

The continuous existence of the more advanced and the less developed economies within the CEAO has raised serious problems of instability particularly when the poorer states have subsidized the richer ones by purchasing their higher priced goods rather than importing similar products from third countries.[5]

The competitive nature of these economies and the predominance of subsistence farming has subjected their intra-regional and external trade, to domination by agricultural and livestock products. Although pre-community inter-state trade more than doubled between 1966 and 1970 (Table 8), trade liberalization under the UDEAO led to an asymmetrical pattern of exchange in which the more industrialized states like the Ivory Coast and Senegal exported far more to the less developed states than they imported. The intra-regional trade balance for the less developed states worsened.

This is surely unsatisfactory from the point of view of the less developed states, considering the fact that intra-regional trade was the most visible indicator of inequality in the distribution of benefits in the UDEAO. This trend accounted for the defection of Benin and Togo from the CEAO. Ndongko and Vivekananda writes:

> "It should be noted, however, that even such informal cooperation would raise grave problems as in the case of UDEAC. There is a basic anti-thesis between, on the one hand, stimulating existing geographic centers in which infrastructure investment is already available (like Cameroon) and which the background for self-sustaining cumulative progress has been created and might trigger off such progress. On the other hand, a program aimed at coming to the rescue, for humanitarian reasons, of the worst areas (like the Chad and Central African Republic) because of the impact of free international trade between unequal partners. So the same effect can be observed in intra-regional trade, or even within the regions of one country ". [5a]

The main export items consisted of groundnuts and groundnut oil, coffee, cocoa, tropical woods, palm products, beef cattle, and as far as mineral products are concerned, iron ore and phosphates. During the period 1961-1966, groundnuts and phosphates accounted for 85 percent of Senegal's exports, iron ore represented 90 percent of Mauritania's total exports, groundnuts and livestock accounted for more than 80 percent of Niger's exports and 50 percent of the exports of Upper Volta were accounted for by livestock. (Table 9)

Agricultural products received higher prices in the French market than in the international market before the creation of the CEAO,. Such pricing policies gave financial advantages to the member states and stimulated their exports.

The French price-support scheme was replaced by EEC aid, which was intended to increase productivity and to diversify production in the area. Increasing importance was attached to new crops such as cotton in Niger, Dahomey, and Mali and to staples such as rice.

The imports commodity distribution in the CEAO member states was dominated by foodstuffs and manufactured goods. These accounted for over 68% of the total imports between 1961 and 1966. Specifically, foodstuffs, beverages, and tobacco averaged 28 percent of the total imports. Despite the fact that imports of capital goods increased at an annual rate of 7 percent of total imports, they averaged about 25 percent of the total imports during this period. (Table 10) "The considerable expenditures on consumer goods was the reason for the increased production of import substitution goods within the grouping and the expansion of intra-regional trade in food stuffs and manufactures."[6]

A considerable proportion of the external trade of the member states is with the EEC and with France. The external trade with the EEC between 1962 and 1966 averaged 68 percent.[7] The proportion of member states' imports from France actually declined from 69 percent in 1961 to 49 percent in 1966 and the proportion of exports decreased from 71 percent to 53 percent. The Ivory Coast and Senegal, the economically advanced member states, accounted for approximately 80 percent of the CEAO's trade with France.[8]

This brief examination of the salient economic features of the member states has revealed the extreme, continuous economic dominance of the Ivory Coast and Senegal in respect to GDP, GDP per capita, intra-regional and external trade as compared to the other states in the CEAO. This situation has had a tremendous impact on shaping the objectives, the various policy instruments, and the institutions of the CEAO since it was created in 1972.

As with other existing regional economic organizations in West Africa, the dominant goal of the CEAO has been to encourage and foster the economic and social development of its member states and that of the collective community as a whole. The objectives of the CEAO have attempted to overcome the short-comings of the UDEAO.

The specific objectives of the CEAO have been:

(i) an organized commercial zone to substitute for the progressive/proportional linear reduction of import duties and of taxes that existed in the defunct UDEAO;
(ii) initiating intervention to establish an active, prosperous, balanced regional market to generate benefits to all members of the community and to the collective;
(iii) a free market for products or commodities that have comparable production potentials, except for the existing domestic (natural) taxes on certain local products or imported goods;
(iv) a system for cattle and meat that prevented import from third or non-member countries and was subject to a 'single tax' system.
(v) a preferential system of industrial products originating from the member states subjected to only the Regional Cooperation Tax (la Taxe de Cooperation Regionale - TCO) that substitutes for all external taxes;
(vi) a unified regional common market to be regulated by a progressive customs tariff with a common fiscal system to improve commercial relations with third countries;
(vii) the compensation of deficits in revenue from imported industrial goods produced within the zone of the special preferential systems; and
(viii) an active regional policy of economic cooperation to encourage and facilitate the development of transportation and industrialization to take advantage of the increased market size of the community.

The institutions of the CEAO have included the Conference of the Heads of States and Governments, the highest branch; the Council of Ministers with two ministers from each state; the General Secretariat with the Industrial Development, Trade

Promotion, Agricultural Development and Community Office for Cattle and Meat departments; and an Arbitration Court for regulating economic and social disparities between member states.

The budget is approved each year by the Conference of the Heads of States. The receipts, or revenues, from contributions of member states for the first four years (1974 - 1978) were: the Ivory Coast 35.1 percent, Senegal 35.1 percent, Niger 9.6 percent, Mali 8.5 percent, Upper Volta 6.4 percent, and Mauritania 5.3 percent. The budget is augmented or increased by subventions from member states, non-member states, bilateral and multilateral organizations, and by loans.

Permits for the financing of development projects and programs of the community are granted by the Community Fund for Development. Resources for the fund are collected from import revenues from each member state and from external aid. The share contribution of each state to the fund has been a function of the value of industrial products exported to other member states. The size of the fund and the share contribution of each state are fixed by the Conference of the Heads of States.

New structures planned were the Community Office for Agricultural Development (Bureau Communautaire du Developpement Agricole - BCDA); a Community Office for Cattle and Meat (l'Office Communautaire du Betail et de la Viande - OCBV); an Interstate Statistical Service to coordinate all national customs codes and statistics; and an Interstate Accounting Agency to centralize the contributions to the Community Fund, to make quarterly payments, and to regulate expenditures on development programs.

A Community Office for Industrial Development responsible for identifying and studying projects of interest to at least two member states was to be set up. This office was to find promoters and the necessary finances, with the assistance of the Development Fund, in the form of grants, capital participation of not less that 29 percent of that of the company undertaking the industrial investment, and medium and long-term loans.

A Community Office for the Promotion of Trade, responsible particularly for acting as a liaison with competent national bodies for the export of commodities to third countries, was to be established with the assistance of the Community Fund for Development. A Community Plan for the Development of Transport and Communications was planned. Also, appointments to technical committees within the General Secretariat were to be made by member states and by the Secretary General.

The protocols of the treaty are concerned with the technical aspects of cooperation and of the functioning of the community. They are concerned with the production and commercialization of cattle and meat, the promotion of agricultural development, industrial development and trade, cooperation in the areas of transport and statistics, customs procedures applicable to the circulation of goods within the community, and the financial and accounting rules relating to the functioning of the community.

The provisions of the treaty were to be progressively applied. The treaty was ratified by the end of 1972, and it came into force on January 1, 1973. The other provisions came into force on the following dates: January 1, 1974, the Regional Cooperation Tax, the Unified Statistical and Customs Code, and the customs procedures defined by an Annex Protocol; January 1, 1976, the harmonization of customs legislation and regulations and the taxes on importations; January 1, 1985, the establishment of a Common External Tariff.

Several important considerations should be kept in mind when attempting to analyze the performance of CEAO. First, the signatories to the Bamako Treaty and the protocols, individually and collectively, professed to expand their national markets through the progressive elimination of tariff barriers to interstate trade within the community. Second, they professed to ensure the gradual integration of their national economies through a new, active regional policy of economic cooperation particularly in industrial, commercial, customs and transportation development based on the reciprocity of benefits and costs. Third, it was recognized by the CEAO that any progress towards effective economic cooperation within the community could only be accomplished by considering the economic situation and the individual interests of each state. Finally, the participation of each state was to enable it to realize the expected benefits from the community.

The allocation of expenditures between recurrent and capital budgets of the Secretariat for the period from 1974 to 1979 (Table 6.5) reflect a considerable proportion of the capital budget has been devoted to the construction of the CEAO General Secretariat building, i.e., 450 million francs CFA in 1974 and 986 million in 1976. Substantial subventions were made by the Ivory Coast (500million Frs. CFA) and Senegal (200 million Frs. CFA) in 1977 for this project.

International aid has consisted notably of UNPD (126 million, for the period 1978 - 1980), UNIDO assistance (valued at 285 million for 1978 - 1981), and the International Trade Center (14 million for OCPE).

Capital expenditures between 1974 and 1979, more than quadrupled while those of the recurrent budget tripled because it has been necessary to ensure the normal evolution of the community. The allocation of budgetary contributions by each member state in 1979 was as follows: 28 percent for the Ivory Coast, 22 percent for Senegal, and 10.5 percent each for Mali, Mauritania, Niger and Upper Volta. The provisional amount of 1,092 million Frs. for the first phase of construction of the CEAO Secretariat was made in January 1979. The amount for the 2nd and 3rd phases was estimated in June 1979 at 2,350 million CFA Frs. (Table 6.5)

The organization and promotion of interstate trade has been the major objective of the CEAO. The CEAO created a community market with a common external tariff. Two categories of products have dominated interstate trading relations.

(a) Unprocessed products produced by the member states with no industrial character. This class of products has circulated in the community and has been subjected to all taxes (except domestic taxes, specific or ad valorem tax). The list of the unprocessed products, which has been modified from time to time by the Council of Ministers, consisted of: coffee, grain or millets, pear, wood and cotton, natural phosphates, petrol, and rubber. Such products as cattle and meat have had a special protocol agreement.

(b) Industrial products produced by more than one enterprise in the Community are subject to a double tax system called preferential tax system is the Regional Cooperation Tax. The rates have differed from one state to another. The Regional Cooperation Tax (RCT) came into force on 1st January 1976, and was fixed for 200 products and groups of products. For example, the rate of RCT for beer, fixed in June 1975, is presented in Table 6.6.

Interstate trade in industrial products had expanded considerably by the end of 1976, with the Ivory Coast and Senegal accounting for about 20 billion francs CFA out of a total of 20.8 billion francs CFA. The value of the total exports and imports of each member state in 1976 is presented in the Table 6.7.

By December 1978, some 618 industrial products were produced by 175 enterprises or companies and were subject to the Regional Cooperation Tax (94 were allocated in the Ivory Coast, 56 in Senegal, and none in Mauritania). A detailed analysis of the number of industrial products produced in the member states under the various agreements relating to different groups or categories of products is presented in Table 6.8. The Ivory Coast and Senegal were the major producers, while the rest of the member states were the main consumers.

The Committee of Exports in June 1978, extended the same tariff or tax rate of unprocessed products to traditional crafts effective January 1, 1979. Due consideration was given to the existing protocol-agreement between Senegal and the Ivory Coast signed on January 1, 1974. The list of unprocessed products (which appear as Annex H of the CEAO Treaty) had been extended by October 1979 to include other products such as live animals, meat, fish, milk, legumes, fruits, green coffee, tea, cereals garri, cocoa, tobacco, salt and hydrocarbons. In addition, by the end of the same year, approximately 188 enterprises were producing goods which were subject to the Regional Cooperation Tax. The distribution of these enterprises between the member states of CEAO is shown in Table 15.

The complete elimination of tariff barriers between the member states, was to be reduced to a zero rate in twelve years time. To this extent, the reduction of the RCT rates, in respect to ordinary soap produced by CPCN for some member states by the end of 1979, is presented in Table 6.9. By December 1979, the special agency, the Community Office for the Promotion of Trade (l'Office Communautaire de Promotion des Exchanges - OCPE) had been established to carry out the functions of disseminating information, publicity and assisting national centers of external trade.

The revenues derived from the RCT by the community increased from 4 billion Frs. CFA in 1976, to 14.5 billion Frs. CFA in 1979. This was an increase of 240 percent during the first four years of the introduction of the tax. The number of products to which the tax was subjected increased from 472 in 1978, to 503 in 1979 i.e. an increase of 44 percent. The harmonization of all customs tariffs of the member states previewed for January 1, 1980, was effectively implemented by that date. The establishment of a common fiscal and customs tariff system for the community has been instituted since January 1, 1986.

It will be recalled that the resources of this fund were to come from customs duties on imports of each member state and also from external aid. The resources of the fund were to be used to subsidize state budgets, to establish enterprises in member states upon their request and to help those states which had suffered from the negative economic and social impact of the creation of the community. The resources of the fund for 1975 and 1976, came from the annual contribution of member states and were determined by the magnitude of their participation in the community's trade in industrial products. These amounted to 1,054,7 million frs. CFA and 2,280 million Frs., respectively. (Table 6.10)

Part of the fund was used to compensate those states that had lost customs revenue as a result of the introduction of the RCT, and part was used to carry out feasibility studies of possible community projects which were to be located in the less developed members of the regional grouping. For example, the total amount of the first fund (1975) of 1,0547 million frs. CFA was devoted uniquely to the study of 35 agricultural and industrial development projects in some member states and the community. An analysis of the allocation of the Fund's resources between the different projects is presented in Table 6.12.

The resources of the second fund (1976) amounting to 2,280.0 millions frs. were utilized as follows: 1,520.0 million Frs CFA for compensation for loss of customs revenue; 38.0 million for 'Tiers Restant'; and 720.0 million for the building of the General Secretariat. The remaining sum of 650 million Frs. CFA was distributed among the less developed members of the community as shown in Table 6.13. The resources of the Third and Fourth Community Fund for Development, and the contributions of the member states for the years 1977 and 1978 are presented in Table 6.14. Between 1976 and 1978, the amounts of 858.0 million frs CFA and 1,532.0 million Frs CFA (i.e. a total of 2,390.0 million Frs CFA) respectively were used to compensate the member states of the CEAO for loss of customs revenue as shown in Table 6.15.

The balance of the fund, in 1977 and 1978, was earmarked for feasibility studies of community projects, the offices of the General Secretariat, study of development possibilities in the four less industrialized states of Niger, Mali, Upper Volta and Mauritania. Some of the resources of the fund for the years 1976 and 1977 were distributed among the less industrialized member states of the Community as shown in Table 6.16.

The resources of the Community Fund for Development between 1979 and 1980, increased from 4,203 million Frs. CFA to 6,760.0 million Frs. CFA, (i.e. an increase of 60 percent). Approximately 2,802.0 million Frs. CFA and 4,506.0 million frs CFA were set aside in 1979 and 1980, respectively, for compensation of those member states whose economies had been disrupted as a result of the creation of the community. The resources for the feasibility studies of Community projects and programs, offices of the General Secretariat and development possibilities in the four less industrialized states increased from 1,401 million Frs CFA in 1979 to 2,253 million Frs. CFA in 1980.

Economic cooperation between the CEAO member states has taken place in several areas. Total grants in the amount of 1,283 million Frs. CFA were allocated to the Community Office for Agricultural Development between 1975 and 1978. Of this amount, 297.7 million went to Upper Volta, 214.8 million to Mali, 201.5 million to Mauritania and 514 million to Niger. In addition, a three year investment program (1979 - 1981) of 1,587 million Frs. CFA, was adopted at Bamako by the 4th Conference of the

Heads of State in October 1978 with 1,377 million allocated for food production, 100 million for hydrology and 109 million for various programs.

An initial allocation of 21.5 million CFA Francs was allotted to the Community Office for Industrial Development, charged with the responsibility for implementing and coordinating the studies of different projects such as mill technology, solar energy and the exploitation of the phosphates at Boureun. An initial allocation of 21.5 million Frs. was allocated for the office. A Three Year Program (1979-81) at the cost of 864 million francs was initiated with 100 million CFA Francs earmarked for the school of textiles, 300 million CFA Francs for the school of mines, 154 million CFA Francs for intervention programs, 60 million CFA Francs for the pharmaceutical industry and 30 million CFA Francs for mill technology.

The Community Office for Cattle and Beef was allocated the sum of 748 million CFA Francs between 1975 and 1978. Of this amount, some 370 million CFA Francs was earmarked for cattle development and 170 million CFA Francs for animal health. The Community Office was created and charged with the responsibility of a realistic study of a project for the creation of a Community company for the purchase and commercialization of fish products in Mauritania, and also fish breeding ponds at Natio Kobadara near Bouake.

During the three year period (1975-1977), a total amount of 1,661 million was allocated to Mali, Niger, Mauritania and Upper Volta. The actual payments to Mauritania and Upper Volta were below the percentage average of the four less developed states taken together. (see the enclosed table).

Cooperation in the domain of rural development was accelerated by the Department of Rural Development (in the General Secretariat) which regrouped three defunct agencies - the Community Office for Rural Development, the Community Office for Cattle and Beef, and the Community Office for Fish Products. With respect to the defunct Community Office for Rural Development, the three Year Program (1978 - 1981) envisaged an expenditure of 1,587 million CFA Francs with 1,200 million CFA Francs was for cereal production, 109.5 million CFA Francs to assist production cooperatives and 100 million CFA Francs for the hydraulic program.

Eighty six percent of the financing of the former Community Office for Cattle and Beef was achieved between 1979 and 1981 as compared with 79 percent during the period 1978 - 1979. Actual expenditures on beef marketing was 417.5 million CFA Francs; 149 million CFA Francs on animal health, 122 million CFA Francs on feed lots in Mali; 35 million CFA Francs for study of a Stabilization Fund for the prices of cattle and beef.

Created during the 3rd Conference of the Heads of States in June 1977, at Abidjan, the Solidarity Fund began operating in June 1979. The resources of the Fund were initially fixed at 5 million Francs CFA for the years 1977 and 1978. They were later reduced to 1.5 million for the year 1979, and then increased to 8 million for 1980. The total share contributions of the member states is presented in Table 6.17.

The main function of this fund was to guarantee loans for all profitable projects. The first effective program of intervention in five states began in July, 1980. (Table 6.18). All of the member states except the Ivory Coast benefited from the Solidarity Fund. Upper Volta, Mali, Mauritania and Niger, the four less developed states together received some 94.56 percent of the allocation while Senegal, the only developed state which benefited, received 5.44 percent.

Clearly, Senegal and the Ivory Coast have made considerable financial sacrifices with a view to ensuring a balanced development of the CEAO community. At the same time, these advanced states have produced the largest share of the products consumed by the less developed members of the Community. The choice of effective policy instruments and institutions by CEAO member states and the common historical, administrative, colonial and economic experiences have largely accounted for the viability and stability of the Community since its creation in 1972.

3. Economic Community of West African States (ECOWAS)

The birth of ECOWAS was the result of numerous efforts to establish an economic community in West Africa. These efforts were started by the late President Tubman of Liberia who first put forward the call for free trade on January 7th, 1964, to the Ivory Coast, Guinea, and Sierra Leone. A number of bilateral and multilateral discussions took place at the ministerial level among representatives of Ivory Coast, Liberia, Sierra Leone and Guinea who met in Monrovia, on August 24th, 1964, and agreed to appoint a committee of experts and ministers to examine this proposal.

The ministerial report which was discussed at a meeting in Monrovia during February, 1965, accepted the report and approved the idea. The result was the appointment of "an interim organization for economic cooperation" to establish a permanent organization for West African Economic Cooperation. This agreement was signed in Freetown (Sierra Leone) on May 28th, 1965. The interim organization was given the task of the "establishment of a Multi-lateral System of Economic Cooperation of a regional character with a view to removing trade barriers and encouraging the harmonious development of the respective states."[9]

The Interim Organization commissioned ten studies in the following areas:

(1) studies on economic development targets of the cooperating states with specific reference to agricultural and industrial development;
(2) studies concerned with trade and customs problems;
(3) studies regarding markets and marketing difficulties;
(4) studies concerned with monetary, financial, and payment arrangements;
(5) studies into the existing fiscal system;
(6) studies concerning barriers to economic cooperation;
(7) studies concerning the harmonization of economic and political commitments of member states to other states and international institutions with the requirements of economic cooperation among the parties;
(8) studies concerning the allocation of industrial and agricultural projects of area importance among the cooperating states; and
(9) studies to determine the most suitable type of economic cooperation for the contracting parties.

The Administrative Secretariat of the Interim Organization opened in Monrovia in September, 1965, with Mr. Donald George as the Administrative Secretary.[10] The United Nations Economic Commission for Africa organized two sub regional meetings, one in Niamey (Niger) from October 10-22, 1966, and the other in Accra (Ghana) between April 27- May 4, 1967. The Articles of Association were discussed at the Niamey meeting the. At the Accra meeting, on May 4, the draft of the Articles of Association of the proposed economic community was signed. The signatories were: Dahomey, Ghana, the Ivory Coast, Liberia, Mali, Mauritania, Niger, Nigeria, Senegal, Sierra Leone, Togo, and Upper Volta. Gambia later joined the Community.

The Articles of Association provided a framework for the Interim Organization for the drafting and ratifying of a treaty establishing the Economic Community of West Africa. The Articles of Association [11] carried the three articles of critical importance.

Article 1
Aims of the Community

A. The aims of the Community shall be:

(1) to promote through the economic cooperation of the member states a coordinated and equitable development of their economies, especially in industry, agriculture, transport and communications, trade and payments, manpower, energy and natural resources;

(2) to further the maximum possible interchange of goods and services among its member states;

(3) to contribute to the orderly expansion of trade between the member states and the rest of the world;

(4) by all these efforts and endeavors to contribute to the economic development of the continent of Africa as a whole.

Article 2
General Undertakings

A. In order to achieve the aims of the Community, the member states shall:

(1) work in close cooperation with one another and endeavor to coordinate and harmonize their economic policies both within and outside the community;

(2) keep each other informed and furnish the community with the information required for the achievement of its aims;

(3) within the community, establish among themselves consultations on a continuous basis and carry out studies in order to determine the areas and lines of economic development to be undertaken jointly or in common;

(4) negotiate within the community the progressive elimination of customs and other barriers to the expansion of trade between them as well as restrictions on current payment transactions and on capital movement;

(5) take measures which render their products relatively competitive with goods imported from outside the community and seek to obtain more favorable conditions for their products in the world market;

(6) endeavor to formulate and adopt common policies, and negotiate and conclude agreements among themselves or through the medium of the Community, designed to serve the achievement of its aims; including the development jointly or in common of specific transport and communications services, the development and the joint use of energy, joint research, training of manpower and the implementation jointly or in common of all other projects designed to promote the objectives of the community, as well as common trade and payments arrangement, and

(7) ensure, both within and outside the community that the common policies that have been adopted and the agreements that have been concluded for the achievement of the aims of the Community are carried out.

B. Member states shall take steps, particularly the provision of budgetary and other resources, required for the implementation of the Decisions and Recommendations of the Community, duly adopted.

Article 3
Cooperation Among Member States and With Other Bodies

A. Individual member states shall be entitled to take, both within and outside the community, measures of economic cooperation without the agreement of other member states, provided that such measures do not prejudice the aims of the Community.

B. Member states which belong to or join other systems of economic cooperation shall inform the Community of their membership and of those provisions in their constituent instruments that have a bearing on the purposes of the Community.

At a meeting of the Interim Council of Ministers held in Dakar (Senegal) on November 21- 24, 1967, a Treaty drafted by an ECA consultant was discussed.[12] The underlying concept of the Treaty was to develop cooperation among member states in all fields. At a Heads of State meeting held in Monrovia between April 23 and 24, 1968, the ECA Secretariat presented *inter alia* the Treaty establishing the West African Economic Community.

Following a number of diplomatic moves initiated jointly by Togo and Nigeria between 1968 and 1972, proposals for the creation of the Economic Community of West African States (ECOWAS) were drawn up by the Ministers for the Lome meeting in December 1973. This meeting was attended by delegates from Dahomey, Gambia, Ghana, Guinea, Guinea-Bissau, the Ivory Coast, Liberia, Mali, Mauritania, Niger, Nigeria, Senegal, Sierra Leone, Togo and Upper Volta.[13]

There was general agreement at this meeting of the basic principles of a sub regional economic community including trade liberalization, removal of customs barriers, harmonization of financial and monetary policies, the efficient utilization of national resources, infrastructural links, communications and energy resources, raising the standard of living, increasing and maintaining economic stability, fostering closer relations among its members, and of contributing to the economic development of the African continent.

ECOWAS was created on May 28, 1975, in Logos, when the Heads of States and Governments of all the 15 West African States signed the Treaty. The signatories to the Treaty: Dahomey, Gambia, Ghana, Guinea, Guinea-Bissau, the Ivory Coast, Liberia, Mali, Mauritania, Niger, Nigeria, Senegal, Sierra Leone, Togo and Upper Volta. These countries represented an economic linkage between former Anglophone and Francophone colonies and the dependants of West Africa. By the early part of July, 1975, the ECOWAS Treaty had come into effect after ratification by the following member states: Nigeria, Liberia, Togo, Ghana, the Ivory Coast, Guinea, Upper Volta, Gambia, Dahomey and Niger.

The 15 member states of ECOWAS constituted the West African subregion as defined by the United Nations Economic Commission for Africa. Together they occupied a geographical area of 6,141,153 sq. km. and shared a total population of approximately 200 million inhabitants in mid 1973. As mentioned in previous chapters they vary both in area and in population.

Gambia, the smallest, has an area of only 11,299 sq. km. and a population of less than half a million. The corresponding figures for Niger are 1,267,000 sq. km. and 4,304 million while Nigeria contains 58.1 percent of the sub region's total population within its 923,768 sq. km.[14]

The countries are poor, with per capita GNP ranging from only $70 in Mali and Upper Volta to over $360 in the Ivory Coast and averaging $184.7 for the entire sub region in 1973. The available data in respect to area, population and per capita GNP as of mid 1973 is presented in Table 6.19.

Agriculture alone accounted for about 39.4 percent of the subregion's GNP in 1971, varying widely from country to country. For example it ranged from 18 percent in Senegal to 53 percent in Nigeria. Only about 9 percent of the GNP of the region was derived from the manufacturing. For states like Gambia and Mauritania, the contribution of manufacturing was as low as 2.3 percent and 2.9 percent, respectively. The products of most of the ECOWAS member states has reduced the possibility of trade is to a very narrow range of goods like oil, mineral ores, coal, livestock, fibers, a few food stuffs, beverages, and a few industrial products. (Table 6.20)

The ECOWAS member states are heavily dependent on foreign trade. In 1971, exports and imports as percentages of GNP averaged 24.4 percent and 23.2 percent, respectively, with individual country figures ranging from 6.3 percent and 19.6 percent for Upper Volta to 51.7 percent and 53.7 percent for the Gambia. (Table 6.21) Primary commodities dominated export trade while manufactures featured prominently in import trade. The bulk of foreign trade has been with the developed countries, particularly those of the enlarged European Economic Community.[15] Only Mali, Upper Volta, Niger and the Gambia have a significant proportion of their trade with other countries of the African sub-region. (Table 6.22) The first three countries are landlocked and a considerable proportion of their intra-West African trade is transit. Gambia is almost surrounded by Senegal causing the same effect.

The paucity of intra-West African trade reflects both the non-complimentary nature of the products of the states and the absence of any official pre-independence, social, political, and economic ties between the French-speaking and English-speaking African states. The roads and railways were designed to remove primary raw materials and crude minerals from the interior of the sub-region for export to Europe during the colonial period. It can be argued that the creation of ECOWAS was based on the considerable potential socio-economic benefits which can accrue to the member states and the collectivity as a whole, following the gradual removal of political, social, economic, cultural and financial obstacles among and between the states.

The institutions of ECOWAS include the supreme authority of the heads of states and government. The Authority has been the "principal governing institution of the community". It has been "responsible for, and has the general direction and control of the performance of the executive functions of the community". The Authority meets once a year, and its decisions are intended to be binding on all the community's institutions.

The Council of Ministers, under the auspices of the Authority, has had the responsibility for keeping "under review the functioning and development of the community" by making recommendations to the authority, and for "giving directions to all subordinate institutions of the community." When the Council of Ministers fails to reach a unanimous decision on a proposal, the proposal is referred to the Authority. The Council of Ministers meets a year, and may call additional meetings..

The ECOWAS Secretariat is headed by an Executive Secretary, the principal executive officer. He serves a term of four years and is responsible for the day-to-day administration of the community. He is assisted by two Deputy Executive Secretaries appointed by the Council of Ministers.

The External Auditor and the Tribunal of the community ensure "the observance of law and justice and the interpretations of the provisions of the Treaty". The four Technical and Specified Commissions are:

(1) the Trade, Customs, Immigration, Monetary and Payments Commission;
(2) the Industry, Agriculture and Natural Resources Commission;
(3) the Transport, Telecommunications and Energy Commission; and
(4) the Social and Cultural Affairs Commission.

The objectives of the community are contained in Article 2 of the Treaty of Lagos. Specifically, it states:

> "It shall be the aim of the community to promote cooperation and development in all fields of economic activity particularly in the fields of industry, transport, telecommunications, energy, agriculture, natural resources commerce, monetary and financial questions and in social and cultural matters for the purpose of raising the standard of living of its peoples, of increasing and maintaining economic stability, of fostering closer relations among its members and of contributing to the progress and development of the African continent."

In line with its objectives, the ECOWAS has briefly outlined priority programs which underscore the importance of collective self-sustaining development based on cooperation among the member states.

The ECOWAS Agricultural Program has had its main objectives the fight against serious food shortages in the West African sub-region, the improvement of rural incomes and living conditions and the provisions of necessary inputs for the Community's industrial program. This has required cooperation in agriculture goals with the exchange of research findings, the formulation of joint programs for both basic and service training, and common agriculture policies in the field of research, training, production, processing and marketing.

The main objective of the food production program has been to alter the present pattern of agricultural production which has been, for the most part, unbalanced in favor of exports, and to bring about qualitative and quantitative improvement in food crop production by replacing a sizeable proportion of the products currently being imported. Agricultural policies of member states are to be harmonized to achieve these objectives.

The policies envisaged under the agricultural plan are associated with:

(a) the preparation, establishment and financing of research programs and projects to improve the genetic potential of food crops;

(b) the effective distribution of suitable agricultural production inputs;

(c) the establishment of a strategic food products storage system and other exports products; and

(d) formulation of sub-regional policies for food loss reduction.

Plans have been for these policies to hopefully lead to the control of famine, the promotion of food crop production, and an increase in the production of other agricultural products.

Concern has been expressed over the low protein intake of the West African population. The main economic activity of wide areas of the sub-region has dealt with livestock. Many obstacles have hampered the yield of livestock production. For these reasons, the ECOWAS food and agricultural program included the development of the livestock industry on a priority basis. The medium-term livestock program included the following:

(a) improvement and development of cattle breeding stations;
(b) improvement in animal health and meat hygiene; and
(c) facilitation of movement and marketing of cattle.

The fishing industry has also received Community attention as a solution to the problem of protein deficiency in the West African diet. Proposed projects are geared toward the development and the improvement of the fishing industry. Emphasis is needed in these projects on the organization of the industry along sub-regional lines since a preliminary study has demonstrated the need for a coordinated approach towards the development of this industry. Some of the activities planned under the medium-term fishing program are:

(a) the establishment of a regional Fishery Research Center;
(b) the establishment of a system of surveillance of territorial waters;
(c) a policy on marine and fresh water fishing; and
(d) a plan for the development of the fish processing industry.

The medium-term forestry program is designed to evaluate the problem of the conservation of natural vegetation cover, the rational use of forest resources, and the aforestation or reforestation of the sub-region. Various attempts are being made by national as well as international institutions to resolve these issues in West Africa. The ECOWAS Forestry Development program has dealt with coordinating these efforts to ensure that projects are properly executed. Among the activities contemplated under the forestry program have been:

(a) the establishment of an advisory board on forestry and wildlife development;
(b) the assessment of the forestry resources of the sub-region; and
(c) location and size of wood-based industries (wood processing, charcoal, pulp and paper, etc).

It has been widely accepted that in regional organizations such as ECOWAS, judicious encouragement of industrial activity is capable of broadening the trade base and thus contributing to the rapid economic development of its member states. ECOWAS has, as one of its major objectives, the development of the industrial sector of the economies of the sub-region. Chapter V of the Treaty emphasized the need for the harmonization of industrial policies and for the establishment of complementary industrial enterprises. The process of establishing regional industrial cooperation and, to an even greater extent, economic integration has had inevitably many obstacles. One such obstacle has been the low level of trade between the countries of the same region. For instance, in the ECOWAS sub-region intra-community trade has been only 4 percent.

Successful industrial cooperation without accelerated industrial growth in the sub-region has appeared impossible. Most integrational groupings among developing countries have come into being primarily as regional commercial arrangements, but while trade liberalization of intra-regional trade is indispensable, it has been an inadequate device for stimulating the process without the simultaneous integration of production. The exchange of goods in the ECOWAS sub-region has depended on the availability of surplus goods over and above the needs of individual member states. The domestically-oriented import substitution strategies currently operating have not generated the needed surpluses for trade expansion because concerted efforts are not made at the community level to integrate production.

Since the Community has attempted to increase the industrial base of member states, the industrial program has tried to arrest the unnecessary competition of uncoordinated industrial policies within the sub-region. The ECOWAS Industrial Program has foreseen the establishment of industrial enterprises whose viability depends on markets larger than the small markets offered by individual member states. To achieve a balanced development and an equitable distribution of the benefits derived from Community action, the allocation of enterprises would be governed mainly by:

(a) the comparative advantage enjoyed by the member state concerned; and

(b) the need to pay special attention to the situation of the least developed member state.

The process of harmonization of industrial development was planned in three stages. The first stage involved the exchange of information such as feasibility studies (evaluation of prospective technical partners and research findings) and the commissioning of joint research projects. Cooperation on the transfer of technology, the development of new products, and the identification of viable projects is envisaged.

The second stage related to the industrial climate in an effort to prevent disruption from dissimilar policies on industrial incentives, company tax, and Africanization. The third stage related to cooperation in the development of manpower. The exchange of skilled, professional and managerial manpower has been encouraged. Member states have planned to provide opportunities in their educational institutions for community citizens.

The rationals, therefore, behind the ECOWAS Industrial Program have been:

(a) the expansion of production opportunities including improved utilization of existing production capacities in the sub-region;

(b) acceleration of the process of industrialization in the sub-region through the promotion of the Community Industrial Program;

(c) improved use of the sub-region resources, reflected in increased efficiency and cost reduction; and

(d) maximization of national income of each member state.

Article 2 of the Treaty of Lagos declared that the aim of the Economic Community of West African States was to promote cooperation and development in all fields of economic activity including industry, agriculture, and commerce. The Community envisaged the establishment of a Customs with a common external tariff, a common commercial policy towards third countries, and the elimination of tariff and non-tariff barriers to trade between member states. Chapter III of the Treaty detailed a 15-year time table for the liberalization of intra-community trade and for the Customs Union.

In a decision of the Authority of the Heads of States and Government in May 1979, member states were to consolidate import duties and non-tariff barriers on goods of Community origin for a period of two years. During this period, the member states were to schedule the reduction and elimination of import duties and non-tariff barriers over the period 1981-1989 in accordance with Article 12, 13, and 18 of the Treaty.

The Authority of the Heads of State and Government in May 1980, adopted the Trade Liberalization Program in conformity with Article 12 and 13 off the Treaty. The program prescribed the total elimination of all tariff barriers to unprocessed products as of May 28, 1981. Community designated priority goods would be liberalized faster by the more industrially advanced member states in all cases; however, all member states would begin the elimination of tariff barriers to industrial products on May 28, 1981, and by May 28, 1989. It was to be completed throughout the Community

In accordance with Article 14 of the Treaty, member states are:
(a) to undertake during the 8 year period beginning 1981, the gradual establishment of a Common Customs Tariff in respect of goods imported into member states from third countries, and
(b) to align their national tariffs with the Common Customs Tariff over the 5-year period beginning May 1988, in accordance with an agreed schedule.

The Authority of the Heads of States and Government has further made decisions to aid the liberalization program. These decisions are the rules of origin for Community Trade Purposes. The rules defined the products originating from member states which qualify for trade liberalization within the Community.

The rules of origin stipulated that goods to be freely traded in the Community must be:

(a) wholly produced, as defined in Article V of the protocol, in a member state; and
(b) produced in a member state other than by any of the operations and processes listed in Article IV of the protocol or with the material from a foreign or undetermined origin whose CIF value does not exceed 60 percent of the total cost of the material employed, or with the material of community origin whose value must not in any case be less than 40 percent of

the total cost of material employed, or with the raw material of community origin representing in quantity at least 60 percent of the whole raw materials used or produced for material of a foreign or undetermined origin and having received in the process of production a value-added of at least 35 percent of the F.O.B. price of the finished product.

A desirable level of indigenous ownership and participation in firms producing goods to be freely traded in Community was also stipulated as well as principles relating to re-exports. A decision was made fixing the desirable level of national participation in the equity capital of industrial enterprises whose products benefited from preferential duty.

As part of the finalization of ECOWAS rules of origin, the Authority has decided that industrial enterprises producing Community originated goods should have the following proportions of their equity capital invested in nations of member states - 20 percent as from May 28, 1981, 35 percent as from May 28, 1983, and 51 percent as from May 28, 1989.

The Authority has adopted a compensation procedure for revenue loss suffered by member states as a result of the implementation of the Trade Liberalization program. The contribution of a member state to the compensation budget would be in relation to its share of intra-community export trade. The Authority also decided to deduct 20 percent of the compensation due to the more industrialized member states (i.e., the Ivory Coast, Ghana, Nigeria, and Senegal) to be allocated to the less industrialized member states over a period of 5 years; thereafter, the 20 percent would be allocated to all member states for another period of 5 years.

As in all regional economic groupings, the main objectives of the ECOWAS Program for trade liberalization was to ensure the development of intra-community trade in a significant manner; and the achievement of a Free Trade Area within an eight year time period between May 1981 and May 1989. The program was intended to contribute to the overall Community objective of a rapid economic development of member states through:

(i) taking advantage of the market potentials which are not available to a single country but only generated by the creation of an economic union; and
(ii) designing and implementing policy measures aimed at ensuring that member states actually do take advantage of such opportunities provided by the Community such as negotiated regional investment, uniform market conditions for the stabilization of competition, harmonized trade-related fiscal policies, negotiated joint trade promotion measures, and development of regional trade-inducing industries.

The Trade Liberalization Program has undoubtedly been the most important activity of the Economic Community of West African States. The sub-regional trade, though limited in volume, has had the potential for the development of intra-community trade from its present low volume. ECOWAS has proposed trade promotion measures to improve market intelligence and market situations.

The ECOWAS Telecommunications Program which forms part of the African Telecommunication Decade was one of the major areas of the priority program activities defined by the Council of Ministers at its meeting in Dakar on November 1979. The program related to the improvement and extensions of the telecommunications network within the sub-region. The priority objectives of the Telecommunications Program were: to open up circuits to members states which have no reliable telecommunications facilities with the outside world; to close discontinuities on existing main Pan African routes; to provide circuits to neighboring member states according to the degree of priority given to national telecommunications; and to recommend ways and means of completing the routes covered in these priorities.

The Authority of the Heads of State and Government established a special fund for the improvement and development of telecommunications within ECOWAS. The special fund had two main objectives:
(1) to guarantee loans requested by member states to develop their telecommunications network; and
(2) to grant subvention to member states who request help for improving the maintenance of telecommunications network

equipment, training and refresher courses for technicians, and procurement of spare parts and measuring instruments.

The ECOWAS Telecommunications Program when fully operational would link the state capitals with more reliable telecommunications systems. The ECOWAS traffic routing plan, which has not become operational, was to ensure transit within the sub-region and the adoption of a uniform system of telephone, telex and telegraph tariffs for intra-community traffic, and to stimulate the development of intra-country trade.

During 1980/81, the problems of the effective implementation of the ECOWAS Telecommunications Program were examined. These were essentially: the technical options for the proposed network; the general and special technical specifications of the tender documents; telecommunications tariffs for the sub-region; an ECOWAS telecommunications routing plan to be gradually established by 1984; the adoption of the Status of the Special Fund for Telecommunications; and the provision of the initial capital which was fixed at $8.5 million, (to be subscribed to in the following manner - $3.5 million to be contributed by member states on the basis of the existing ECOWAS formula and $5 million by the ECOWAS fund.)

As all these measures were accomplished, invitations to tender bids for the supply of equipment and the construction of technical buildings were undertaken during the second half of 1981. Several joint missions were undertaken in connection with the identification of sources of funding by the Secretariat and the ECOWAS Fund. A meeting of the Funding Agencies was held in Freetown on May 20, 1981. At that meeting, the institutions indicated the extent of financial commitments that they were prepared to make towards the funding of ECOWAS programs and of the Telecommunications projects.

Various financial institutions made the following offers:
(a) Commercial Banks BIAO (Paris): $50 million, Morgan Grenfell (London): $8 - 10 million, Credit Bank (Brussels): $20 million Skandinavizka Euskilda Batiken: $5 million, and
(b) the European Development Fund (EDF): $7 million; and

(c) African Development Bank (ADB): $7.7 million. These offers made it possible to proceed with the implementation of the Telecommunications Program as planned.

The ECOWAS Transport Program aimed to the coordination and development of a modern and efficient system of transportation within the West African Sub-region. It was to develop transit between member states of the Community in order to facilitate intra-community economic and social activities. The importance of facilitating the movement of people, goods and services within the Community placed the transport program within the priority program whose other aims related to the free movement of persons and the liberalization of trade. The problems posed by the poor transportation system at the national level gave an indication of the magnitude of the perplexities confronting the Community and necessitated immediate action in order to facilitate the development of the economy of the sub-region.

Transportation has been crucial in national as well as regional economic and social development as it is vital in the inter-related activities of production, distribution, equalization of prices, effective mobility of resources and direct contribution to the gross national product of a country. It provides, through the different modes, effective channels to facilitate the flow of economic and social agents and products within a given economic space. On the other hand, transportation broadens the information base and sphere of use within and beyond the national frontier and effectively reduces the economic space in terms of time.

There is no doubt that an adequate transportation - network is a critical factor in the achievement of the noble objectives of ECOWAS. The attainment of those objectives depends on, among other things, the orientation of the transport network to facilitate effective interaction through trade and other economic exchanges within the sub-region. Having realized the potential of the Community and the vital role that transportation can play in bringing them to fruition, member states have adopted the Transport Program to develop and coordinate the various aspects of transportation in order to break down the colonial legacy which has handicapped economic and social interaction among ECOWAS states.

The Transport Program adopted these strategies: the development and modernization of a transport infrastructure in the sub-region (roads, rail, maritime, river and air transport); transport legislation of member states to facilitate the movement of goods, services and persons; and making land-locked and isolated countries accessible as rapidly as possible.

The completion of the transport program would facilitate the movement of persons, goods and services and remove the main transport obstacles of the sub-region which lie in the present fragmentation of its transport system into sub-systems which are isolated from one another. These systems consisted mainly of access routes from the coasts to the hinterlands. The realization of the program would bring to the Community enormous benefits derived from a comprehensive network of roads, railways, inland water and air connections, which are homogeneous and continuous and ensure easy movement of trade in all directions.

The Transport Program's objectives for the period were carried out. Although the design of the Transport Program involved many different modes, the first phase was on road transport. The Transport Commission agreed on the alignment for the Trans-West African Highways - both the Coastal Lagos-Nouakchott and the Sahelian Dakar-Niamey links. That commission also determined the state of execution of the various stretches.

The National Road Transport Units were organized to supervise road matters including the development of the road sector. The Vienna Conventions on Road Traffic and on road signs were adopted to ensure conformity within the Community and with international practice. Other actions were the adoption of right-hand drive practices throughout the sub-region; progressive introduction of international road signs on all international and national highways; adoption of minimum safety equipment requirements and standardization of equipment; introduction of compulsory periodic vehicle inspection; uniform categorization of driving licenses and harmonization of rules governing the possession of these licenses; types of vehicle documents required for interstate traffic; limits on axle-load for road design and vehicles as a temporary measure pending fuller study; draft ECOWAS Insurance Certificate; draft agreements relating to inter-

State Road Transport and Road Transit; and a mandate to the Executive Secretariat to draft an ECOWAS Highway Code.

In the areas of monetary and fiscal matters, the Community has concentrated on economic and fiscal policies, maintaining balance of payment equilibrium in member states, and effective monitoring of developments in the economies of member states. The Treaty provided for a committee of West African Central Banks to oversee the system of payments to be channelled through the West African Clearing House. A Capital Issues Committee charged with ensuring the mobility of capital within the community by inter-locking the capital markets or stock-exchanges is provided for in the treaty.

The legal documents of the Community provided for a Fund for Cooperation, Compensation and Development which is intended to:

(a) provide compensation and assistance to any member which suffers losses resulting from the application of the provisions of the treaty including losses from the location of community enterprises;
(b) provide grants for financing community or national research and development; and
(c) grant loans for feasibility studies and guarantees for foreign investments in respect of enterprises established in pursuance of industrial policies in the community.

The ECOWAS secretariat has commissioned three major research projects on trade customs and tariffs, transportation and communications, and a general economic survey of member states. It is hoped that they will facilitate decision making (and implementation) aimed at alleviating poverty in the sub-region.

According to the Treaty, the policies to be followed in order to achieve the goals previously discussed can be summarized as follows.:

(a) The elimination between member states of customs duties "and other charges of equivalent effect" on imports and exports;

(b) The elimination of quantitative and administrative restrictions on trade among members;

(c) The establishment of a common tariff structure and commercial policy towards non-member countries;

(d) The elimination of obstacles restricting the free movement of persons, services and capital among member states;

(e) The harmonization of the agricultural policies and the promotion of common projects in the member states notably in the fields of marketing, research and agro-industrial enterprises;

(f) The evolution of common policies on, and joint development of transport, communications, energy, and other infrastructural facilities;

(g) The harmonization of economic, industrial, and monetary policies of members, and the elimination of disparities in the level of development of members; and

(h) The establishment of a Fund for Cooperation, Compensation and Development.

The policies enumerated above are aimed at the establishment of an economic union in West Africa, while the implementation of policies (a) and (b) establish a free trade area; (c) establishes a customs union; (d) establishes a common market; and the implementation of (e) to (f) establishes an economic union.

The performance of the Community has illustrated three main facts. First, despite the unavoidable initial problems, the conceptualization phase and the establishment of the functional structures of the institutions of the Community were successfully brought to a close at the May 1980, Summit in Lome. Second, the far-reaching decisions made by the Authority at the Summit marked the end of the period of formulating the major Community policies and measures that were required to give practical form to the framework for cooperation as defined by the ECOWAS Treaty. The organization embarked definitively upon the implementation phase of decisions that were bound to change not only certain aspects of the system of national administrations, but also, and more significantly, the lives of the various socio-economic groups of the sub-region. Third, in spite of the extremely encouraging achievements made during this initial period, the potential elements of danger that could, in the short-run, compromise the smooth operation of the Community, had already surfaced. These related to the manner in which the member states fulfill their obligations to the Community and their attitude towards the effective implementation of Community decisions.

It is for these reasons that it was considered necessary to fix as an objective for the period May 1980 to May 1981, the consolidation of the Community achievements, especially since the main guidelines and the bulk of the Community Program for the 1980 - 1989 Decade had already been adopted. The three objectives for the period 1980/1981 were: effective application by all the member states of the existing Community decisions; implementation of measures defined in the priority Program in accordance with the agreed time-table, and the strengthening of the administrative institutions of the Community by attracting qualified and competent middle and senior-level cadres to bring the existing staff to full strength.

As stated, the Community priority Work Program was concerned with the trade and customs cooperation and related matters; transport and communications; immigration matters; and industrial cooperation; and agricultural cooperation.

As concerned trade liberalization and promotion, the achievements were in the form of:

(a) finalization of a trade liberalization program which included a list of priority industrial products, the definition of Community Enterprise, a liberalization scheme and development program for traditional handicrafts, an indicative list of non-tariff barriers, and classification and harmonization of indirect taxes;

(b) finalization of ECOWAS Rules of Origin - concerning fish and fish products;

(c) printing of trade and customs documents;

(d) introduction to the use of the trade and customs documents;

(e) organization of customs administration authorities of member states,

(f) road legislation including the adoption of an interstate road transit convention,
(g) formulation of a computerization program, and
(h) formulation of a comprehensive trade promotion program.

The definition and the preparation of the list of handicraft products to enjoy the Community's preferential tariff was undertaken by the ad hoc committee on trade liberalization. A definition of traditional handicrafts and a list of these products was written. The Committee proposed that the fiscal regime applied to these products would be the same as that of unprocessed products, namely total elimination of tariff and non-tariff barriers without compensation for loss of revenue.

There has also been the establishment of the list of priority industrial products eligible for accelerated liberalization because of their vital role in the development of intra-Community trade, and in the promotion of industrial cooperation within the Community. Based on studies provided by the Executive Secretariat, the ad hoc committee on trade liberalization drew up a list of priority industrial products which reflected the ten priority industrial sectors identified by the Council in November 1979. The ad hoc committee recommended that the list not be considered as definitive but rather as subject to future modification.

The definition of Community Enterprise was required for the granting of Community status to enterprises under the ECOWAS industrial program, and for purposes of operating the trade liberalization program. The executive Secretariat, in conformity with the Work Program approved by the Industry, Agriculture and Natural Resources Commission, undertook a study with the assistance of UNIDO into the industrial legislation of all member states and developed a draft proposal on ECOWAS Protocol on Community Enterprises.

The trade liberalization and promotion program, whose implementation covered the ten year period May 1979 - May 1989 was from the administrative and political view point, unquestionably one of the most immense and complex undertakings of the Community. It culminated in the establishment of a free trade area in the sub-region in May 1989, and was designed to regulate, on a gradual basis, the vast potential ECOWAS market of some 150 million consumers which is expected to expand to cover 200 million people by the year 2000.

The first phase of this program was completed in 1981. It placed emphasis on the structures, procedures and customs documents, and fiscal measures required at the national level for the smooth implementation of the Program. Important decisions were made by the Community in 1979 and 1980 and attention since then has been directed to their implementation.

Certain trade and fiscal measures under the trade liberalization program were necessary for the first tariff reductions in 1981 as provided for in the Lagos Treaty.

A Community Enterprise has required certain conditions: participation of citizens from at least two member states; ownership of majority shares by Community citizens; operations to be substantially carried out within two or more member states; the direct promotion of industrialization policies and programs of the Community; contribution to the level of employment within the Community; training of citizens and up-grading of skills in relevant administrative, technical, managerial and other fields; and adequate environmental and pollution controls.

Such an enterprise would be granted any or all of the following privileges: exemption from expropriation except for reasons of public policy; no share-owner to be compelled to cede his interest in capital to any other person; benefits accorded an enterprise not to be altered subsequent to its disadvantage except under some specified conditions; and where, in exceptional circumstances, an enterprise is taken over or its capital ceded to another in the public interest, adequate compensation to be paid.

There were to be no restrictions on: remittance of capital, transfer of profits; transfer of payment in respect of principal interest and other loan charges, transfer of fees and other charges incurred in the ordinary course of business, entry into member states of requisite managerial and technical personnel if such expertise does not exist within the Community. There were to be facilities available for expatriate remittances abroad for maintenance of their families and contractual obligations (such as insurance premiums, provident and pension funds), tariff and non-tariff protection, and free movement of factors of production within the Community.

The Executive Secretariat worked jointly with UNCTAD on the trade regimes of member states. The outcome of this study was submitted for further analysis to the ad hoc committee of Trade Liberalization which developed a list based on the submissions of member states regarding their trade regimes, on documents of the GATT (General Agreement on Tariffs and Trade), on the Secretariat, and on the Tokyo Round of Trade Negotiations. While recognizing that member states are allowed, under the approved trade liberalization scheme, to determine the elimination of these barriers, the ad hoc committee proposed an outline of a probable schedule to assist member states to eliminate all non-tariff barriers.

In conformity with the Council directive to decide the tax nomenclature of member states, the Executive Secretariat appointed a team to study fiscal cooperation measures. This team studied the tax structures of member states and classified indirect taxes. This classification, which covers import duties and taxes of equivalent effect as well as internal indirect taxes levied on all goods, facilitated the proper application of the provisions of Articles 13 and 17 of the Treaty. Those provisions related to the taxes that were to be eliminated within one year once the general tariff elimination began, and to the taxes that were to be phased out over the stipulated eight-year period. The report of the study team indicated a need for the regulation of indirect taxes within the Community to eliminate discriminatory taxes and the possibility of member states reintroducing taxes under other assumed guises.

Defining the origin of fish products was a problem. The ad hoc Committee on Rules of Origin, to which legal experts in maritime law from member states were co-opted, prepared a definition of the origin of fish products obtained from the territorial waters of member states. The problem was to formulate a definition taking into account the international characteristics of this sector, the internal situation of member states, their financial and human resource potentials, and the territorial waters now extended as a result of new international regulations.

The provisions of Article III, paragraphs 3 and 4 of the Protocol on the definition of the concept of products originating from member states, imposed strict conditions on the manning of the vessels used (at least 50 percent of the crew should be nationals of member states) and their ownership (at least 50 percent of the capital should be owned by nationals of member states). It did not promote intra-Community trade and the development of this sector. The ad hoc Committee on Rules of origin, therefore, proposed transitional measures for the period May 1981 to May 1989. These measures were designed to make the conditions prescribed in the said Article of the Protocol on Rules of Origin more flexible, especially regarding the participation of nationals in the ownership of vessels. The adoption of these transitional measures necessitated the suspension of the provisions of the Protocol during the period in question.

During the 1980/81 period, plans were made to publish the customs documents including the transcribed tariffs of member states into the ECOWAS Customs and Statistical Nomenclature; the Common Statistical Standards and Definitions; the Customs Declaration; the Certificates of Origin, and the Movement Certificates. These documents were available January 1, 1981.

There have been some problems in respect to, for example, the ECOWAS Common Customs Nomenclature. The printing of national tariffs and the entry into force of the Common Customs Nomenclature. Considerable efforts made by the Executive Secretariat to ensure that entry into force of the Common Customs Nomenclature with the transcription of the national tariffs occurred in line with the agreed time-table. However, despite the various reminders sent by the Secretariat, member states took considerable time in transcribing their tariffs and forwarding them to the Secretariat.

The Nomenclatures were sent to the members states by the end of December 1979 with the request that they be returned to the Secretariat within three months after the transcription of the national tariffs. The transcribed tariffs were to be received by the Secretariat not later than the end of March 1980, to allow time for printing and distribution before July 1980. This time-table was adopted so as to leave sufficient time before their effective application began in January 1981. Unfortunately, only one state was able to meet the required three month limit. In fact, half of the transcribed tariffs did not arrive at the Secretariat until July 1980.

It was found necessary to solicit the intervention of the Chairman of the Authority of the Heads of State in respect to the member states which were late with their submissions. When we had still not received all the tariffs by November 1980, we decided to print those tariffs already in hand. At the end of December 1980, the time-table for the checking of the proofs of the printed tariffs was communicated; again the dispatch of the national experts by the states to check the proofs of their tariffs was not completed within the stipulated time. Indeed, the last such official was dispatched by his country at the end of April 1981.

As concerns the entry into force of Common statistical Standards and harmonized Customs Documents of ECOWAS, the Secretariat forwarded them to all the member states at the beginning of January 1981 for their immediate implementation. These documents were The ECOWAS Common Statistical Standards and Definitions; the Declaration Forms (for home use, for exportation, for re-exportation, for warehousing, and for temporary admission), and the ECOWAS Certificates of Origin (for industrial products, for unprocessed products and for traditional handicraft products.

A mission was sent out to the member states to assess the application of these documents which constitute an essential element in the implementation of the trade liberalization program. It is regrettable to note that none of the reports received on the status of implementation by member states of these Community policies and measures was encouraging. It appears that none of the documents enumerated above, which had to be introduced into use as a prerequisite for a smooth application of the trade liberalization program, has been effectively implemented by any member state.

In order for the trade liberalization program to proceed without undue delay, Council needed to set a deadline for all member states to effectively put into use these vital documents, including the transcribed Customs Nomenclature. This same deadline should apply to the outstanding matters on which the Trade and Customs Commission has asked for further study and action. These matters were: classification of tariffs and indirect internal taxes; assessment of fiscal implications of the trade liberalization program, and derogation requests from CEAO and MRU.

An essential factor contributing to the trade liberalization program and the related compensation mechanism would be a reliable and up-to-date information and data base. A preliminary assessment of facilities within member states has pointed to the need for an improved statistical systems operating in the sub-region. A program aimed at remedying the situation has been accorded priority status since the compensation procedures for the loss of revenue called for the rapid and frequent submission of up-to-date, accurate trade and revenue data.

While emphasis was placed on information on trade and fiscal revenue initially, a computerized program is to be designed for a statistical base for other types of economic and social statistical data. The program is planned to involve a progressive movement towards the use of a computerized system linking a central Community data bank with modernized statistical units at the national levels. The draft program, prepared with the assistance of the UNCTAD Secretariat, is being presented to the Trade and Customs Commission.

The Council of Ministers requested action be taken to finalize the TRIE Convention at its November 1980 session. This document, designed to facilitate the transportation of goods within the Community, was prepared by the Secretariat on the basis of similar conventions and agreements being operated within the sub-region and elsewhere. The draft TRIE Convention was submitted to the Trade and Customs Commission in May, 1981.

In the application of the Protocol on the Free Movement of persons within the Community, a definition was needed of Community citizen. The draft definition prepared by an ad hoc Committee was based on the three possibilities for the acquisition of citizenship as those by birth, descent, or naturalization. The proposed definition was submitted to the Commission for consideration at its May, 1981, session in Free Town.

The Protocol on the Free Town Movement, signed on May 29, 1979, has so far been ratified by only nine member states and is being implemented by an even fewer number of member states. It is strongly felt that by now the Protocol should have been ratified and the first phase fully implemented throughout the sub-region. A check on those member states actually implementing the Protocol, in relation to the measures to be instituted to effect the proper application of the Protocol, revealed that nowhere have the provisions of the Protocol been fully observed.

Compliance with all the provisions of the Protocol is necessary for at least two reasons. First, the administrative measures envisaged under the Protocol are designed to ensure the smooth functioning of that Protocol within each member state.

Second, those measures would also form part of the control system for monitoring the effects of the Protocol. It should be recalled that it is upon results of the monitoring and assessment of the operation of the first phase abolition of visa that the subsequent phases - right of residence, and, later, right of establishment - can be introduced.

The smooth implementation of the priority program of the Community, as well as a cohesive development of the Community, have necessitated an effective cooperation in the monetary field, given the special circumstances prevailing in the West African sub-region. The Executive Secretary, therefore, commissioned the International Monetary Fund to carry out a study on the convertibility of the national currencies of the member states. The report of this study was presented to a meeting of the Directors of Research of the Central Banks of the Member States of ECOWAS.

A program of monetary cooperation was submitted to the Committee of Central Bank Governors at its May 1981, meeting in Accra and were forwarded to the Council of Ministers' May 1981 session in Freetown. The purpose of the monetary cooperation program proposed by the Central Bank Governors is to achieve the convertibility of the currencies of the members states of ECOWAS by 1989.

This ambitious objective would require far-reaching political and economic measures on the part of the member states and institutional adjustments at the sub-regional level. In particular, it is necessary to: prepare an economic program aimed at correcting external structural imbalances; establish a balance of payments support system; and bring about closer consultations between the Central Banks in order to monitor the management of the economies of the countries of the sub-region.

A program for the planning of a modern postal system has been adopted to ensure an efficient mail distribution system, turn the sub-region into a single postal zone, and institute a training program for postal services personnel. A total contribution of $3.6 million from member states would be necessary for the implementation of this program.

It has been acknowledged that for a group of developing countries like the ECOWAS member states the mere creation of a free trade zone is unlikely to generate much intra-Community trade. What is more important is ensuring the development of a sound and modern production base. In pursuit of this strategy, the broad outlines of an industrial work program was adopted and its implementation was begun in 1980.

The first phase of the industrial program of ECOWAS dealt with the preparation of the legal text regulating the development of the industries that are retained as priority industries within the sub-region, and the enterprises that are granted Community Status. This legal text (entitled "ECOWAS Protocol relating to Community Enterprise") was drafted and circulated to all member states in preparation for the meeting of the Industries Commission in May 1981, in Freetown. Once adopted, the text served as a basis for the design of a sub-regional industrial program of ECOWAS.

The development of a modern agriculture, capable of contributing to food self-sufficiency, constitutes one of the major concerns of ECOWAS member states. In order to strengthen and develop effective actions at the national level, ECOWAS drafted a common agricultural policy to be examined by the Industry and Agriculture Commission at its May 1981, session.

The proposed common agricultural policy covers the following: development of an efficient agricultural production system; organization of the agricultural market - both intra and extracommunity transactions in agricultural produce, research into agricultural and agro-industrial activities; agricultural training programs; agricultural financing, including the creation of an ECOWAS Agricultural Support Fund; and establishment of national technical and administrative support services for the agricultural sector.

The world economic crisis reflected in persistent global inflation has continued to play havoc with the balance of payments situation of the member states. The economic conditions have been so poor that the capacity to develop the West African economy has been undermined on a more or less permanent basis. One area for concerted action has been in the energy sector. While oil imports have become a dominant factor in the ever rising import bills of member states, the ECOWAS region possesses the ability to cut down drastically, or to totally eliminate, its crushing dependence on external sources.

The preliminary proposals for an Energy Program include: a desk study supplemented with quick field surveys of the entire energy question (demand pattern, existing supply situation, extent of resource endowment and available plans for energy development); implementation of an emergency 'survival' program to give an immediate relief within the sub-region; in depth study of the energy sector aimed at the identification of all possible medium and long-term Community actions; and implementation of the full Community Energy Program which will include exploration and exploitation of both conventional and non-conventional sources of energy, as well as the organization of the sub-regional energy production and distribution system.

By this Community action, it was hoped an organized and long-term solution would be developed for the energy problem. The draft Energy Work Program was presented to the Transport, Telecommunications and Energy Commission meeting in Freetown in May 1981.

The Fund finalized, in the course of 1980/81, the policy measures vital to its operation. The outlines of general policies relating to loans, investments, guarantees and subventional general conditions relating to loans agreements were examined by experts of the member states and adopted by the Board of

Directors. As already pointed out, the Fund devoted much of its activities to seeking funds to finance the Telecommunications Program. This phase ended with the meeting of funding institutions on May 20, 1981, in Freetown.

The Special Ministerial Defence Commission drew up a draft Protocol on Mutual Assistance in matters of defence in conformity with the directives of the Heads of State conference held in Lome on May 1980. This document was submitted to the Summit in Freetown on May 1981.

It should be pointed out that despite the achievements of ECOWAS, there have been a number of problems facing the Community. All members of the Community are still underdeveloped, and the standard of living in some of the countries, particularly the landlocked countries like Mali and Niger that are also located in the arid and semi-arid portions of the sub-region, has been deplorably low. This state of affairs stemmed from the fact that they lack the right quantity and quality of water upon which their economic prosperity depends. Their socio-economic conditions have also been aggravated by such factors as extreme heat and inadequate energy supplies. This calls for their total reliance on the Community for financial technical, and material assistance.

Since the financial, material and human resources of the Community has been inadequate to meet its commitments, solving the problems of the disadvantaged countries within the Community is prohibitive. Perhaps the solution lies in the exploitation of such special assistance program as Special Program for the Least Developed; Special Program for the Landlocked; Special Program for Agricultural Improvement; the EEC-ACP arrangements and programs through existing regional organizations. This could be coupled with the evolution of an effective system for the distribution of gains and costs of economic cooperation with a view to alleviating the present economic and social situation. In this way the problem countries do not become greater liabilities but, rather, assets to the Community.

A further problem area is the low level of trade between member countries, i.e., intra-ECOWAS trade. For example, the percentages of the volume of trade between ECOWAS countries to that of ECOWAS export trade with the rest of the world for the years 1964, 1970, 1973, and 1974 were, respectively, 2.9, 4.4 and 3.3. The barriers between West African countries have been: the heavy reliance of ECOWAS countries on revenue from trade, both import and export; the difficulty of converting one currency to another, inadequate credit facilities and the relatively low level of production of both manufactured and agricultural products. All of these discourage trade. The volume of trade among member states of ECOWAS is likely to remain small and the benefits accruing from integration limited.

Table 6.23 indicates very strongly that the revenue from imports and exports duties constituted a very significant proportion of total government receipts. Yet, since intra-ECOWAS trade is a relatively small proportion of total export trade of the sub-region, the elimination of tariff (and other taxes) within the Community may not have a great impact on the revenue derived from customs duties. Since the Community must maintain a common external tariff equal to, but not higher, than the arithmetic average of the tariff of the member states, potential "***danger***" exists for countries whose customs duties are now very high; a sort of compensatory financing will have to be worked out and implemented. Although the "Fund" is set up to play this role, it is by no means easy to work out a system that will be acceptable to countries who may suffer huge losses.

There are ten different currencies in ECOWAS. The CFA Franc is used in six of the ECOWAS countries, but it is not directly convertible to any of the other currencies in the sub-region. In fact, none of the currencies in the sub-region is directly convertible into another. As a result, the issue of convertibility becomes important for the expansion of trade in the sub-region. (Table 6.24)

The resolution of the convertibility problem cannot ignore the special arrangements between the CAP Franc zone and the French Franc. These special arrangements include guarantees and overdraft schemes. Therefore, the issue of convertibility in West Africa is as economic as it is political.

It should be pointed out that most of the member states of ECOWAS are also members of the West African Clearing House which provides credit facilities for only one month. Credit facilities for longer periods may be required to boost trade in the Community, but this may be a tremendous burden on countries with balance of payment surplus, or on the "***Fund***". The Problem becomes more intricate when we recognize that member state's balance of payments in ECOWAS cannot be treated in isolation from their overall balance of payments positions.

Given the delicate overall balance of payments position of the member states of ECOWAS, credit guarantees by the West African Clearing House (and the Fund) for substantially long periods of time may still be inadequate for improving the overall balance of payments positions of quite a number of the member states. Therefore, the "Fund's" most important role, in this respect, will be to solicit and, perhaps guarantee, international assistance for the deficit countries. This task is by no means easy, and is made more difficult since long-term solutions to the problem must also be sought.

The expansion of trade in ECOWAS and, indeed, between ECOWAS and third countries also depends on the level of production of both manufactured and agricultural products. The manufacturing sector is composed of the traditional small scale industries and the import substitution industries. In each country, both are geared towards the domestic market, but, more importantly, the latter is rarely linked to the domestic economy so that inputs, labor, and even raw materials are imported.

The expansion of production for the larger community market requires larger firms with the advantages of economies of scale. Inconsistent investment makes it almost imperative that such projects be Community enterprises. These are not easy to undertake. Problems of standardization and the commitment of member states to patronize the enterprise must be solved. Also, the general problem of mutual vulnerability must be solved.

In the agricultural sector, production trends have been largely disappointing. Table 31 shows that agricultural per head in a number of ECOWAS countries is on the downward trend. The indices for 1975 are generally lower than the respective 1970 figures. This decline in agricultural production has resulted in increased food importation and other agricultural products. As noted earlier, Nigeria was a major exporter of groundnuts and palm produce and is now a net importer. The situation is, of course, much more serious in the landlocked and arid/semi-arid countries.

Some of the Major constraints on agricultural production in the sub-region are inadequate water supply, migration to the cities, continued use of traditional methods of farming, and diseases such as river blindness, in the fertile river valleys of the Niger and Volta. The solution to these problems entail major efforts by the Community, as well as international assistance on a vast scale. It cannot be denied that unless the problem of the low level of production is resolved the aspirations of the Community will not be fulfilled. The Economic Community will also have to rely heavily on the funds that can be generated internally. Contributions by member states are therefore important. The assessment procedure is such that Nigeria's contribution accounts for over 30 percent of the total. It is doubtful that the economic and political situation in Nigeria will continue to carry this proportion of the financial burden. The present procedure for assessment may, therefore, need to be reviewed such that the internal sources of funds for the Community will not depend too critically on the economic and political developments of a "handful" of member states.

The ECOWAS Treaty also tends to give excessive powers to such representatives of member states as the Heads of State and government (in the Authority), and Ministers (in the Council of Ministers). The absence of such an independent branch as the Commission of the EEC may make the process of making decisions more dependent on the narrow, national interests of individual member states instead of the overall interest of the Community.

Political factors are likely to raise problems. First, the existence of such potential rival groupings as the French-speaking West African Economic Community (the CEAO) within ECOWAS may cause a conflict of interest in the future. Second, the lack of a common ideological orientation accepted by members may, as in the East African Community, lead to problems in the future. Third, the influence of non-African countries and economic interests in all ECOWAS countries may eventually sabotage the ECOWAS idea.

As a concluding note, it has been attempted to highlight the objectives, and achievements, as well as some of the real and potential problems in ECOWAS. The intention, however, is not to paint a gloomy picture of the Community. Rather, it is hoped that these touchy problems will be recognized and given appropriate attention by members of the Community so as to ensure its smooth evolution, viability and stability in the long-run. Indeed, the experience of the defunct East African Economic Community is still fresh in our minds and should serve as a warning.

8 Conclusion

To sum up this chapter of the study, it should be noted that an examination of the salient economic features of some of the major sub-regional economic organizations has revealed the following:

(a) that the economies of the member states of some groupings such as CEAO, ECOWAS, and LCBC are largely competitive in terms of the range of what they produce and sell;

(b) that all the regional organizations depend heavily on foreign trade, which is dominated by agricultural products on the exports side, and by manufacturing and consumption goods on the import side;

(c) that because of the their different colonial orientations and experiences, all the regional organizations have continued to carry out a large proportion of their trade with their former colonizers and very little trade between themselves;

(d) that virtually in all member states of the regional organizations, all the development indicators such as per capita incomes, the share contribution of industry to GDP etc.., are relatively low; thus reflecting low levels of industrialization and standards of living, and

(e) that in each regional organization there are member states which can go it alone (like Nigeria in ECOWAS, Senegal in Entente Council and the Ivory Coast in CEAO). Because of their competitive strength, they may tend to accumulate most of the benefits while relatively less developed partners (like Mali and Mauritania in ECOWAS, and Mauritania in CEAO), would need extra-economic measures to compensate them for the costs incurred as a consequence of being members of the regional groupings.

Footnotes

1. See CEAO Treaty, Bamako, June 3rd, 1972.

2. World Bank, Annual Report 1975, p. 26 and Courier EEC-ACP. Special Issue, March 1975.

3. ECA. A Survey of Economic Conditions in Africa, 1972, Part 1, p. 61.

4. See "Possibilit es d'Industrialisation des Etats Africains et Malgache Associes a la EEC" in BCEAO, Notes d'information et Statisiques, No. 146, December 1967, p. 10.

5a. See Wilfred A. Ndongko and Frankin Vivekananda in " Critical Essays on African and Third World Economic Development " Bethany Books, Post Office Box 7444. 103 91 Stockholm, Sweden, 1988, P. 25.

5. IMF Surveys of African Economies, Vol. III Washington D.C. 1970 p. 38.

6. A. J. Brown, "Economic Separatism Versus a Common Market in Developing Countries," Yorkshire Bulletin of Economic and Social Research, Vol. 13, 1961 pages 31-40 and Andrew Kamarck, The Economies of African Development, (New York and London 1967), pp. 148-65.

7. IMF. Surveys of African Economies, Vol. III, op. cit., p. 43.

8. EEC. Foreign Trade Statistics, Brussels, 1968, p. 30.

9. Agreement to create an "Interim Organization" with a view to the Establishment of a Permanent Organization for West African Economic Cooperation. Signed at Freetown, Sierra Leone, 28th May, 1965 (Published in 599 United Nations Treaty Series (1966), pp. 274-282. Reprinted in English in 54 American Society of

International Law, (1965) International Legal Materials, pp. 916-920.

10. Green, (R.H.), and Krishna (K.G.V.), Economic Cooperation in Africa: Retrospect and Prospect, Nairobi, 1967, pp. 39-40.

11. Articles of Association for the Establishment of an Economic Community of West Africa. Signed at Accra, Ghana 4th May, 1967, published in E/CN 14/399 (24th May, 1967), Annex IV. Reprinted in 6 American Society of International Law, (1967) International Legal Materials, pp. 776-781.

12. United Nations, Economic Commission for Africa, Preliminary Draft of a Treaty for the Economic Community of West Africa and Explanatory Notes, (E/CN, 14/INA/EC/5, 27th October 1967.)

13. Adebayo Adedeji, "Economic Community of West African States: Ideals and Realities," The Nigerian Trade Journal, Vol. 22, April - June, 1975 p. 1.

14. World Bank, Annual Report 1975, p. 26 and Courier EEC-ACP Special Issue, March 1975.

15. Economic Commission for Africa, A Survey of Economic Conditions in Africa, 1972, Part I, p. 61.

Table 6.1. ECONOMIC CHARACTERISTICS OF CEAO MEMBER STATES - 1972

Country	Population	Area (km^2)	GDP (US $) Million	Principal Products and Exports
Ivory Coast	5,400,00	322,463	1,836,000 (360)*	Timber (29%) Coffee (23%) Bananas Cocoa (15%)
Mali	5,260,000	1,240,000	370,000 (70)*	Cotton (39%) Rice, Livestock Groundnuts, Fish (33%)
Mauritania	1,205,000	1,032,455	217,440 (90)*	Iron Ore (73%) Livestock and Gum
Niger	4,248,000	1,267,000	400,000 (90)*	Groundnuts (35%) Livestock (12%) Uranium
Senegal	4,080,000	197,161	1,037,400 (270)*	Groundnuts (35%) Phosphates
Upper Volta	5,620,000	2,274,122	392,910 (70)*	Livestock (48%) Cotton, Groundnuts, Coffee
TOTAL	25,813,000	2,861,817	4,252,710	

Source: European Community - Africa - Caribbean, Pacific 'Lome Dossier' in Courier No. 31, Special Issue (Brussels) 1975. World Bank Annual Report.

* Indicates GNP Per Capita

TABLE 6.2. CEAO: PERCENTAGE SHARE OF INTRA-REGIONAL TRADE (1966 and 1970)

Country	1966		1970	
	Imports %	Exports %	Imports %	Exports %
Ivory Coast	32.9	39.8	29.4	34.1
Mali	9.9	11.7	11.2	5.3
Mauritania	4.8	N.A.	10.4	3.8
Niger	4.7	6.9	7.3	24.3
Senegal	25.0	13.1	21.3	
Upper Volta	16.6	28.3	12.1	10.3
*Dahomey (Benin)	6.1	1.2	8.2	2.4
TOTAL %	100.0	100.0	100.0	100.0
TOTAL CFA (million Frs)	8,020	9,150	18,110	18,320

Source: Banque Centrale des Etats de l'Afrique de l'Ouest. Notes d'Information et Statistiques no. 197 Juillet, 1972

TABLE 6.3. CEAO: STATES EXPORTS TRADE STRUCTURES 1961 - 1966
(VALUE IN BILLION FRANCS CFA)

Country	1961	1962	1963	1964	1965	1966
1. Ivory Coast						
Total Exports	43.6	45.0	56.9	74.6	68.4	76.7
Major exports:						
Coffee	20.1	18.7	24.4	31.7	25.9	30.3
Cocoa	9.8	10.5	11.3	14.5	10.9	13.1
Tropical Woods	7.8	8.3	11.4	16.0	15.0	14.9
Bananas	2.1	2.8	3.5	3.2	2.7	2.8
Major exports as per cent of total exports	91	90	89	88	80	80
2. Mali						
Total Exports	3.5	2.5	2.6	4.1	3.9	3.2
Major Exports:						
Groundnuts	1.3	1.0	1.0	0.8	0.5	0.3
Cotton	0.3	0.2	0.3	0.3	0.6	0.8
Cattle	0.3	0.2	0.3	0.7	1.1	0.7
Major Exports as per cent of total exports	54	56	62	44	56	56
3. Mauritania						
Total Exports	0.5	0.7	4.0	11.3	14.2	17.0
Major Exports:						
Iron ore	-	-	2.7	10.6	13.3	15.8
Major Exports as per cent of total exports	-	-	68	94	94	93
4. Niger						
Total Exports	3.8	4.8	5.3	5.3	6.3	8.6
Major Exports:						
Groundnuts	3.0	2.9	3.6	3.8	3.4	5.2
Livestock on the beef	0.4	1.1	1.0	0.6	1.0	0.9
Major Exports as per cent of total exports	89	83	87	83	70	83

Table 6.3, Continued

Country	1961	1962	1963	1964	1965	1966
5. Senegal						
Total Exports	30.7	24.8	20.2	23.5	24.9	28.6
Major exports:						
Groundnuts and Groundnut oil	25.4	24.8	20.2	23.5	24.9	28.6
Major exports as per cent of total exports	86	85	79	85	87	85
6. Upper Volta						
Total Exports	0.9	1.9	3.1	3.3	3.7	4.0
Major exports:						
Livestock on the beef	0.5	0.9	1.0	1.5	1.9	2.0
Major exports as per cent of total exports	56	47	32	45	51	50

Source: EEC, Foreign Trade Statistics, Brussels, 1968.

TABLE 6.4. CEAO STATES: COMMODITY DISTRIBUTION OF IMPORTS (1961-66)
(BILLION FRANCS CFA)

Country	1961	1962	1963	1964	1965	1966
a) Foodstuffs, Beverages and Tobacco						
* Dahomey	1.2	1.7	1.8	1.9	1.9	2.0
Ivory Coast	6.4	6.4	6.9	10.0	10.3	12.6
Mali	1.7	2.2	1.8	1.5	2.1	1.9
Mauritania	0.4	0.5	0.4	0.3	0.3	0.4
Niger	1.1	1.5	1.0	1.0	1.2	1.4
Senegal	12.2	12.1	13.0	15.8	14.8	13.8
Upper Volta	1.3	1.8	2.2	2.5	2.2	2.5
TOTAL	24.3	26.2	27.1	33.0	32.8	34.6
b) Raw Materials and Fuel						
* Dahomey	0.7	0.7	0.7	0.7	0.6	0.5
Ivory Coast	2.8	2.4	3.2	4.1	4.2	4.8
Mali	0.8	0.9	1.0	1.0	1.0	1.2
Mauritania	0.4	0.4	0.3	0.3	0.2	0.3
Niger	0.5	0.6	1.0	1.2	1.0	1.5
Senegal	2.7	2.8	2.8	2.7	6.3	4.5
Upper Volta	0.6	1.0	1.6	1.5	2.6	1.6
TOTAL	8.5	8.8	10.6	11.4	1.59	14.4
c) Capital Goods						
* Dahomey	1.5	1.3	1.5	1.2	1.4	1.5
Ivory Coast	10.8	9.2	12.1	18.4	16.4	17.3
Mali	1.6	4.2	1.9	2.5	2.4	1.4
Mauritania	3.0	3.1	4.9	2.3	3.3	2.9
Niger	0.8	3.1	2.8	4.5	5.5	6.5
Senegal	6.4	6.5	6.7	6.7	5.8	6.0
Upper Volta	1.7	1.9	1.6	1.8	1.2	1.6
TOTAL	25.8	29.3	31.5	37.4	36.0	37.2

TABLE 6.4, Continued

Country	1961	1962	1963	1964	1965	1966
d) Other Manufactured Goods						
* Dahomey	2.9	2.9	4.2	4.1	4.5	4.2
Ivory Coast	18.1	16.4	19.4	27.9	27.3	28.6
Mali	4.7	4.1	3.8	4.0	5.0	4.5
Mauritania	3.9	4.9	1.9	0.9	2.3	2.1
Niger	2.3	1.6	1.7	1.6	1.6	1.6
Senegal	17.0	16.8	16.1	17.1	15.7	15.0
Upper Volta	3.5	3.9	3.8	4.0	3.0	3.5
TOTAL	52.4	60.6	51.1	59.6	59.4	59.5
GRAND TOTAL	111.0	111.9	120.3	141.4	144.1	145.7

Source: EEC, Foreign Trade Statistics, Brussels, 1968. N.B.
 * Note CEAO member

TABLE 6.5. CEAO BUDGET (1974 - 1979)

Year	Recurrent Budget (%)				
	MM Frs.	(%)	MM Frs.	(%)	MM Frs.
1974	248.0	(33.07)	502.0	(86.93)	750.0
1975	259.8	(29.30)	526.8	(70.70)	886.6
1976	429.0	(30.08)	997.1	(69.92)	1,426.1
1977	481.2	(24.92)	1,467.1	(75.08)	1,948.8
1978	660.0	(33.59)	1,965.0	(66.41)	2,665.0
1979	912.9	(28.25)	2,318.2	(71.75)	3,231.5
TOTAL	2,990.9	(27.78)	7,318.2	(72.22)	10,767.1

Source: Bulletin de l'Afrique Noire, No. 888 of 10th November, 1976, No. 894 of 21 March 1979, and No. 1022 of 31 October, 1979.

TABLE 6.6. REGIONAL COOPERATION TAX FOR BEER (1975)

Company	Rate of RCT					
	Ivory Coast	Upper Volta	Mali	Mauritania	Niger	Senegal
BRACODI	--	67%	17%	20%	17%	10%
SOLIBRA	--	67%	17%	20%	17%	10%
BRAVOLTA	0	--	10%	20%	17%	10%
SOBOA	0	67%	17%	20%	17%	--

Source: Official Journal of CEAO, 13th December 1975, p. 40.

TABLE 6.7. CEAO: INTER-STATE TRADE - 1976

		IMPORTS						
	MM Fr. CFA	Ivory Coast	Upper Volta	Mali	Mauritania	Niger	Senegal	CEAO
exports	Ivory Coast	--	161.2	135.9	7.02	43.3	2,696.6	3,038.1
exports	Upper Volta	2,106.7	--	26.6	--	9.9	350.6	2,393.9
exports	Mali	4,161.4	1.7	--	0.7	4.7	2,989.6	7,158.2
exports	Mauritania	231.5	--	8.0	--	--	3,913.4	4,153.0
exports	Niger	1,191.8	302.6	0.02	--	--	179.4	1,404.8
exports	Senegal	2,622.4	0.0	1.1	1.9	---	--	2,635.6
	TOTAL	10,315.9	194	182	3.6	5.8	10,030.1	20,783.9
	% Total	49.63%	0.93%	0.87%	0.18%	0.279%	48.26%	100%

Source: Bulletin de l'Afrique Noire, No. 994; March 21st 1979, p. 19356.

TABLE 6.8. CEAO - GROUPS OF PRODUCTS SUBJECT TO RCT. 1978

Product Group Subject to RCT	Ivory Coast Entr.	Ivory Coast Prod.	Upper Volta Entr.	Upper Volta Prod.	Mali Entr.	Mali Prod.	Niger Entr.	Niger Prod.
Primary Products	16	31	2	5	4	14	1	2
Textiles and Leather	17	102	1	2	2	12	2	14
Chemical Products	26	69	3	9	1	6	1	3
Mechanical Products	17	50	-	-	2	6	1	2
Miscellaneous Products	18	28	2	24	3	6	-	-
Total	94	280	8(1)	40	12(2)	44	5(3)	21
%	53.70%	15.3%	4.6%	6.5%	6.9%	7.1%	2.9%	3.4%

(1) SAP, BROVOLTA, CARVOLT, SOSUHV, FLEXIFOAM, SOVOLTA, SOVOLPLAS, SOPIVOLTA

(2) COMATEX, SEGMA, Gde Confiseve du Mali, SOMABIPAL, SOMAFAM, SOMASCAO, Mamadou Diallo, SONATAN, ITEMA, SOCOMA, SOMAPIL, Azard Freres

(3) SEPANI, NITIX, SPCN, ONERSOL, SONITAN

Source: Bulletin de l'Afrique, No. 994, March 21, 1979, p.19357

TABLE 6.8, continued

Product Group Subject to RCT	senegal Entr.	Prod.	Mauritania Entr.	Prod.	CEAO Entr.	Prod.
Primary Products	10	32	-	-	33	84
Textiles and Leather	12	95	-	-	34	225
Chemical Products	9	35	-	-	10	122
Mechanical Products	11	36	-	-	31	94
Miscellaneous Products	14	35	-	-	37	93
Total	56	233	-	-	175	618
%	32.9%	37.7%	0%	0%	100%	100%

TABLE 6.9 CEAO: COMPANIES SUBJECTS TO RCT: 1979

Member State	Number of Companies	Percentage Share
Ivory Coast	101	53.72
Senegal	58	30.85
Mali	112	6.38
Upper Volta	11	5.85
Niger	5	2.66
Mauritania	1	0.54
	188	100.00%

Source: Bulletin de l'Afrique Noire, No. 1022, 31st October,1979.

TABLE 6.10 <u>CEAO: RCT RATES IN RESPECT OF SOAP (1979)</u>

Country	1978 Rate	1979 Rate	Difference
Ivory Coast	10%	2%	- 8%
Upper Volta	40%	34%	- 6%
Mali	27%	16%	-11%
Senegal	17%	15%	- 2%

Source: <u>Bulletin de l'Afrique Noire</u>, No. 1022, 31st October, 1979, p. 19792.

TABLE 6.11. CEAO - COMMUNITY FUND FOR DEVELOPMENT 1975 - 1976

State	1975			1976		
mm. Frs CFA			Additional			% Sur.
	%	Amount	Subvention	%	Amount	Recet (1)
Ivory Coast	58.1	524.8	52.6	60.760	1,385.7	2.2066 %
Upper Volta	1.8	16.2	9.6	1.321	30.1	0.3331 %
Mali	6.27	56.7	12.7	1.559	30.5	0.5723 %
Mauritania	0.05	0.4	7.0	0.008	0.2	0.9917 %
Niger	0.67	6.0	14.4	0.427	9.7	0.1174 %
Senegal	33.20	300.3	52.6	35.925	819.3	2.9261 %
Total	100%	904.7	150.0	100%	2,280.0	

(1) Pourcentage represente par levement sur l'ensemble des previosons de recettes liquide et parcues a l'importation par les administrations douanieres.

Source: Bulletin de l'Afrique Noire, No. 888 du 10th November p. 17342.

TABLE 6.12. UTILIZATION OF 1975 FUND FOR DEVELOPMENT PROJECTS

Projects	Amount (mm. Frs. CFA)	Location
- Station of Quarantine Plants	155.0	Maradi
- Groundnuts Expansion	125.0	Upper Volta
- 2 Pe Prioieres pour Roboisement	88.0	Mauritania
- Hydrology Centre	45.0	Mali
- Livestock Development	420.0	Community
- Fishing (Peche)	42.0	Community
- Industrial Development	67.50	Community

Source: Bulletin de l'Afrique Noire, no. 888 of 10th November 1976, p. 17242.

TABLE 6.13. DISTRIBUTION OF 1976 FUND BETWEEN SOME STATES

Country	Amount (million Frs. CFA)	% Shares
Upper Volta	206.0	31.69%
Mali	206.0	31.69%
Niger	160.0	24.62%
Mauritania	78.0	12.00%
TOTAL	650.0	100%

Source: Bulletin de l'Afrique Noire, No. 888, 1976

TABLE 6.14. CEAO - COMMUNITY FUND FOR DEVELOPMENT (1977 & 78)

Country	Amount (mm. Frs)	% Share	Amount (mm. Frs)	% Share
Ivory Coast	791.4	61.464 %	1.140.9	49.634 %
Upper Volta	45.3	3.158 %	21.4	.934 %
Mali	17.0	1.324 %	20.1	.976 %
Mauritania	0.9	0.038 %	0.4	.018 %
Niger	6.9	0.538 %	6.4	.979 %
Senegal	426.4	33.121 %	1.109.3	48.259 %

Source: Bulletin de l'Afrique Noire, No. 944 of 21st March, 1979.

Table 6.15 COMPENSATION OF MEMBER STATES (1976-1978)

State	Amount (million CFA Frs.)	% Share
Ivory Coast	385.0	25.13 %
Upper Volta	379.6	24.77 %
Mali	158.0	10.30 %
Mauritania	108.8	7.10 %
Niger	121.9	8.00 %
Senegal	378.2	24.70 %

Source: Bulletin de l'Afrique Noire, No. 944, 21st March, 1979.

TABLE 6.16. DISTRIBUTION OF PART OF 1976 AND 1977 FUND BETWEEN THE LESS DEVELOPED STATES

States	Amount (1976) (million Frs. CFA)	%	Amount (1977) (million Frs. CFA)	%
Upper Volta	206.5	(31.79)	116.4	(27.15)
Mali	206.5	(31.79)	122.0	(28.45)
Mauritania	76.0	(25.72)	85.4	(19.91)
Niger	160.6	(11.70)	105.0	(25.21)

Source: Bulletin de l'Afrique Noire, No. 994 of 31st November, 1979, p. 19358.

State	Provisional Allo-cation; (mm F.CFA)	Actual Amount Received (mil-lon Frs. CFA)	% of the Provi-sional Alloca-tion.
Mali	438	414	94%
Niger	389	357	92%
Mauritania	322	233	72%
Upper Volta	510	294	58%
	1,661	1,299	78%

Source: Bulletin de l'Afrique Noire, No. 1022, 31st Oct. 1979.

TABLE 6.17. SOLIDARITY FUND (1977 - 1980) (million Frs. CFA)

State	1977/78	1979	1980	Total	% Share
Ivory Coast	2,500	750	4,000	7,250	50%
Upper Volta	250	100	450	800	5.5%
Mali	250	100	450	800	5.5%
Mauritania	250	100	450	800	5.5%
Niger	250	200	650	1,100	7.6%
Senegal	1,500	250	2,000	3,750	25.9%
Total	5,000	1,500	8,000	14,500	100%

Source: Bulletin de l'Afrique Noire, No. 1022 of 31/10/79, p. 19794 of 12th November 1980, p. 20550.

TABLE 6.18. ALLOCATION OF SOLIDARITY FUND RESOURCES - JULY 1980
(million Frs. CFA)

State	Amount	Project
Upper Volta	45.00 (11.66%)	Development of middle valley of Black Volta and reactivation of the Poura Mine.
Mali	300.00 (77.72%)	Loan guarantee to the FRAB Bank for the Mali Hotels Company.
Mauritania	10.00 (2.60%)	A study of a mineral water project at Benichab.
Niger	10.50 (2.72%)	A feasibility study of Briqueterie at Zinder.
Senegal	21.00 (6.44%)	Studies of Projects for the transportation of Cassava at Kinkelibah
TOTAL	386.00	

Source: Same as Table 6.17

Table 6.19. ECOWAS: DEVELOPMENT INDICATORS OF MEMBER STATES 1973

Country	Area (sq.km.)	Population Mid-1973 ('000)	Per Capita GNP At Market Prices 1973 ($ US)
Benin	112,622	2,947	110[2]
The Gambia	11,295	493	120
Ghana	238,537	9,313	300
Guinea-Bissau	36,250[2]	800	230[3]
Guinea	246,000	5,243	100[2]
Ivory Coast	322,463	5,600	360
Liberia	111,369	1,452	330
Mali	1,240,000	5,370	70
Mauritania	1,032,455	1,257	190
Niger	1,267,000	4,304	90
Nigeria	923,768	71,262	170
Senegal	197,161	4,070	270
Sierra Leon	72,236	2,787	190
Togo	56,000	2,105	170[2]
Upper Volta	274,122	5,714	70

Source: World Bank Annual Report 1975, p.26, The Courier EEC-ACP No.31 Special Issue, March 1975. 1- Estimated of Mid-1973; 2- Preliminary Estimates; 3- for 1972.

TABLE 6.20. PRINCIPAL PRODUCTS OF SOME ECOWAS STATES

(1)	Benin	Palm Products, cotton, fish, groundnuts (30% - 40%).
(2)	Ivory Coast	Coffee, Cocoa, Timber, Bananas (25%).
(3)	Gambia	Groundnuts (94%).
(4)	Ghana	Gold, Diamond, Timber, Aluminum and Cocoa (61%).
(5)	Mali	Rice, Cotton (30%) Groundnuts, Livestock, Fish.
(6)	Mauritania	Iron Ore, (73%) , Copper, Gum, Gum Arabic, Fish (24%).
(7)	Niger	Groundnuts (24%), Livestock, Uranium.
(8)	Nigeria	Petroleum (88%), Tin, Groundnuts, Palm Products, Rubber, Cocoa, Cotton and Timber.
(9)	Senegal	Groundnuts (35%), Phosphates, Fish, Manufacturing.
(10)	Sierra Leone	Diamonds (63%), Iron ore, Bauxite, Palm Kernels, Coffee, Cocoa, Ginger, Kola nuts.
(11)	Togo	Phosphates (62%), Cocoa (25%) , Coffee (13%).
(12)	Upper Volta	Livestock (48%), Coffee, Groundnuts.

Source: Central Bank of Nigeria, Economic and Financial Review Vol. 10, No. 1, June 1972.

TABLE 6.21. ECOWAS: EXTERNAL TRADE - 1971

Export and Imports of Goods and Services as % of GNP (at Constant 1970 Market Prices.)

Country	Exports (%)	Imports (%)
Benin	34.9	41.4
The Gambia	51.7	53.7
Ghana	14.8	18.9
Guinea Bissau	n.a.	n.a.
Guinea	22.4	25.4
Ivory Coast	33.9	31.6
Liberia	49.8	36.1
Mali	19.4	22.8
Mauritania	45.1	35.1
Niger	16.0	23.5
Nigeria	25.0	20.4
Senegal	16.7	29.2
Sierra Leone	24.9	26.7
Togo	30.6	28.2
Upper Volta	6.3	19.6
Total	24.4%	23.2%

Source: ECA ... A Survey of Economic Conditions in Africa, p.61
Note: n.a. = not available.

TABLE 6.22. ECOWAS STATES - PATTERN OF TRADE (1971) IMPORTS (I) c.i.f. (000) U.S. $: EXPORTS (E) f.o.b. (000) U.S. $

	Country		World	EEC	AFRICA	WEST AFRICA	% of Total with W.A.
1.	Mauritania	I=	63,811	35,269	5,933	3,290	
		E=	90,444	67,252	4,147	2,592	
		Total	154,255	102,521	10,080	5,882	4.81%
2.	Senegal	I=	218,080	135,722	14,308	2,370	
		E=	214,977	78,045	5,660	2,034	
		Total	343,057	213,767	19,968	4,404	1.28
3.	Mali	I=	64,638	35,631	12,566	12,080	
		E=	39,115	10,214	20,025	19,554	
	2)	Total	103,483	45,845	32,591	31,634	30.57
4.	Upper Volta	I=	46,659	30,714	10,166	8,555	
		E=	118,202	5,583	8,950	8,791	
		Total	164,861	36,297	19,116	17,346	26.74
5.	Ivory	I=	399,129	278,491	30,068	14,285	
		E=	455,735	293,715	26,998	21,643	
		Total	854,864	572,206	57,066	35,928	4.20
6.	Niger	I=	53,923	34,659	6,984	5,880	
		E=	38,420	22,620	13,255	13,219	
	1)	Total	92,343	57,279	20,239	19,099	20.68
7.	Gambia	I=	20,459	9,531	781	5,880	
		E=	14,715	13,763	253	13,219	
		Total	35,174	23,294	1,034	19,099	
8.	Guinea Bissau	I=	30,577	8,951	1,834	2	
		E=	1,990	231	181	--	
		Total	32,667	9,182	2,016	2	0.01
9.	Guinea	I=	55,023	40,900	1,066	1,066	
		E=	42,377	12,810	353	273	
		Total	97,400	53,710	1,419	1,339	

Table 6.22, continued

	Country		World	EEC	AFRICA	WEST AFRICA	% of Total with W.A.
10.	Sierra	I=	114,437	55,650	12,721	7,543	
	Leone	E=	98,481	77,924	642	373	
		Total	212,718	133,574	13,363	7,916	3.72
11.	Liberia	I=	149,697	59,936	3,039	2,430	
		E=	213,733	136,493	2,774	2,613	
		Total	363,430	196,429	5,813	5,043	1.39
12.	Ghana	I=	434,283	216,122	24,407	15,901	
		E=	341,965	173,864	3,648	2,433	
		Total	776,248	389,986	28,055	18,334	2.36
13.	Togo	I=	70,055	45,832	5,377	4,301	
		E=	55,240	43,233	1,769	1,324	
		Total	125,295	89,065	7,146	5,625	4.49
14.	Benin	I=	54,747	34,869	7,963	6,288	
		E=	26,877	16,543	6,029	5,405	
		Total	81,624	51,412	13,992	11,693	14.33
15.	Nigeria	I=	1,510,467	878,287	50,146	3,971	
		E=	1,793,170	1,122,287	27,196	25,722	
		Total	3,303,637	2,000,574	77,342	29,693	0.90
	3) Grand Total		(599,886,673)				2.64

(1) For 1970 I= Imports

(2) For 1969 E= Exports

(3) Total Excluding Benin, Liberia, Guinea, Gambia and Upper Volta.

Source: Compiled from ECA: Foreign Trade Statistics for Africa Direction of Trade Series, Nps. 20 and 22; Addis Ababa 1973.

TABLE 6.23. CUSTOMS RECEIPTS AS PERCENTAGE SHARE OF TOTAL GOVERNMENT RECEIPTS (1973)

Country	Customs Revenue as Percentage Share of Total Government Revenues
Benin	48.8
Cape Verde**	7.5
Gambia	52.6
Ghana	26.6
Guinea	n.a.
Guinea- Bissau	n.a.
Ivory Coast**	35.3
Liberia	20.4
Mali	25.4
Mauritania	28.1
Niger	16.3
Nigeria	19.7
Senegal*	30.3
Sierra Leone*	37.0
Togo*	28.1
Upper Volta*	47.2

* estimates

** data for 1972

n.a. Not available

Source: Statistical and Economic Information Bulletin for Africa No. 9 U.N. E/CN 1.4/SE IB.9, International Financial Statistics, January 1978.

TABLE 6.24. CURRENCY OF MEMBER STATES OF ECOWAS

COUNTRY	CURRENCY
Benin	CFA Franc
Gambia	DELASI
Ghana	Cedi
Guinea	Syli
Guinea Bissau	Feso
Ivory Coast	CFA Franc
Liberia	Dollar
Mali	Mali Franc
Mauritania	Onquiya
Niger	CFA Franc
Nigeria	Naira
Senegal	CFA Franc
Sierra Leone	Leone
Togo	CFA Franc
Upper Volta	CFA Franc

Source: IMF, International Financial Statistics.

TABLE 6.25. INDICES OF AGRICULTURAL PRODUCTION PER HEAD IN SELECTED WEST AFRICAN COUNTRIES (1961/65 - 100)

COUNTRY	1970	1971	1972	1973	1974	1975
Ghana	100	102	94	89	71	93
Mali	94	99	78	61	63	67
Nigeria	98	93	89	80	84	84
Upper Volta	106	100	94	83	86	84

Source: Adapted from figures supplied by the Food and Agriculture Organization of the United Nations.

Chapter VII
Problems and Prospects for the Future

1. Introduction

Attempts toward economic cooperation in West Africa have been confronted with a number of problems. As mentioned, the countries in the West African sub-region were administered in the colonial period by Britain and France, and therefore have different colonial traditions and official languages. This means that not only is there a large disparity between member states with respect to population, land area, and resource endowment, but also that differences between the metropolitan powers themselves in terms of policies have helped to mold the social, political and economic structures of these countries.

The success or failure of economic cooperation in this sub-region has depended largely upon the manipulations of the former metropolitan powers. For example, it was Britain's admission into the EEC that paved the way for the present day economic cooperation between French speaking and English speaking countries of the West African sub-region.

In discussing general problems, it has been important to examine the important economic and social conditions that the different policies of the member states must improve. First, there has been the problem of low per capita income in the face of a high rate of inflation. Second, there has been a low level of industrial activity resulting in a negligible volume of exportable manufactured goods and a gap between manufacturing and other sectors of the economy such as agriculture. There has been little or no linkages between the various sectors of the national economies. Imports of intermediate capital and primary goods have been on the increase and thus have affected the balance of payment position of the countries. Third, farm population and agricultural production have been on the decline because of rural-urban migration emanating from the disparity in wages, social infrastructure, and other opportunities between the rural and urban areas of member states.

The implications of this are threefold: (a) food imports have had to be increased (b) export of traditional agricultural commodities have decreased, and (c) agro-based industries have operated at less than full capacities because of the low level, or complete lack of, agricultural raw materials. Agricultural production and other economic activities are also affected by lack of water in the landlocked areas of the sub-region.

Other issues of rural-urban migration have reflected the problems of urbanization. Urban population have increased and cities have become crowded with the attendant problems of unemployment, housing shortages, crimes, etc. An added dimension to the problem of rural-urban migration is related to income disparity that has encouraged a drift from the low to high income countries. Where there is already a shortage of manpower the brain drain tends to aggravate the situations. In some other instances, shortages of highly trained and middle-level manpower have required foreign personnel at very high cost.

The poor infrastructure linking the sub-region has slowed the pace of development. The existing road, rail, and telecommunication systems only have served the individual countries instead of linking the various countries. Furthermore, the levels of economic development among the members of the organizations discussed in this paper have varied with the availability of natural resources. While the Ivory Coast and Nigeria are richly endowed with oil, Mali, Mauritania, and the Niger Republic are poor in every aspect. Ghana, despite the Akosombo Dam project and a great many mineral reserves, has had a severe balance of payment problems.

Members of the community, when compared on an economic scale, have had a wide variation. This has lead to the implementation of different scales of personal taxation and revenue collection through the imposition of customs dues on both imports and exports among the members. This, to a large extent, has frustrated the common objectives of many organizations: to promote through the economic cooperation of the member states, a coordinated and equitable development of their economies especially in industry, agriculture, transport, communications, trade and payments, manpower, energy and natural resources.

Apart from the general problems of economic cooperation which have been briefly examined above, a number of sensitive and crucial problems are closely examined in this chapter. These problems are related to the multiplicity of and multi-membership in regional organizations, trade liberalization, financial and monetary harmonization, industrial cooperation, free mobility of labor, distribution of gains and costs of cooperation, coordination of different legal systems, ideological differences among the states, and political instability. An attempt has also been made to suggest alternative policy solutions to these important problems which have affected the evolution, viability, and stability of the various economic organizations in the West African sub-region.

2. Multiplicity of and Multi-Membership

One substantive and complex issue that has required serious attention has been the existence of a multitude of multilateral and bilateral agreements among the various groupings. The interlocking relationships among member states of the ECOWAS with other regional organizations whose objectives have conflicted with those of ECOWAS, or whose continued existence may jeopardize the progress of ECOWAS is illustrated in Figure 1.

The multiplicity of regional economic organizations has tended to divide the West African sub-region into sub-organizations with varying memberships. (Figure I) Undoubtedly, such multiplicity of regional organizations has effected the serious economic problems as a result of the obligations which member states have assumed, either individually or collectively.[1]

Although at first glance the creation of multiple regional economic organizations has appeared to be beneficial to the countries concerned, it cannot be determined, in light of the experiences of other defunct and existing groupings, if the most expedient path to rapid development lies in such economic arrangements.[2] Such groupings may have, to a large extent, intensified the "balkanization" process and partially dictated the rate at which the economies could develop. In the long run, it is questioned to what extent the multiplicity of regional economic organizations in West Africa has been of permanent significance. Some groupings, such as the CEAO and the Entente Council have been anxious to preserve their links with Europe and with France. Thus, they may have backed their continuous existence for potential economic benefits even though these benefits have been minimal.[3]

Other alternatives are still open to the West African states due to their active participation and involvement in world affairs. The issues involve a complex mass of political and economic judgements. Is the present multiplicity of regional organizations likely to foster and to produce the stimulus necessary in the economic and political stability in West Africa? The Entente Council, CEAO, OCAM, and UMAO grew out of a traditional colonial policy - the assimilation of commercial, financial, administrative, and economic policies of France.[4]

In the post-colonial phase, Africa's dominant political mood seemed increasingly colored by Pan africanism, by more or less explicitly expressed longings for greater unity and cooperation at all levels and by an angry resentment of all forms of neo-colonial controls which have resulted in considerable economic and political instability of the West Africa sub-regions.[5] Given this mood, it is possible that the existence of multiple economic groupings, for all their immediate advantages, may have become the target for criticism and concern by those interested in the future and integrity of Africa as a continent capable of achieving some measure of economic independence.

There has been no doubt that it is possible to resolve the apparent conflict between ECOWAS and CEAO, if both Senegal and the Ivory Coast, (the largest and more influential member states of CEAO) take the initiative in order to recognize the positive need to change this status and become groups functioning under the aegis of ECOWAS. This resolution has depended partly upon the effectiveness of the diplomatic efforts undertaken by Nigeria and Togo to negotiate with the Ivory Coast and Senegal, and partly on the latter's opinion of ECOWAS as an appropriate group for solving the economic problems associated with CEAO.

With respect to other groups, it can be argued that OCAM has been a superfluous group, an anachronism rooted in colonialism.[6] Many French speaking African states like Congo, Cameroon, Zaire, Chad, and Madagascar have withdrawn from the organization. It will certainly disintegrate in the long run if the remaining member states put greater emphasis on the economic benefits derived from the other groups to which they belong than on the present cultural and political benefits which OCAM has provided them. The Conseil de l'Entente group of Benin, the Ivory Coast, Niger, Togo, and Upper Volta, with its headquarters in Abidjan, has been an active body with limited economic objectives.

In view of the fact that economic objectives must override all other goals of cooperation between African states if the entire economy of the West African sub-region is to be transformed, it seems logical that a rational policy must be pursued by African heads of state to discourage the present multiplicity of regional economic groups with dual membership. This is due to the present situation of multiple regional objectives in West Africa that will not foster and sustain the rapid economic development of the independent African states. The development may even be hindered.

3. Trade Liberalization

The obligations of the member states concerning trade liberalization have included the complete and gradual elimination of custom tariffs on either all products or on a select few in some cases. It has been pointed out that CEAO, as a Customs Union, may proceed at the same pace as ECOWAS. There may be potential conflict of loyalty between the two regional groups. In particular, those Francophone states which belong to both groups may remain loyal to CEAO and discontinue their support of ECOWAS, if their international trade and collective economic interest can be catered to solely by the CEAO.[7]

Certainly, a Customs Union similar to the kind envisaged in the ECOWAS Treaty, involving the gradual elimination of all tariffs, may be incompatible with CEAO's preferential system, partly because of the potential loss of revenue to be incurred by all the member states of the latter group as a consequence of lowering and eventually abolishing all external tariffs, and partly because the function of the ECOWAS Fund for Development Cooperation and Compensation and the payment system between the member states is vague.[8] More importantly, the issues center on the nature of adequate compensation of the economic distortions arising from trade liberalization within ECOWAS, of which CEAO is a sub-grouping.

There is no doubt that CEAO is likely to commit acts of derogation under Article 59 of the ECOWAS Treaty which defines the relationship of member states of the community with other region treaties. The states concerned should take immediate steps to identify their incompatibilities and to resolve them.

Article 1 of the trade agreement on livestock, meat, and other agricultural products has stipulated that the contracting parties shall permit, subject to the obligations accepted by one of the parties in a customs union, a free trade area or any other international agreement for the importation into their respective countries of duty free and other taxes of equivalent effects on the products originating from a Conventional Basin Area listed in Annex A of the agreement. These products, which are mainly foodstuffs, are: tinned meat, livestock, vegetables, meat, barley, banana, avocado pear, pineapples, millet, beans, onions, melon, sorghum, mangoes, yams, offals, maize, oranges, and sweet potatoes.[9]

Furthermore the contracting parties, shall undertake negotiations of the progressive removal of all obstacles to free trade in the products of the Convention Basin listed in Annex B. These products are: sausages, sausage meat, hides and skins, milk and dairy products, cotton seed oils, poultry, groundnuts, eggs, fish, tanned skins, tinned fruits and vegetables, wheat, and rice.

Article 2 of the trade agreement states that specific quantities of the products listed in Annexes A and B shall be negotiated. They may be modified at the request of any of the contracting parties. Any ensuing modifications shall come into effect 30 days after the contracting parties have agreed. However, such modification shall not affect, in any way, contracts already concluded under the terms of the trade agreement between exporters and importers of the countries concerned.[10]

The analysis of the trade liberalization provisions of the various treaties and trade agreements reveals, so far, that while in the case of ECOWAS, CEAO and the LCBC (for List B products), the elimination of trade barriers between member states will be progressive and gradual, the LCBC (List A products) provisions call for immediate and complete removal of all quantitative restrictions on these products (specified in the relevant schedules), originating from the member countries. These differences, with respect to timing, in the application of tariff reductions on goods originating from member states of each regional grouping, could have far reaching economic and commercial implications for the various states.[11]

The establishment of a customs union may engender trade practices which may result in problems like smuggling and dumping. These practices could frustrate the objectives of the Union and create instability in the group. Consequently, various safeguard measures which are intended to counteract such practices have been inserted in the treaties of ECOWAS and UDEAC. None are provided in the treaty of CEAO. The implementation of the trade agreement (Article 1) is subject to the obligations accepted by any of the member states in other economic arrangements only in the case of the LCBC. More importantly, Article 59 makes it possible for member states of CEAO to still regard their group as a positive and real alternative to an integrated wider West African grouping which is represented by ECOWAS.

Certainly, while the member states of CEAO are conscious of the fact that they have common economic interests and problems with other members of ECOWAS, they may be hesitant to transfer complete alliance and legitimacy to ECOWAS, partly because they are not too sure of the real commercial benefits to be derived from the Community and partly because their more established grouping is built on strong mutual political, cultural and economic experiences. There is already free trade between CEAO member states, (including the financing of industrial projects from the Common Fund and the operation of a common regional development tax).

There is no doubt that the trade provisions of CEAO's treaty limit the capability of its member states to participate effectively in ECOWAS. This has been done by consciously limiting free trade to only non-industrial products and by creating an industrial preferential scheme based on a system which replaces import duties on goods from within the community with a lower regional cooperation tax levied on similar imported or locally made goods.

Consequently, the trade provisions of CEAO can be said to conflict with the provisions of Article 58(3) of the ECOWAS treaty.

The Lagos Treaty established the rules against trade deflection (Article 16), and dumping (Article 19), regarding ECOWAS. Trade deflection takes place if, as a result of trade liberalization, imports into a member country increase because duties and charges levied by the exporting member states on raw materials for the manufacture of the products in question are lower than the corresponding duties and charges levied by the importing member state, and if this increase in imports causes or is likely to cause serious injury to domestic production.

Under those circumstances, the community, through its Council of Ministers, will review the question of trade deflection and its causes, with a view to taking the corrective measures which are deemed necessary. The preferential treatment which member states have promised each other in the field of trade applies to goods originating from within the member states.

A close examination of the above mentioned safeguard clauses of the trade liberalization provisions of the regional groupings, revealed that the sources of problems such as dumping in ECOWAS (Article 16 and 19) and the economic disturbances may be extremely difficult to identify and deal with adequately in practice. First, to the extent that there are no safeguard provisions in the LCBC trade agreement and the CEAO treaty, it would be possible to re-export products originating from the Lake Chad Basin through Nigeria and Niger to other members of ECOWAS and CEAO. Second, products imported from the other UDEAC member states into Cameroon and which are difficult to distinguish from the latter's products, may be re-exported through the Basin area into Nigeria and Niger, and finally to other member states of ECOWAS and CEAO. The same problems will arise in the case of products originating from those member states of ECOWAS and CEAO, which are not members of the LCBC.

Consequently, it will be extremely difficult to differentiate between products and animals originating, first from the Lake Chad Basin area and those from the rest of the national territories of the member states of the Commission, and second, from those originating from the other member states of ECOWAS and CEAO, which are not members of the LCBC.

Most of the economies of the member states of the four regional groupings, particularly those of the LCBC, have been largely competitive with respect to the agricultural sector. For example, meat, yams, wheat, maize, and livestock, which are produced in the Conventional Basin area, are also produced in the rest of the national territories of the member states of LCBC. This situation has made the problem of distinguishing the products more complex and challenging.

In accordance with Article 20 of the ECOWAS Treaty, member states shall accord to one another, in relation to trade between them, the most favored nations treatment, and under no circumstances, shall tariff concessions granted to a third country, under any agreement with a member state, be more favorable than those applicable under the treaty. Furthermore, any agreement between a member state and a third country, under which tariff concessions are granted, shall not derogate from the obligations of that member state under the ECOWAS treaty.

The implication of this provision is that Nigeria and Niger, which are member states of ECOWAS, CEAO and LCBC can extend preferential treatment to Cameroon and Chad, which are also members of LCBC but not members of ECOWAS and CEAO, only if the tariff concessions being extended are higher than those which Nigeria and Niger are extending to member states of ECOWAS and CEAO.

Considering the fact that the ECOWAS treaty called for a gradual reduction of tariff barriers by member states against other member states over a period of fifteen years, the implication is that Nigeria and Niger cannot immediately implement Article 1 of the LCBC trade agreement. This called for the immediate elimination of duties and other taxes on the products (list A of the annex of the trade agreement) which originated from the Conventional Basin Area. This is complicated by the fact that, in accordance with Article 5 of the LCBC trade agreement, Nigeria and Niger are subjected to the obligations assumed under the ECOWAS treaty.

Analysis of the trade liberalization provisions has revealed that the multiplicity of regional organizations may result in numerous commercial problems because of the trade obligations which member states either individually, or collectively, assumed under the different treaties and protocol agreements that established the organization of the groupings of which they are members. The obligations of the member states in the different groupings included the complete or gradual elimination of custom tariffs on all or selected products and a common external tariff wall against third countries. Some sensitive commercial problems are bound to arise in the course of fulfilling these obligations.

Taking agricultural products as an example, it is easy to see how difficult it will be to implement free trade among member states since each member state is characterized by a different level of agricultural productivity and also since every state, for political and economic reasons, would like to have a firm base in agriculture. It is, therefore, plausible that the trade provisions of the multilateral and bilateral agreements of the various organizations may be incompatible.

Consequently, there may be a problem with regard to the extension of the principle of the "most favored nations treatment." Also, it may be difficult to identify which products originate from which area within each economic grouping. And, in the absence of special "treatment" to non-member states, there is the likelihood of smuggling and dumping across inter-union borders to the non-member states. Closely related to this is the problem of deciding the nature of administrative machinery which could control the movement of goods between the different groups so as to prevent the dumping and smuggling.

In the light of the foregoing trade problems, the policy measures which can minimize and possibly eliminate trade diversion and dumping, in the long run, would appear to be as follows: (1) the member states of the LCBC and CEAO can dissolve these groupings and maintain their respective memberships in ECOWAS and the UDEAC. For example, the apparent conflict between ECOWAS and CEAO can be resolved if both Senegal and the Ivory Coast take the initiative and pressure the other states to recognize the positive need to form a group functioning under the aegis of ECOWAS. This would depend partly on the effectiveness of the diplomatic efforts undertaken by Nigeria and Togo to convince the Ivory Coast and Senegal, and partly on the latter's regard for ECOWAS as an appropriate organization for solving the economic problems associated with CEAO.

In the case of the LCBC, the similarity of those sections of the national economies of the member states - Nigeria, Niger, Chad, and Cameroon - which fall within the Basin area, and their low rates of industrial development, including backward infrastructures, would bring about a low degree of complementarity of trade in the commodities of member states of the commission. Because of similar climatic and soil conditions, the range of agricultural activities has limited member states to importation of substitute types of consumer goods most of which are basic necessities.

The agricultural products to be traded within the Conventional Basin are mainly food items (livestock on the hoof, meat, fish, cereals, etc.) which are produced in virtually all parts of the region. Thus, the national territories of the member states which fall in the Conventional Basin have been competitive rather than complementarity. Such a situation does not help to stimulate trade within the commission.

To this extent the LCBC may become a superfluous regional organization which does not generate sizeable economic benefits to the member states and the Basin area as a whole. In the long run, therefore, the commission may become redundant, particularly because of the greater commitments and obligations of Nigeria and Niger in ECOWAS and CEAO, respectively.

Considering the foregoing problems, the policy measures which can minimize and possibly eliminate trade diversion, dumping and smuggling in the long run appear to be as follows: First, the member states of the LCBC and CEAO can dissolve these organizations and maintain their respective memberships in ECOWAS and the UDEAC. Such a decision would, no doubt, result in wasted resources in the short run, particularly in respect to those projects which are now jointly financed by the member states of CEAO and LCBC.

Second, the jurisdiction of the trade agreement, in the case of LCBC, can be extended to the entire territory of each member state, particularly as the Conventional Basin will soon be producing more foodstuffs than can be consumed by its population. However, since the products imported into Cameroon and Chad from Nigeria and Niger may, due to differentials in the price levels, be re-exported to other member states of the UDEAC, this policy, as indicated earlier, could place Cameroon and Chad in the undesirable position of middlemen. The same would be true of goods imported into Nigeria and Niger from Cameroon and Chad.

Third, a certificate of origin could be provided for each product imported from one member state into another member state within each of the regional groups. This requires that any consignment of goods from any member state be accompanied by a certificate of origin which should be signed by customs or any other recognized authority. This certificate should accompany the goods and be presented along with the import declaration of the importing state.

The name of the authority empowered to issue the certificates of origin and the specimens of their stamp and signature should be made available to all members of each groupings. Furthermore, information supplied on the certificates of origin should not necessarily be accepted by the customs authority of the importing member state and they may if they so wish, request the evidence of the origin of the product imported.

The customs authority of each member state should , upon specific request, send to the other authority the following information: (1) confirmation of the authenticity of certificates of origin; (2) proof that the goods subject to the trade liberalization provisions arrived at their destination, and (3) all other information not already mentioned in the certificate of origin and arising from the documents in their possession. The customs authorities of all the member states should meet frequently to discuss problems arising from the implementation of this procedure.

All payments for goods exchanged between the various member states of the regional groups should be made in convertible currencies, mutually agreed upon by all the member states, through a Clearing House, (see details in Chapter 6) which should be operated by a committee of central banks of the member states of all the regional groupings and in accordance with the foreign exchange regulations in force. It is proposed that a unit of account, to be used in the settlement of bills, should be equivalent to one special drawing right (SDR).

Apart from the cost of administration, the implementation of the third policy proposal could be laborious and excessively demanding in terms of time, dedication, and manpower. Nevertheless, if the member states of the regional groups are willing to minimize and eventually eliminate the economic disturbances like dumping, smuggling, etc., which arise from trade liberalization, then all efforts must be made to implement this third proposal.

Assuming that the "most favored nations treatment," is extended to other member states of UDEAC and ECOWAS by Nigeria and Cameroon a possible trade arrangement between Nigeria and the UDEAC on the one hand, and between Cameroon and ECOWAS on the other, could take the following forms.[12]

1) A selective approach under which Nigeria and Niger, after consulting other member states or the CEAO and ECOWAS merely indicate their willingness to reduce tariffs applied to individual commodities (or to relax non-tariff restrictions) originating from other regional groupings. It would be necessary to ensure that the goods are not re-exported to their countries. This could be done through the use of certificates of origin as suggested earlier. The market sizes of ECOWAS and CEAO, separately, are much greater than that of the LCBC; this organization may in the long run, and depending on which of the two trade arrangements is chosen, be found to serve no useful purpose to its members. This is particularly true as, of the four member states of the LCBC, Cameroon belongs to the UDEAC, Nigeria and Niger belong to ECOWAS, and Niger belongs to CEAO.

2) Assuming that regional organizations like CEAO, ECOWAS, and LCBC continue to exist, then an alternative trade arrangement could be that which ensures that all goods originating from the LCBC and which are imported into Nigeria are not re-exported to other member states of ECOWAS and CEAO.

This would require issuing certificates of origin to importers and exporters of products which are either to enjoy immediate free entry or gradual tariff reductions, under the LCBC trade agreement, as already discussed in detail above.

4. Financial and Monetary Harmonization

Problems of financial and monetary harmonization have arisen partly from the existence of multiple monetary and currency zones in the African sub-region and partly from the fact that, at the present time, some national currencies are neither convertible nor have they had stable exchange rates.[13] Since financial and monetary considerations have been important in the realization of the objectives of the regional economic organizations, this section examines the problems of the desire of the African states to harmonize their monetary, financial and fiscal policies, and to suggest some policy alternatives.

In order to understand the origins and importance of these problems, it is pertinent to briefly examine the colonial monetary and financial systems and policies in Africa. Attention is given to those policies of the French and British in West Africa where there is a multiplicity of regional economic organizations.

Any consideration of colonial monetary policy should note that the two major colonial powers, France and Britain initiated and maintained unique monetary systems and policies in their colonies. In the case of Britain, the 1880 Demonetization Ordinance for British Controlled Territories in Africa restricted the currency to gold and silver, British sterling, French twenty-Franc pieces, and gold dust.[14] By 1893, nearly all coins in circulation were sterling and cowries were in use among Africans only for small transactions. In West Africa the British further consolidated their control of their colonies by establishing the West African Currency Board in 1922, with its headquarters in London.[15]

This Currency Board issued currencies for the West African territories with the same denominations as the British Currency; pounds, shillings, and pence. These currencies were fully backed, not by gold, but by securities purchased from the United Kingdom government with foreign currencies earned by the sale of the colonies' exports. The British argued that the prices of African exports were so notoriously low and unstable that such an arrangement was necessary to guarantee the acceptability of the colonial African currencies for foreign trade. In practice, however, the purchase of the United Kingdom securities by the Currency Board, with funds generated from the sale of exports produced in the colonies, constituted an ironic set-up in which the colonies were actually lending capital to the British government. To this extent, therefore, the West African Currency Board system drained funds which could have been available for productive investment in Africa.[16]

The French colonial monetary policy established a close association between the currency of the colonial territories and that of the French Franc. All the French speaking countries belonged to the Franc zone which was a monetary area sharing a common currency.[17] The local French Franc, which circulated in both West Africa and Equatorial Africa, was issued by the French West African Bank and backed by France. In 1941, when Equatorial French Africa opted to support free France during World War II, its monetary links with Francs and French West Africa were broken. This led to the creation of new bank issue (the CFA Franc) for French Equatorial Africa and Cameroon.[18] The maintenance of an 'Operation Account' in the French Treasury by each French African colony was obligatory. Every colony was required to deposit into this account all the foreign currencies which came from the sale of each country's exports. The use of the resources was to be made with the permission of the French Central Bank.[19]

The attainment of independence in the early 1960s by many African countries led to the creation of autonomous currencies and financial institutions, notably the central bank, in many ex-British West African territories. But the renegotiation of the cooperation agreements between France and her ex-colonies in Africa only led to a relaxation of the rigid rules which had hitherto governed the functioning of the Operation Account. The new CFA Franc still has unlimited French guarantee.[20]

The colonial monetary system, as well as other forms of financial arrangements, was certainly easy to operate and relatively trouble-free. This was because it guaranteed the convertibility of the local currencies into metropolitan ones.

However, the absence of a common currency and central bank for all the independent African states which would facilitate the inter-state commercial transactions, centralize monetary reserves, mobilize African financial resources for development, and ensure the stability of the exchange rates and the freedom of transfers within the continent, has led to the continuous subordination of the financial and economic interest of many African countries and of those of some metropolitan powers.

To the extent that this existing relationship has continually dictated the pattern and pace of African economic development, in addition to impeding intra-African trade and payments, the urgent need for financial, monetary and fiscal harmonization between the African states has become a matter of concern to many policy-makers in the continent.[21] The colonial financial system cannot respond adequately to the intensified pressures involved in quickening the pace of economic development in many of the independent African countries. Such a system was primarily developed to facilitate commerce between the metropolitan centers and the African periphery rather than to mobilize resources for economic development.[22] Consequently, the African leaders have tended to insist on the inclusion of specific provisions for financial, monetary and fiscal cooperation and harmonization in the treaties establishing the major regional economic groups.

The specific provisions are intended to eliminate those obstacles which have impeded rapid national and regional economic development, the expansion of intra-African trade and financial transactions, and the efficient mobilization and allocation of investments in the African sub-region.

A long term objective of many African regional groupings has been the complete harmonization of financial, fiscal, and monetary policies. For example, in the case of ECOWAS, Article 36 of the Lagos Treaty called for the harmonization of the fiscal policies of member states, and the maintenance of balance of payments equilibrium. It is stipulated in Articles 37 and 38 of the same treaty that a Clearing House shall be established to facilitate intra-community financial and commercial transactions.

These are important provisions considering the fact that the financial and fiscal environments within which the member states operate would have a significant effect on the cost of production. For example, the privileges some firms enjoy under the different national investment codes or incentives systems may have a great impact on their production costs and the retail prices at which they sell their goods. To the extent that such a situation is undesirable, the question arises as to the problems which would be encountered by the policy-makers in the course of harmonizing the different financial, monetary, and fiscal systems prevailing in the various African states.

Because of the diversity of the economic and financial conditions in different member states of the regional organizations and between the organizations (particularly in the case of ECOWAS), and also because of the fluctuations in the relative strength of the different national currencies and their inconvertibility, priorities policies and objectives on of the member states will inevitably come into conflict. The nature of the diversity of monetary conditions among West African states is indicated in Table 7.1 which provides information on the central banks in the member states of ECOWAS/CEAO, and LCBC, the currency units, and the value of each currency per U.S. Dollar as of July 21, 1976.

It can be seen that the existence of multiple monetary zones and national currencies, and the guarantee of the value of some currencies by former colonial powers, particularly France, will surely create difficulties in the harmonization of monetary and financial policies within ECOWAS and LCBC and between other regional groups. (Table 7.1) The problems are further accentuated by the existence of different levels of Central Bank discount rates which vary from one member state to another. (Table 7.2)

The short term conflicting economic policies of the member states of the different groups, which were aimed at achieving stabilization, a high rate of economic growth, full employment, and a balance of payment equilibrium, will definitely militate against immediate achievement of the (or implementation of) objectives of financial, monetary and fiscal harmonization and eventual integration. In particular, the problem of inconvertibility of the national currencies of some West African states will definitely present a major obstacle to the rapid promotion of inter-state and intra-regional trade especially within ECOWAS, LCBC, and CEAO.

Because of the differences in financial and monetary indicators and policy instruments between the African states, one uniform Central Banking policy which could ensure the immediate and effective harmonization of monetary and financial practices between all the member states of each group, and between groups, may not be feasible. But while the technical measures to implement Central Banking measures may have to be different in view of the diversity of national and regional circumstances, it will be pertinent for all central banks to agree on a general policy strategy. This is necessary considering the fact that the ultimate objective of the central banking policy, within and between the regional groups, should be eventual harmonization of their financial and monetary systems.[23]

Initiating individual Central Banking policies will be vital for each central bank to ensure that the choice of the policy instrument does not interfere with the autonomous policies of the other central banks in each of the regional groups. To this end, the utilization of similar techniques of monetary control and policy measures would surely make it possible for the central banks to lend support to each other's policies. This would facilitate the initiation and coordination of a central banking strategy within, and between, the different regional groups.[24]

Institutions such as the African Center for Monetary Studies, the purpose of which is to provide Africans with the means of analyzing contemporary financial and monetary problems of the continent, will pave the way for eventual harmonization of financial, monetary, and fiscal policies between the different regional groups.

More importantly, the establishment of the West African Clearing House with the objectives of (1) promoting the use of member states' currencies for commercial and financial transactions within and between the regional groupings, (2) encouraging member states of different regional groupings to liberalize trade among themselves and (3) promoting monetary and financial cooperation and consultation among the regional groups, will facilitate and hasten, to some extent, the harmonization of economic policies in the financial, fiscal, and monetary areas. The West African Clearing House will foster efficiency in the use of the scarce foreign exchange reserves of the member states of the various regional groups by eliminating the commissions and transfer charges which are being paid to banks outside Africa (especially in New York, London, and Paris) for carrying out payments for commercial and financial transactions within and between the regional groups. Such clearing houses will reduce the frequency of settlement of accounts in foreign currencies and help to minimize the delays in trade and payments among the member states.

The West African Clearing House should adopt a settlement period of one month. The currency for settlement of all types of transactions could be the U.S. dollar, French Franc, German Mark, Swiss Franc, or the Sterling, which are all convertible currencies.[25] At the end of each settlement period, each national central bank should be advised of its net credit and debit position with respect to each member state. Those central banks which are in debt should make payments to the appropriate national central banks within five days of receipt of notification from the Clearing House.

It would also be necessary to create a West African Unit of Account (WAUA), which should be the equivalent of one SDR. Such a unit of account should be utilized in transactions within and between the different regional groupings. The parity of the currency of each state should be expressed in terms of WAUA. With a view of facilitating the use of the WAUA, the day-to-day rate of exchange of the currency of each national central bank should be stated in terms of that currency per unit of account (that is the equivalent of one SDR. The West African Clearing House should then be able to work out the exchange rate among the different national currencies.

With respect to fiscal harmonization, the adoption of a common investment code for all member states of each regional group would eliminate the possibilities of either foreign or domestic investors taking advantage of and exploiting existing differentials between the various investment incentives of the member states.[26] Such a common investment code must clearly identify the underdeveloped areas in each regional group which may require special incentives in order to attract adequate private investment and skilled manpower.

In the course of the harmonization of financial, fiscal, and monetary policies within and among African regional groups, all remnants and vestiges of colonial monetary and financial institutions, deemed to be inimical to the attainment of these objectives will have to be removed and the Euro-African relationship restructured. This is necessary because the policies of some existing central and commercial banks in many African states are still largely influenced and dominated by Paris and London because of the extensive guarantees of commercial and capital transactions.

Such a restructuring and reorientation of financial and monetary relationships between Paris, London, New York and Africa, would enable the member states of the regional groups to establish an African monetary zone rather than the Franc, Sterling and Dollar areas to which many African states are associated with or belong to as members. In the long run the national currencies, especially in most of the French speaking African states and in Liberia, will be freed from external colonial domination and influence, thus facilitating the eventual harmonization of the different financial, monetary, and fiscal policies which now prevail in the African continent.

5. Industrial Cooperation

To the extent that free trade can encourage specialization and subsequent rapid industrialization of the regional economic organizations, it is necessary to examine the provisions relating to industrial harmonization and cooperation, the attendant problems, and to suggest policy alternatives. This is necessary because the economies of the West African States have, since the attainment of political independence, been dominated by agriculture. In most cases, industries have been on a limited scale. Although primary products have accounted for a large proportion of total exports and have made varying but significant contributions to the GDP of the African countries, the expansion of primary products for export has not generated considerable positive effects which can ensure self-sustained collective economic development of these countries.[27]

One of the major policy objectives in many African countries has been rapid and sustained economic development. A possible policy option would be the structural transformation of the national economies through the promotion of industrialization. However, industrial expansion would quickly face the problem of the limited size of the national markets.[28] In these circumstances, the search for wider markets which could accommodate large-scale industries, or at least provide an adequate domestic demand base partially explains the efforts of many African states to forego economic cooperation.

The larger market size and the subsequent specialization of labor and production would result in economies of scale which should reduce the excess industrial capacity existing in many West African states. This would enable the establishment of more efficient collective industrial projects and complexes. Currently, many of the African countries industries operate in isolation.

The need for industrial harmonization and cooperation at the sub-regional level in West Africa was recognized by a ECA Industrial Coordination Mission which argued that: "real Industrial growth depends primarily on stimulating activity at a number of key growth points. This means the installing now of modern industries strategies for economic development, with their growth effects. It has been shown that "such industries are mainly large scale with a minimum size, which, although smaller than is the case in the industrialized countries, are still considerable and beyond the scope of existing or foreseeable national markets."[29]

It is for this reason that many African governments and policy-markers have made relentless efforts to ensure that the provisions for industrial cooperation and harmonizations are included in the treaties and protocol agreements of regional groupings. The provisions of the treaties relating to industrial cooperation and harmonization stem from the importance of industrialization as the basis of rapid economic development. In the case of ECOWAS, industrial development and harmonization is the subject matter of Articles 28 to 32 of the Lagos Treaty. There is provision for a three stage approach to industrial cooperation.

Briefly, during the first stage there is to be an exchange of major feasibility studies and industrial reports as well as joint research bodies. In the second stage, member states pledge to create uniform industrial climates through the harmonization of their investment incentives and industrial development plans. To this extent, the Community will avoid unhealthy rivalry and the waste of scarce resources. The third stage will see the promotion of joint or complementary projects, the exchange of skilled professional and managerial personnel in the operation of projects within the community and the provisions for training of Community citizens in educational and technical institutions.

As concerns CEAO, Article 14 of the Bamako Treaty set up a Community Fund for Development which is intended to finance industrial projects which are jointly initiated by all member states. This Fund is intended to pay compensation to the landlocked states of Mali, Upper Volta, and Niger which may suffer from the economic distortions arising from the establishment of CEAO.[30]

Apart from the provisions for industrial cooperation, Articles 33 to 35 of the ECOWAS Treaty envisages cooperation in the development of common agricultural policies which will eliminate unnecessary competition and wasteful depletion of natural resources. This will require the exchange of information on experiments, research findings, and rural development programs. This implies the control of production levels of primary export crops, a common export sales policy, and the establishment of agro-based industries. In the LCBC, cooperation between the member states is envisaged in the areas of animal husbandry, fisheries, and agriculture.

It should be noted, however, that the socio-economic disparities between member states have threatened industrial harmonization in some other regional groupings like UDEAC. These disparities could also pose the same problems in ECOWAS and CEAO. The membership of Nigeria and Niger in LCBC and ECOWAS, of Niger, Senegal, and the Ivory Coast in CEAO and ECOWAS, and of Cameroon and Chad in LCBC and UDEAC could create considerable problems in the allocation and financing of industrial and agricultural projects, within the four different regional groupings.[31]

These problems would arise in respect to allocation of public and private investments, industrial incentives, compensatory measures, and international development assistance. For example, the other member states of ECOWAS and CEAO may not support the location of Community industrial projects in the territorial areas of Nigeria or Niger that falls within the Lake Chad Basin for the simple reason that the benefits generated from such projects may eventually accrue to Cameroon and Chad which are not members of ECOWAS and CEAO.

Serious objections would be raised especially if the projects are to be financed by the Fund for Cooperation, Compensation, and Development (Articles 50 to 52) of the Treaty of ECOWAS, or the Fund for Development and Cooperation of the CEAO. The same problems will arise when it comes to the encouragement through the provisions of various regional investment and industrial incentives measures for private investors to locate their plants in the less developed parts of the Community or Union. The question arises whether private businesses operating in the Lake Chad Basin will be subject to CEAO or ECOWAS business taxes.[32]

More intriguing is the fact that it will be extremely difficult to determine whether the long run structural dislocations of the economy of that part of the Nigerian territory which falls within the Lake Chad Basin are caused as a consequence of that country's membership in ECOWAS or the LCBC. The same problem will be posed in the case of similar structural dislocations of the economies of the part of Cameroon, Niger, and Chad territories that fall within the Lake Chad Basin.

Like the problems arising from the allocation and financing of domestic public and private (domestic and foreign) investments, the multiplicity of and dual membership in the regional economic groupings will also tend to raise the problems of inefficient allocation and possible duplication of international development aid between member states of the same regional groupings and between those countries which belong to more than one regional economic grouping.[33]

The foregoing problems could arise from the eventual implementation of the industrial cooperation and harmonization provisions of the various treaties and protocol agreements of the different West African regional economic organizations. This would call for effective policy measures which must be carefully examined and thought out before being introduced. The nature of some of these policy measures will now be examined.

In view of the foregoing problems, it will be absolutely necessary to carefully identify the sources of economic dislocation suffered by any state by virtue of its membership in the regional groupings. When the sources of the economic dislocation have been identified, appropriate policy action could then be taken with a view to ensuring that the member states in question are fully compensated for the costs of losses in incomes, reduction in employment levels, etc. In the case of projects located in the Lake Chad Basin Commission, the problem of leakages of some of the benefits to non-member states could be reduced if the source is identified. The same approach will also apply to the direct benefits arising from executing such projects and subsequent third party positive effects which may be generated.

The problem of the duplication of public and private investments within and between the regional groupings could be resolved by two actions. First, a policy of balanced industrial development policy grouping must be properly defined and the appropriate policy instruments clearly tailored out. Second, the economic dislocations resulting from the formation of each of the groupings must also be carefully identified.

International assistance has been an important complementary factor which may influence the pace of development of the regional groupings and the member states. Given this, and considering the problems confronted by aid donors in allocating resources to countries belonging to different regional groupings, it would be necessary to classify development aid into two groups: (a) aid which benefits all member states belonging to the same regional grouping and (b) aid which benefits only one member state of a regional economic organization.[34]

In the light of the foregoing classification, it is proposed that multilateral aid should fall under group (a) and should be used to finance regional projects. These are projects which could generate benefits which are not limited to the territorial boundaries of any one member state. Bilateral aid should be classified under group (b) and should be allocated to projects which would benefit only one member state of a regional grouping.

Because the allocation of bilateral aid between member states is influenced largely by non-economic considerations, like the existence of diplomatic relations between donors and the recipients, such aid may tend to aggravate existing and potential economic and social disparities between the member states of the same regional economic organization. Bilateral aid donors could channel a large proportion of their development assistance through multilateral international aid agencies to the regional groupings since the allocation of multilateral assistance is influenced largely by economic factors.

This may not be possible considering the fact that virtually all bilateral aid donors have so far been interested in extending and consolidating their spheres of economic, political, and cultural influence over individual aid recipients. The extent of the sphere of influence is often determined by the magnitude of the development assistance which bilateral aid donors have made available in the past to the aid recipients and their commitment to continue to do so in future.

Since multilateral aid is influenced mainly by economic considerations and the need to promote regional cooperation, this type of aid could help in reducing the economic and social disparities aggravated by bilateral aid. This could be done by assigning the regional offices of the multilateral international aid agencies and distribution channels to the poorer member states of the regional organizations. This would tend to generate employment and income in those states where the agencies are located. The regional offices of multilateral aid agencies could expect only limited financial participation in inter and intra-regional projects from the poorer states, relative to that from the richer states of the same regional groupings.

In the case of regional organizations where there is multi-membership, the multilateral aid donors can avoid the problem of duplication of development assistance by ensuring that they finance only those projects which could generate intra-regional benefits. For example, Nigeria, Niger, Chad, and Cameroon are members of the LCBC, but are also members of ECOWAS (Nigeria and Niger), and UDEAC (Cameroon and Chad), so it will be essential for the multilateral aid donors to finance those projects which cut across all the three regional groupings. Infrastructural projects will be the most appropriate in this case.

The problem of leakage of aid benefits may not exist for the multilateral aid agencies since within the framework of regional groupings, their role would largely be that of initiating and financing inter and intra-regional group development projects. For the bilateral aid donors, the leakage of aid benefits to other member states of the same grouping would surely present a problem. This could be handled by ensuring that the recipient country restricts the benefits of bilateral aid to its national territory. This would be a plausible condition for continuous receipt of bilateral aid from the donor country.

To the extent that the primary objective of many regional economic organizations is the integration of several diverse markets with a view to eliminating regional disparities and fostering the free movement of goods and services within a more expanded market,[35] an alternative policy measure for effecting a balanced regional allocation of private investment is licensing.[36] A licensing arrangement is a contract between a foreign manufacturer (the licensor) whereby the manufacturer, with an ownership of an industrial property right, licenses its use to another while retaining some measures of control over the production, use, and sometimes the sale, of the finished products.

One particular kind of licensing system often used in developing countries is patent licensing. It confers on the license for a specified period a limited purpose, a specifically restricted territory and, often for monetary consideration in the form of royalties, one, several, or all of the rights of patentee/licensor. In the context of regional distribution of industries within and between the different West African regional economic groupings, two types of patent licenses could be used. One is the internal type between a licensor and licensee within the same grouping and the other is the external type between two or more groupings.

The use of the former, for example by ECOWAS, will cause technology and technical expertise to move from the more technologically developed member states like Nigeria, the Ivory Coast and Senegal to the less technologically developed ones like Mali, Niger, Mauritania, and Gambia. If it is centrally coordinated and integrated, it could even eliminate existing and potential industry distribution inequality between the member states; by directing new enterprises to "depressed or backward areas," within the regional grouping.

There is no doubt that in order to realize the objective of balanced regional distribution of industries, it would be necessary to (a) initiate an effective immigration and labor policy which will enable investors to move from the technologically advanced states to the less developed ones to locate new enterprises, and (b) establish an adequate and efficient capital market which can finance such new business ventures.

As concerns external-type licensing arrangements between the regional groupings, there may be opportunities for abuse if these arrangements are left unchecked and unguided. The usual entrepreneur would normally set up his business enterprise in an area where he can maximize sales, find opportunities for economies of scale, locate adequate and inexpensive skilled manpower and have access to sources of raw materials and existing efficient transportation facilities. This may aggravate existing economic and social disparities within the regional organizations because of the eventual concentration of industries in relatively technologically advanced states as Nigeria and the Ivory Coast in ECOWAS and the Ivory Coast and Senegal in the CEAO.

To the extent that the system of integration industries can be viewed as the primary method of achieving regional balance, it would be necessary for the decision makers in each grouping to designate a major industry, or number of important industries, for each of the member states with the specific requirement that no one state would be awarded a second such industry until all member state have benefitted from such an initial allocation.

In order to maximize results, prevent abuses, and secure balanced development within and between the regional organizations this policy must be both regionally and supra-regionally coordinated and implemented, and not left in the hands of private investors. Such coordination will ensure that inter grouping payment of royalties and other fees does not have an adverse effect on each grouping's overall balance of payment. This is also necessary for the harmonization of inter-grouping common policy on industrial incentives and the maintenance of a balance of payments equilibrium.

In making the above proposals, it has been argued that public and private investment and multilateral aid should be directed to ensuring that the fundamental structural disparities which either existed between the member states before the creation of a regional grouping, or have been aggravated by bilateral aid or private investment, are corrected as the economic union evolves. Such corrections should necessarily be compatible with the equitable distribution of economic and social benefits and costs resulting from economic cooperation. Inequitable distribution has very often led to the break up of some regional groupings like the defunct Caribbean Free Trade Area or like the collapse of the East African Economic Community.

The proposals put forward for industrial harmonization may not resolve all the problems arising from the allocation and financing of different types of investment in a regional setting but it is hoped that they would help reduce those problems resulting from the allocation of investments in the regional economic organizations.

6. Free Mobility of Labor

The successful implementation of the objectives of the various regional economic organizations has depended on the availability of skilled manpower in the member states. Many West African states have suffered from the acute shortage of labor for production especially with respect to quality and quantity. For this reason, the authors of many of the Treaties establishing the various regional economic organizations have deemed it necessary to insert the appropriate provisions which are intended to encourage the free mobility of labor within each grouping.

Because of the potential effects of free labor mobility on the economies of the member states, the nature of the relevant provisions that relate to the mobility of citizens and persons within and between African regional groupings, and any attendant problems, must be examined and policy proposals suggested. The mobility of persons and citizens between member states of the same regional organization and between groupings have been a concern although internal labor mobility which takes place within each member state may not necessarily raise serious problems for the organizations.

Of all the provisions in the Treaties of West African regional organizations there is no doubt that those relating to the free mobility of citizens and persons between the member states are heavily "loaded". This is true of the provisions of ECOWAS (Article 27), and CEAO (Article 14). In the case of ECOWAS, Article 27 conferred on citizens of member states the right to be regarded as Community citizens. To this end, member states are expected to abolish all obstacles to their (citizens') freedom of movement and residence within the Community. Article 27 (paragraph 2) of the ECOWAS Treaty further stipulated that following the conclusions of any bilateral agreements, Community citizens will be exempted from holding visitors' visas and residence permits. Community citizens will also have the legal right to work and undertake commercial activities within the territories of member states. Although the nature of the free mobility of persons and citizens is not clearly spelled out in Article 14 of the CEAO Treaty, there is no doubt that the objectives and intention of the provisions are the same as those of Article 27 of the ECOWAS Treaty.

The mobility of persons and citizens, either temporary or permanent, implies that the migrants come into a society which is already organized and structured in the various facets of economic, cultural, political and social activity.[37] More often than not, unskilled labor constitutes a greater proportion of the migrants as compared with traders, office workers, top business executives, skilled workers, professionals and academicians.

Generally, the mobility of persons and citizens, as stipulated in the relevant provisions of the Treaties of the organizations, may in the absence of any protective and rational policies give rise to such negative effects as: increased crime rate among the migrants, destitution and vagrancy, the spread of diseases, the break up or disruption of family and communal life, and a reduction in normal birth-rates, unsatisfactory employment conditions, rapid expansion of slums with poor housing and health facilities, and potential damage to the economy of the migrant and that of the receiving countries.[38]

These problems may have far reaching economic, social and political implications for the receiving country's labor and social welfare policies relating to the national labor legislation, introduction of zonal and sectoral minimum wage laws, working conditions, and manpower training. The problems could be more complex in the context of dual membership in the African regional organizations. Since some member states of ECOWAS (Nigeria) and CEAO (Niger) are also members of LCBC, there is the possibility that citizens of Cameroon, Gabon, Congo and the Central African Republic (member states of the UDEAC) may migrate through the Lake Chad Basin into Nigeria and Niger and, finally, to other member states of ECOWAS and CEAO.

The same would be true of labor migration from Nigeria and Niger through the LCBC into Cameroon and into other member states of the UDEAC in search of better employment opportunities, the possibilities for establishing business ventures, and perhaps even permanent residence in these states that are not members of the same organization with their country of origin. Those that migrate may be highly qualified and well trained, but they may flood the labor market of the state receiving them.[39] This could lead to a high rate of unemployment with subsequent undesirable economic, social and political repercussions.[40]

Although linguistic and cultural differences may limit the magnitude of the mobility of such persons, this may be so only in the case of migration between French speaking and English speaking African states, particularly in the short run. Real problems would remain in the long run with respect to completely free mobility of people. The changes in the political boundaries of Africa, following the attainment of independence by most member states of the regional groupings, account for most of the obstacles which may prevent the regional groupings from achieving the objectives of complete and unimpeded free mobility of citizens and persons. During the process of economic, cultural and social planning, the need for well trained foreign nationals in the domestic labor market is obvious.[41] Consequently, many member states of the regional organizations are bound to face the dilemma of deciding how to give priority to their nationals without disrupting the harmonious expansion of economic and social activities.

Despite the frequent rhetoric about the need for African economic cooperation and unity, many West African states are not yet ready to tolerate, voluntarily, the presence of trained and enterprising foreigners in their territories. In many cases, and sometimes as a distraction from domestic problems, some African governments have resorted to the expulsion of aliens. For example,in recent years, nationals of Nigeria have been expelled from Ghana,[42] those of Upper Volta from Ghana, Ghanians from Sierra Leone and Dahomians from Upper Volta, despite the fact that these states are all members of ECOWAS. As a consequence, there has been continuous deterioration in bilateral relations between many African states.

The most effective weapon that many African states have continuously used against foreigners is the Immigration Law which, again, is another obstacle to the free mobility of persons and citizens. The Immigration Laws of most African states have specific procedures and requirements with respect to entry into the country and the subsequent employment of non-indigenous workers. These workers need to obtain the appropriate permission or approval, either in the form of an identity card, a work permit, or a residence permit.

Even in situations where foreigners are allowed to enter a member state to participate in the development of the recipient's economy, they are very often faced with the existing national investment legislations which have reserved certain sectors of the economy and categories of enterprises for its citizens. This is true in the case of the Ghanian Business Promotion Act No. 334 of August 1, 1970.[43] The Nigerian Enterprises Promotion Decrees of 1972 and 1974 exclusively reserved for Nigerian citizens, companies, and associations the establishment and operation of certain enterprises.[44]

Despite the existence of the foregoing complex problems that has impeded the complete mobility of citizens and of skilled and unskilled manpower, the phenomenon cannot be divorced from the general problems of economic development in the West Africa sub-region. The economies of some West African states could have long collapsed, had it not been for the positive contributions of so called "***foreigners***".

The social, human, and economic problems arising from the free movement of persons will constitute a great challenge to all the West African regional organizations and their respective member states. To be sure, this is not a problem which can be handled alone by individual member states or by the regional groupings which are directly affected. It is absolutely necessary that the appropriate policy measures which are chosen to handle the complex problems should be collectively designed to ensure maximum effectiveness.

There are two alternative but largely complementary courses of policy action which could be pursued by the member states and the regional groupings on a collective basis. On the one hand, the incidence of migration can be reduced by creating in the states or the groupings of origin of the migrants real opportunities for remunerative permanent employment and a sustained standard of living of those who could potentially migrate.

Alternatively, in the long-term interest of the migrants, the member state, and the economic grouping where this migration takes place, it would be necessary for the various regional groupings to collectively provide legislative measures, which would be directed inter alia, to: (a) discourage any migration, including permanent, that may not likely result in the employment of the migrant. (b) ensure the appointment at the place of employment of welfare and placement officers who are familiar with the language and cultures of the migrants. (c) facilitate the transmission of voluntary family remittances from the migrant to his country of origin and to ensure that provision is made for the accumulation of deferred income to be paid to the migrant on his final return to his country, and (d) ensure that the migrant worker and his family return to their home of origin on completion of his contract period.

The implementation of the provisions of free mobility of persons within the regional groupings has to be pursued with caution and in stages. First, the acquisition of entry visas could be facilitated by reducing all the requirements that generally delay the issues of entry visas by competent national immigration authorities.[45] When there is complete free trade and free capital movement between the member states of the same regional grouping, then the complete elimination of entry visas would become automatic.

The early stages of industrial, fiscal, financial, and monetary harmonization between the member states of each grouping might require the utilization of skilled manpower from another member state. This will reduce high labor costs paid to expatriate labor from third countries . When the industries have begun operation, the free mobility of labor would take place with a minimum negative effect on the social, economic, and political situation of the member states and the regional groupings.

7. Distribution of Costs and Benefits

West Africa has been one of the least developed parts of the African continent and the most dependent on developed countries for economic development. The period of colonization laid the foundation for the present practice of externally-oriented and mono-cultural economy in West Africa. The West African economy is dependent and disarticulated. Internal attempts for the accumulation of capital and technology are easily vulnerable to external intervention.

West Africa is ill-equipped to absorb the shock of economic integration. To this extent, the distribution of costs of regional economic cooperation, and the leaders' perception of the likely benefits to be derived therefrom have become a focal issue of survival for each West African economic community. This was most obvious in the East African Community. For example, it was argued by Uganda and Tanzania that Kenya benefitted most from the common services of the said Community. This allegation, and other related issues like unbalanced distribution of investments, and "ineffectiveness of the East African Development Bank as an equalizing device,"[46] contributed immensely to the demise of the Community. Basically the situation in East Africa was a re-distribution crisis.

Besides the above, other redistribution issues that became politicized related to gains or losses from transport and tourism. This is clearly narrated by A. Hazlewood:

> A number of issues concerning transport and related issue of tourism, caused tensions between the Partner states (of the East African Community). The Kenya

> tourist industry benefited from access to the game parks of Northern Tanzania. They were generally included in a circuit for Nairobi-based tourists, using Kenyan vehicles. Although payments were obviously made for the use of Tanzania's hotels and game parks, and for other goods and services,nonetheless it was strongly contended by Tanzania that she received only minor benefits from the traffic.[47]

It was obvious, therefore, that Tanzania leaders' perceived the transport services of the Community as having a negative effect on its national development because the traffic between Kenya and Zambia crossing Tanzania's was in Kenya's interest but at Tanzania's cost.

The less developed partners in the LCBC, CEAO, or ECOWAS are likely to be more sensitive over the issue of the sharing of costs and benefits. There is also the geographical trend in a Community whereby the highly qualified professionals migrate from the less developed areas to more lucrative states for higher remuneration and an easier life. This trend aggravates the economic asymmetry between the member states.

In an attempt to solve this problem, it would be necessary to bear in mind that: (a) an orderly development of productive activities through the regional economic organizations in the West African sub-region is necessary for correcting the fundamental, structural disequilibrium in the internal and external sectors of their economies, and (b) such corrections need to be compatible with equitable distribution of costs and benefits among members of the various sub-regional economic organizations and other intergovernmental bodies that are at different stages of economic development.

8. Harmonization of Legal Systems

The importance of the judicial arm of a regional economic organization cannot be over stressed. Adjudication prevents possible breakdown of the organization through its mediation of disputes between member states and its timely interpretation of the community laws and regulations. A well constituted and generally accepted adjudicating body is imperative for community survival. ECOWAS, for example, has seen the Tribunal Common markets and Customs Unions in Africa disintegrate partly because of inefficient and inadequate provisions for peaceful resolution of conflicts.

An equally serious legal problem is the prevailing plural legal systems based on those of the old colonizing countries of Britain, France, Spain, and Portugal. The adopted British, French, Portuguese or Spanish legal systems have to be standardized both between themselves and between them and varying African laws. Unifying the varying legal systems is necessary because, as duly observed: "economic development may be regarded by a piecemeal system of law, and it may be fostered, if there is one unified system of law, which enables all persons in the territory (union) to enter freely into commercial transactions."[48]

Thus a single legal system, though an idealistic concept, would enhance West African economic cooperation by removing the present discrepancies in company laws, taxation laws, transportation laws, and immigration laws of the member states of the different organizations.

As has already been stated, the emergence of a unitary legal system in the West Africa sub-region is mythical. A realistic solution will be the harmonization of the diverse municipal laws with the laws of each organization. In ECOWAS, the English and French speaking member states sometimes differ in their conception and interpretation of certain provisions of the Lagos Treaty. L. Adegbite, in his study on this controversy, observed that the Ivory Coast regards the provisions of the Lagos Treaty as an:

> authority superior to that of the laws. They would thus be binding, with certain exceptions, on municipal courts without further parliamentary intervention.[49]

On the other hand, the Nigerian constitution (1979) has duly provided for the incorporation of Treaty into Municipal Law. By virtue of section 12(i) of the Constitution, no Community Law will be implemented in Nigeria "except to the extent to which any such Treaty has been enacted into law by the National Assembly." Thus, the Nigerian style of legalizing Community Law is more time consuming than that of the Ivory Coast. Such differences are bound to retard the implementation of Community Laws and its process.

9. Ideological Differences and Political Instability

The political problems that beset economic cooperation efforts in West Africa are due to the general political instability and the ideological differences in the region. The West African states fall roughly into "**conservative/radical/socialist**" ideologies. Nigeria, the Ivory Coast, and Senegal presently represent a conservative outlook, although these are African states that have previously had liberal economic policies towards foreign investments. In these areas, there is a higher concentration of multinational activities than in the "**radical/socialist**" groups of Guinea, Mali, and Mauritania. Differences in ideology result in diverse and conflicting approaches to development planning and allocation of investment resources.

Further, the generic political instability seen in constant changes in governments disrupts or, at best, delays integration plans and schedules. Ghana and Benin have between themselves shared over three governments in a decade. The fratricidal conflicts in Ethiopia, Spanish Sahara and Chad have antagonized immediate neighbors and pitted distant friends in West Africa against one another, thereby removing the social and economic background conditions for a successful economic cooperation arrangement in the West Africa sub-region.

It should be kept in mind by the policy makers that before any attempt is made at solving these problems, care must be taken to clearly define and delineate the responsibilities of the individual member states and those of the cooperation as a whole. Furthermore, although each member state in solving its socio-economic problem is at liberty to adopt a strategy suitable to it's needs, care must be taken to avoid conflict within the regional organizations.

10. Conclusion

As a concluding note, it should be pointed out that this study does not provide a story of great success. In a number of ways, it is a story of weakening regional economic cooperation rather than of a strengthening of economic and political ties among nations of West Africa. The idea of economic cooperation is an idea for bringing countries together for their mutual benefits. The story here is one largely of a multiplication of economic organizations, and not of a "coming together" for self-reliance and self-sustaining at the sub-regional level. Strangely enough, the present boundaries of West Africa are colonial boundaries which have, in many cases, cut across viable ethnic or tribal lines. These boundaries were largely boundaries of administrative convenience and did not reflect economic reality.

Since independence, countries of West Africa (as in other parts of Africa too) have psychologically developed a strong will to defend their colonial boundaries considering them as more durable than any interterritorial links envisaged by regional economic organizations.. The declarations made by such eminent African statesmen as President Nkrumah, Toure, and Nyerere, of a Pan african approach to African problems has been an illusive fantasy.

Hazlewood explains this strange behavior among nations in this way.

> What has to be remembered is that, at independence political power was transferred to the territorial not the supraterritorial units. The inheritors of political power have an interest in maintaining the authority and boundaries of the national states inviolate. Their interest in interterritorial links is much less direct. It is, therefore, not surprising that while the interterritorial links of colonial times crumble, the practical achievement in the establishment of new links between independent states - despite much talk - is still meager."[50]

One of the key factors that any regional economic organization must take into consideration is ideological compatibility. The lesson for the West Africa sub-region from the East African Common Market is that the search for an economic organization must begin with a search for ideological compatibility. This factor has been shown to be most purposeful in a number of prospering regional economic organizations of which ASEAN (Association of South East Asian Nations) is a good example. The ASEAN has brought together: Thailand, Malaysia, Singapore, Indonesia, and the Philippines, with Brunei earmarked as its sixth member after its independence in 1982.

Political organizations often produce a greater degree of cohesion than purely economic organizations. The problem with the West Africa region is that ECOWAS, which acts more as an economic umbrella under which nations of a different political persuasions have gathered, may prove to be a force of greater intensity than other regional economic organizations. An economic organization among states satisfies the ideological needs too. It is against this background that the scenario can be drawn of a new association of states extending across Africa, from the Seychelles possibly to as far as Zaire, and including both Mozambique and Zimbabwe.

The break-up of existing economic organizations in West Africa will not necessarily separate their members forever. Equally the maintenance of the existing economic organizations may not be beneficial to their members forever. New groupings are bound to appear and disappear in West Africa. But the most durable group may well be a collection of countries where ideological beliefs truly intersect economic interests.

Nevertheless, it is hoped that this study has exposed the important economic and political issues that many African states rarely consider before signing multiple protocol agreements which very often have conflicting objectives with respect to the treatment of third countries and the obligations which they collectively have to assume.

Despite the complex problems arising from the multiplicity of and dual membership in West African regional economic organizations, and others that have not been touched upon and which constitute a considerable drawback to the realization of effective economic cooperation at the regional level in West Africa, one compelling and irreversible reality is obvious - the vicious circle of underdevelopment to which West Africa is continuously subjected, with its attendant economic, social, and political ills, can be improved only by joint endeavors at the regional level and the harmonization of national economic policies.

African states in the West Africa sub-region, therefore, have no alternative but to collectively work, effectively and relentlessly, for unity of purpose on economic cooperation issues and for solutions to problems among themselves. The deciding factor must be the existence of a political will among the West African leaders to unite economically since it is one of the most important preconditions for successful regional economic cooperation. This must be demonstrated by the preparedness of African states to give up some of their sovereignty over the management of their national economies. The short term costs of such an action could be considerable. The long term benefits of a single regional grouping could, other things being equal, over-shadow the costs.

Footnotes

1. W.A. Ndongko, "The Economic Implications for Cameroon of the LCBC Proposed Trade Agreement," Quarterly Review of Information, Economic and Financial Studies, Yaounde, No. 5, September 1976, p. 25.
2. Teveedjre, Albert, Pan africanism in Action, Cambridge: Harvard Center for International Affairs, Occasional Papers in International Affairs, No. 11, 1965, Passim.
3. Lewis, H.W. (eds). French Speaking Africa: The Search for Identity, New York: Walker & Company, 1965.
4. See for example, Yansane A.Y., "Some Problems of Monetary dependency in West African States of French Colonial Legacy," op cit; Passim.
5. For a more detailed development of this mood, see Walterstein Immanuel, Africa: The Politics of Unity, New York, Vintage Book, Random House, 1967.
6. "Independence Within ECOWAS: 1," West Africa, 10th October 1977, pp. 2078-2079.
7. "Independence Within ECOWAS" West Africa, 10 October 1977, pp. 2078-2079
8. See the provisions of Article 50 to 52 of the ECOWAS Treaty, creating this Fund.
9. West Africa, 10th October, 1977, p. 2079.
10. For more details see LCBC Trade Agreement on Livestock, Meat and other Agricultural Products Among Member States of the Lake Chad Basin Commission, Ndjamena, 1971.
11. See W.A. Ndongko, "The Economic Implication for Cameroon of the LCBC Proposed Trade Agreement," op. cit., passim.

12. These arrangements have been discussed in W.A. Ndongko, "The Economic Implications of Multimembership in Regional Economic Groupings," Africa Spectrum, No. 3, 1976.

13. Osagie, Eghosa, "Monetary Disintegration and Integration in West Africa," Nigerian Journal of International Studies, No. 1 Vol. 1, July 1975, pp. 19-27.

14. Newlyn, W.T. and Rowan, D.C., Money and Banking in colonial Africa, (Oxford University Press, Oxford 1954).

15. Adomakoh, Abert. "The Evolution of Currency and Banking in West African Countries," Basle Center Publication Series A. No. 42, 1962.

16. The limited Role of the Currency Board System in fostering the economic development of British West Africa could be attributed to its limited scope of operation as defined by the British Secretary of State in the Regulations defining the Constitution, Duties and Powers of the West African Currency Board" of 2nd September 1949.

17. Robert, S.H., The History of French Colonial Policy: 1870-1925, London: Frank Cass and Co., Ltd., 1963.

18. Newlyn, W.T. and Rovan, D.C., op. cit., Passim.

19. This is in contrast to the economic and monetary balkanization in English speaking Africa where the British were unwilling to provide similar leadership to her former colonies. However, the encouragement of continuous economic and financial dependence on France by the former French African colonies greatly limited the extent to which the so-called independent state can autonomously manage their national economies.

20. Frank G. Andre, "Les Flotterments du Franc Francais et la Monnaie Africaine," Marches Tropicaux 25 January 1975.

21. In Nigeria, for example, an effort to remove the deficiencies in the function of the financial system has led to the setting up of the Financial System Review Committee, to recommend ways and means of rectifying the deficiencies.

22. Cox-George, N.A., Finance and Development in West Africa, London 1961, Passim.

23. The attainment of this objective will be facilitated by the creation in 1968, an Association of African Central Banks. This idea was first introduced on May 25th 1963 when African Heads of State, and Governments, meeting in Addis Ababa unanimously resolved to set up a monetary and Economic Committee to study a large range of monetary and financial matters. Following the

meeting of the Governors of African Central Banks, in Addis Adaba in Feb. 1966, it was resolved to create an Association of African Central Banks. The Article of Association of the AACB came into force on 17 Dec. 1968 after having been signed by the fourteen required institutions.

24. Enufuwosu, C.E., Developmental Roles and Policies of African Central Banks," Central Bank of Nigeria, Economic and Financial Review, Vol. 10, No. 3, Dec. 1972, pp. 1-12.

25. Taylor, A.B., The West African Clearing House (Mimeo). Also for see Falegan, S.B. in "Clearing and Payments Arrangements within the West African Sub-Region," prepared for Conference by NIIA, August, 1976.

26. See Hymer, S. "The Multinational Corporation and the Law of Uneven Development," in Bhagwati, J. (ed) Economics and the World Order, (New York, MacMillan Company, 1972).

27. Samir Amin, "Underdevelopment and Dependence in Black Africa: Origins and Contemporary Forms," Journal of Modern African Studies, Vol. 10, No. 4, December 1972.

28. See W.A. Ndongko, "Trade and Development Aspects of the Central African Customs and Economic Union," Cultures et Developpement Louvaine, Vol. VII, No. 2, 1975, pp. 344-345.

29. Quoted in Arthur Hazlewood (ed), African Integration and Disintegration, (Oxford University Press, London, 1968).

30. A.Y. Yansane, "West African Economic Integration: Is ECOWAS the Answer?" Africa Today, Vol. 24, No. 3, July - September 1977, pp. 47-50.

31. For our purpose, a community, union or commission project is defined as one which is approved by all member states of each regional grouping, as serving the purpose and objectives of economic cooperation and integration and which need access to the markets of the grouping in order to maintain efficient operation.

32. Hymer, Stephen, "The Multination Corporation and the Law of Uneven Development" in J. Bhagwati (ed) Economics and the World Order, (New York; MacMillan Co., 1972).

33. For a more detail analysis of this problem see W.A. Ndongko "International Development Aid within the Context of Regional Economic Groupings," CERES: FAO Review on Development, Rome, Vol. 10, No. 1, January - February 1977 and Development and Cooperation, Bonn, No. 2, 1977.

34. Ibid., passim.

35. For example, see Article 2, Treaty of the Economic Community of West African States (ECOWAS) ILM, Vol. 14, No. 5, September 1975.
36. The raison d'etre of a licensing system is that industrial property rights like all other factors of production are capable of ownership and also must for varied economic reasons move from one area of supply to demand. This so-called industrial property rights - patents, know hows, trade marks, secret processes - enjoy protection under national or international laws.
37. In the case of ECOWAS, Articles 27 and 31 of the Lagos Treaty should prove useful. The former provides that the citizens of member states shall be regarded as community citizens and for the abolition of all obstacles to their freedom of movement and residence within the community, while Article 31 stipulates personnel exchange training and joint ventures.
38. Amin, Samir (ed) Modern Migrations in Western Africa. Oxford University Press, London, 1974, p. 66.
39. The problems were identified by the InterAfrican Labor Conference (Elizabethville, 1950) see CETA Report: Migrant Labor in Africa South of the Sahara, Abidjan, 1961, p. 21.
40. See Piault, M.P. "The Migration of Workers in West Africa," in CCTA Publication No. 79 Migrant Labor in Africa South of the Sahara, Abidjan 1961, pp. 324-325.
41. Panofsky, H.F. "The Significance of Labor Migration for the Economic Welfare of Ghana and the Voltaic Republic in CCTA Publication No. 79, op. cit., passim. This is particularly true of such countries like Ghana where the Economic Survey of 1958 reported: "Migratory labor continued to play a great part. Nearly 20,000 out of 130,000 employees in establishments were Africans of non-Ghanian origin. The mining industry employed 6,600; construction 4,200; transport, electricity, water and sanitary 800 each. Many more were known to be employed in agriculture and casual work."
42. Nigerian Institute of International Affairs Bulletin, Vol. 1, No. 3, January 1972, p. 21.
43. See Samir Amin (ed) op. cit., pp. 175-176 and West Africa, No. 3079, 5th July 1976, p. 966.
44. Some of these enterprises include: advertising, pool betting and lotteries, assembling of musical instruments, blending and bottling of hot drinks, bread and cake making, candle manufacture, cinemas and other places or entertainment, hair

dressing and hauling of wood over roads, see Schedule 1, of the 1972 Promotion Decree.

45. It should be noted that at a recent ECOWAS Heads of State Summit in Dakar, a decision was taken to remove this requirement so as to enable the Community's citizens to visit member states for a temporary period of 90 days.

46. A. Hazlewood "The End of the East African Community: What are the Lessons for Regional Integration Schemes?" Journal of Common Market Studies, Vol. XVII, No. 1, September 1979, p. 45.

47. Ibid., p. 48.

48. London Conference on Future of Law in Africa. (1960).

49. L. Adgbite, "Need for Integration of Legal Systems Among ECOWAS States," presented at the International Conference on ECOWAS, NILA 23-27 August 1978.

50. A. Hazlewood, (ed) African Integration and Disintegration, Oxford University Press, 1967, p. 3.

TABLE 7.1. CENTRAL BANKS AND CURRENCY UNITS OF WEST AFRICAN STATES

REGIONAL GROUPING	CENTRAL BANK	CURRENCY UNIT	EXCHANGE RATE US AT 2132/76
I. <u>ECOWAS/CEAO</u>			
1. GHANA	BANK OF GHANA	NEW CASH	1.1538
2. NIGERIA**	CENTRAL BANK	NAIRA	0.6265
3. SIERRA LEONE	BANK OF SIERRA LEONE	LEONE	1.1210
4. GAMBIA	BANK OF GAMBIA	DALASI	2.2421
5. GUINEA	NATIONAL BANK OF GUINEA	SILY	21.86
6. GUINEA BISSUA	--	PESO	32.160
7. MALI*	Banque Catea-EDU MALI	MALI FRANC	49.065
8. LIBERIA	NATIONAL BANK OF LIBERIA	LIBERIAN DOLLAR	1.00
9. MAURITANIA*	BANQUE CENTRALE DU MAURITANIA	OUGUIYA	49.065
10. BENIN 11. IVORY COAST* 12. NIGER** 13. SENEGAL* 14. TOGO 15. UPPER VOLTA*	BANQUE CENTRALE DES ETATS L'AFRIQUE DE L'OUEST (BCEAO)	C.F.A. FRANC	245.33

* Denote CEAO Member states

** Denote LCBC Member States

Source: Compiled from (a) IMF, <u>International Financial Statistics</u>, April 1976 and <u>The Financial Times</u>, 23 July, 1976.

TABLE 7.2. CENTRAL BANK DISCOUNT RATES IN SOME AFRICAN STATES

COUNTRY/GROUPING	1971	1972	1973	1974	1975
1. BENIN (ECOWAS/CEAO)	3.50	3.50	5.50	5.50	8.00
2. GHANA (ECOWAS)	8.00	8.00	6.00	6.00	6.00
3. MAURITANIA (ECOWAS)	3.50	3.50	5.50	5.50	5.50
4. NIGERIA (ECOWAS/LCBC)	4.50	4.50	4.50	4.50	3.50
5. SENEGAL (ECOWAS/CEAO)	3.50	3.50	5.50	5.50	8.00
6. CAMEROON (UDEAC/LCBC)	3.50	3.00	3.50	5.50	8.00
7. GABON (UDEAC)	3.50	3.50	3.50	5.50	8.00
8. NIGER (ECOWAS/LCBC/CEAO)	3.50	3.50	3.50	5.50	8.00

Source: IMF. International Financial Statistics, Feb. 1976.

Fig. 1 Multilateral and Bilateral Groupings in the West African Sub Region

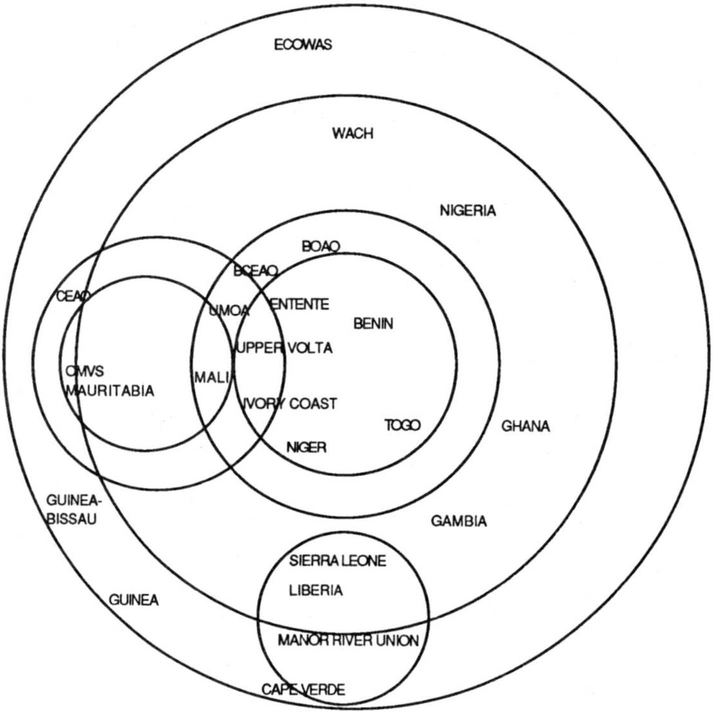

NOTES:

ECOWAS	-	Economic Community of West African States
WACH	-	West African Clearing House
CEAO	-	West African Econimic Community
OMVS	-	Organization for the Development of the Senegal River
UMOA	-	West African Monetary Union
BOAD	-	West African Development Bank

VIII. References

I. Africa
Economic Cooperation and Integration

Abdel-Salam, D.H., "The Evolution of African Monetary Institutions," Journal of Modern African Studies, 8,3, October 1970, 339 - 362.

African Bibliographic Center, Economic and Regional Integration in Africa, Washington: African Bibliographic Center, 1973, p. 49.

African Development Bank, The African Development Bank, Abidjan, 1965.

Ajala, Adekunie, Pan-Africanism: Evolution, Progress and Prospects, London: Andre Dentsch, 1973, 442 p.

Allo, Anthony M., "The Changing Legal Status of Boundaries in African: A Diachromic View," in Ingham, K., Ed. Foreign Relations of African States, London 1974, 111 - 128.

Economic Cooperation and Integration in Africa: Three Case Studies, United Nations. Department of Economic and Social Affairs, New York, 1969.

Hazlewood A. "Problems of Integration Among African States," African Integration and Disintegration, Ed. by A. Hazlewood. (Oxford University Press, London).

Simmons A. "Economic Integration in Africa" M.S.U. Business Topics, Winter, 1969.

"Africa and Economic Cooperation," African Target/Objectives Africans, Vol. 4, No. 6, June 1970, pp. 10-11, 25.

Decker, G., "International River Basins and Regional Development in Africa." Paper presented at AID Conference on Regional African Development, Nov. 1969.

Anguile, Andre G. and David Jacques, F. l'Afrique sans Frontiers (Monaca, Paul Bory, 1965.)

Arkhurst, F.S., "Problems of Economic Integration in Africa in the Seventies and Eighties, 1970.

Balogh, Thomas, "The Mechanism of Neo-Imperialism, The Economic Impact of Monetary and Commercial Institutions in Africa," Institute of Statistics, Oxford Bulletin, 24, 3: August 1962.

Botchmay, Francis A. "A Reconsideration of PanAfricanism Reality," PanAfrican Journal, S.I. Winter 1970, 34.48.

Brown, A.J. "Should African Countries form economic unions?" Economic Development in Africa (ed) E.F. Jackson, (Oxford University Press, 1965).

Brunsching, H. Myth et Realities de l'Imperialisme Colonial Francais, 1871-1914, (Paris, Armand Colin, 1960).

Cervenka, Zdenck, The Organization of African Unity and its (New York, Frederick A. Praeger, Inc. Publishers, 1969).

Cervenka, Zdneck, Towards a United Africa: The First Ten Years of the O.A.U., (London: C. Hurst, 1975), 250p.

Chikwe, J., "Africa: United and Differentiation," World Marxist Review, January 1972, 84-90.

Constantine, F., "L'Integration Regionale en Afrique Noire Esquisse Sur Dix Annees de Recherches," Revue Francaise de Science Politiques, 22, 5 October 1972, 1074 - 1110.

Djalloh, A. Abdul, Political Integration in French Speaking Africa, Berkeley: Institute of International Studies, University of California, 1973.

Ndongko W. A. and Franklin Vivekananda.
Economic Development of Cameroon. Bethany Books, P.O. Box 7444, 103 91 Stockholm, Sweden 1989

Ndongko W. A. and Franklin Vivekananda.
Critical Essays on African and Third World Economic Development. Bethany Books, P.O. Box 7444, 103 91 Stockholm, Sweden 1988

Economic Commission for Africa, "Coordination of Development Plans in Africa," U.N. Economic Bulletin for Africa, 1, 1964.

Escdebe, P.O. "Origins and Meaning of Pan-Africanism." Presence Africaine, 73, First Quarter, 1970-109-127.

Ewing; A.F., "Prospects for Economic Integration in Africa," Journal of Modern African Studies, III, 3, 1965.

G.A. "Les Flotterments du Franc Francais et la Monnaie Africaine" Marches Tropicausc: January 1974.

Guha Amalendu and Franklin Vivekananda, Development Alternatives, Bethany Books, P.O. Box 7444, 103 91 Stockholm, Sweden 1985

Green, R.H., "African Economic Unification: Some Perspectives paths and problems," Economic Bulletin of Ghana, 2, 1965.

Green and Krishna (eds), Economic Cooperation in Africa: Retrospect, (Oxford University Press, London, 1967).

Green, R.H. and Seidman, Ann, Unity or Poverty: The Economics of Pan-Africanism, Harmondsworth: (Penguin Books, 1968), P. 363

Gruhn I.V., "The Commission for Technical Cooperation in Africa," Journal of Modern African Studies, 9, 3 October 1971, 459 - 469.

Hance William A., Population, Migration and Urbanization in Africa. (New York, Columbia University Press, 1970.)

Hazelwood, Arthur (ed). African Integration and Disintegration Case Study on Economic and Political Union, (London, Oxford University Press, 1967).

Karmach, A.M., The Economics of African Development, (New York, Praegen,, 1967.)

T.M.F. Surveys of African Economics (Vols. I and II), World Bank, Washington D.C. 1968.

Jackson, E.F. (ed) Economic Development in Africa, Basil Blackwell, Oxford, 1951.

Langley, Jabe Ayodele, "Pan-Africanism in Paris, 1924-1936," Journal of Modern African Studies, 7 April 1969, 69-74.

LangMamurer, R.J. "Regional Integration and Cooperation in Africa: A History of Disappointment," Inter-Economics No. 9/10, 1977.

Mattews, R.O. "Inter-state Conflicts in Africa: A Review," International Organizations, Vol. 24, No. 2, Spring 1970.

Martin, Jane H., Bibliography of African Regionalism, Boston: Boston University, African Studies Center, 1969.

Mutherika, B.W.T. Towards Multinational Economic Cooperation in Africa (New York, Praeger Special Studies 1972).

Myteka, L.K. "A Genealogy of Francophone West and Equatorial Regional Organization." Journal of Modern African Studies, 12 2, 1974.

Ndongko W.A. "From Economic Domination to Association: Africa in the EEC," Presence Africaivle, Paris, No. 99/100, 1976.

Regional Trade and Economic Arrangements: Alternatives to Africa, Association with the EEC," Internationales AFRIKA FORUM, Munich, No. 1, 1977.

The Economic Implications of Multimembership in Regional Economic Groupings AFRIKA SPECTRUM, Hamburg, No. 3, 1976.

Ndongko, W.A.: "The Economic Origins of the Association of African States with the European Economic Community," PanAfrican Journal, New York, Vol, V. NO. 3, Fall,1972 and

African Studies Review, Michigan, Vol. XVI, No. 2, September 1973.

Ngango, Georges: Les Investisements d'Origin Exterieure en Afrique Noire Francophone: Statut et Incidence sur le Developpement (Paris, Presence Africa, 1973).

Ndongko, W.A.: "Trade Liberation within the Setting of Multi-membership in African Regional Economic Groupings," (Mineo).

Newlyn, W.T.: Money in African Context, (Oxford University Press, 1967).

Nkrumah, Kwame: Neo-Colonialism: The Last State of Imperialism, (New York: International Publishers, 1965).

OCAM, La Cooperation Interafricaine au Seinde l'OCAM et ses Institutions Specialises. (Yaounde - Cameroon, 1972).

Okigbo, P.C.N.: Africa and the Common Market, London, 1967.

Regional Green H. and Seidman, A.: Unity or Poverty? The Economics of PanAfricanism (Middlesex - England, Penguin Books, 1968).

Robson, Peter: Economic Integration in Africa, (London, Allen & Unwin, 1968); and Evantson, III: North-Western University Press, 1968.

Robson, P. and Lury, D. (eds): The economics of Africa, George Allen & Unwin, London, 196_.

Roland, Julienne: "Problems of Integration in French Speaking Africa" in Arthur Hazlewood (ed), African Integration and Disintegration. (New York: Oxford University Press, 1967).

Ranoleje, A.M.R. and Sanders, A.J.G.M.: "The Structural Pattern of African Regionalism." Comparative and International Law: Journal of Southern Africa, 2,2 July 1971, 155-197; 4, 3 November 1971, 293-323; 5, 1 March 1972, 35-55; July 1972; 171-188; 5, 3 November 1972, 299-388 and 6, 1 March 1973, 82-105.

Rothehild, D.: "African Federations and the Diplomacy of Decolonization," Journal of Development Areas, 4, 4 July 1970.

Sohn L.B.: Basic Documents of African Regional Organizations. Vol. I, II and III, Oceana, New York, 1972.

_______, African Regional Organizations: History Literature and Basic Documents, Dobbs Ferry, New York, Oceana, 1971, 4 Vols.

Tevoedjre, Albert: Panafricanism in Action, Cambridge: Harvard University, Center for International Affairs, Occasional Papers in International Affairs, No. 11, 1965.

Thomposon B. Vincent: Africa and Unity: The Evolution of Pan Africanism, London, Longmans 1969.

Touval, Seadia: "Treaties, Borders and the Partition of Africa" Journal of African History, 7, 2, 1966.

UNECA: Background Paper on the Establishment of a Common Market UNECA, Niamen, 1963.

UNECA, African Trade Statistics, No. 3, December 1967.

UNECA, IntraAfrican Trade, E/CN/.IV/STC/20, 1963.

UNECA, Reports of Industrial and Integration Unions to West, East and Central, North and Control (Equatorial) Africa. E/CN.IV/246, 247, 248, 320, 1963 to 1966, Addis Ababa.

Economic Cooperation in the African Region in African Target Objectives Africains, Vol. 3, No. 6, Sept. 1970.

Ewing, A.F.: "African Economic Cooperation Revisited" in Journal of World Trade Law, Vol. 4, March-April 1970.

Forch, Rene: "Steps Towards Unity in Europe and in Africa," Africa Progress Through Cooperation, edited by John Karefa - Smart, Dodd, Mead & Co. 1966.

Friedrichs Dieter: "Association Problems of African States," Intereconomics, No. 8, August 1970.

Gambari, Ibrahim: "Which Way Africa? African Progress, Vol. No. 3, June 1971.

Gedamu, T. "Economic Cooperation in Africa," The Challenge of Development "Nairobi", (East African Publishing House, 1968).

Hazi-Vasilewa, J.: "InterAfrican Economic Cooperation," African Boundary Problems, edited by Carl Gosta Widstrand, Uppsala, The Scandinavian Institute of African Studies, 1969.

Helmsyhroff, H.: "Integrations and Disintegrations: Tendenzen in Schwarzafika der ersten dekade inder Unabhangigkeit." International Africa Forum, Vol. 6, No. 9, September - October 1970.

Obote Milton, A.: Problems of progress through cooperation," Africa, Progress Through Cooperation, edited by John Karefa - Smart, (New York, Dod, Mead and Col, 1966).

Philip, Kjeld.: "Regional Cooperation in Africa" in Mawazo (Kampala), Vol. 3, No. 3, June 1972.

N'Dongo, Sally: La "Cooperation" Franco-Africaine, Paris, F. Maspero, 1972.

"Economic Commission for Africa," Africa, No. 1, May 1971.

Legum, C.: PanAfricanism, Pall Mall Press, London, 1961.

Decreane, P.: Le PanAfricanism, Paris 1959.

Hoskyns, (C) PanAfricanism in Accra, Africa South, Cape Town, Vol. 3, No. 3, 1959.

Basic Documents of African Regional Organization, Vol. 1. Ed. Sohn (LIB), Oceana, 1971.

Accra Declaration of 1958, Para 8. Recommendation 1.

The Sanniquellie Declaration, 1959, para. 7. Also Legum, Ibid.

Dubois, (V.D.), The Search for Unity in French Speaking Black Africa, New York, 1965.

Jacquot, (M.J.), La Politique Douaniere et la cooperation Franco-Africaine, Paris, 1963.

Delavignethe, (R), l'Afrique Noire Francaise et son Destin, Paris, 1962.

Malembe, (P), Le PanAfricanisme et le Regroupement des Etas Africains et Malagache de Langue Francaise, Louvain, 1965.

Steinfield, (J), Pour UNC Cooperation Economique Africaine Brussels, 1964.

Neres, P.: French Speaking Africa: From Colonial Status to Independence, New York, 1962.

Leduc, (M), Les Institutions Monetaires Africaines: Pays Francophones, Paris, 1965.

_________, "Le Role Anti-Inflationniste des Institutions de la Zone Franc en Afrique de l'Ouest," 1961, Annales Africaines.

Muracciole, L.O.: "La Banque Centrale des Etats de l'Afrique de l'Ouest," 14 (1960) Revue Juridique et Politique d'Outre-Mer pp. 371-430; 16 (1962) Revue Juridique et Politique d'Outre-Mer pp. 375-424.

Green, (R.H.) and Krishna, (K.G.V.) Economic Cooperation in Africa: Retrospect and Prospect, Nairobi, 1967.

Legum, (C) PanAfricanism: A Short Political Guide, New York, 1965.

Sands, (W), "Prospects for a United Maghreb," The Arab Middle East and Muslim Africa, ed., New York 1961.

Rainero, (R), Documenti della Organissasione Africana, Padua, 1967.

Shepperson, (G), "PanAfricanism and PanAfricanism: Some Historical Notes" 23 Phylon: The Attanta, University Review of Race and Culture (1962).

Rothchild, (D.S.) Towards Unity in Africa: A Study of Federalism in British Africa, Washington, D.C., 1960.

United Nations, Economic Commission for Africa Resolution 142 (vii) on Economic Integration, 22 February 1963. Annual Report; 3 March 1964 -23 February 1965. (Official Records of the Economic and Social Council, Thirty Ninth Session, Supplement No. 10 (E/4004; E/Ec.14/343/Rev.1, 1965).

African Integration and Disintegration, Ed. by Hazlewood, A. (Oxford University Press, 1967).

Frank, G.A. (1974), "les Flottements du Franc Francaise et la monnaie Africaine" Marcus Tropicau.

International Monetary Fund (1970) Surveys of African Economies Vol. 3, Washington: ILF, Jeune Afrique (1971) (Paris 18 December).

J.F. Munro: Africa and the International Economy 1800-1960: London, 1976, J.M. Dent/Totowa, N.J.

Alpheus Manghezi: Class, Elite and Community in African Development, Uppsala: Scandinavian Institute of African Studies 1976.

A Bark Needs Strategy for Africa: International Labor Office, Geneva: ILO, 1977.

Liniger-Goumaz, M.: Africa: l'Afrique d'Hier a Demain, Geneve: Edns du Temps, 1977.

Philips M.M. and Patrick O'Meara: Africa, London: (Indiana University Press, 1977).

Rondney, W. 1972, How Europe Underdeveloped Africa. Dar es Salaam: Tanzania Publishing House.

Seers, Dudly 1973, "The meaning of development" in C.K. Wilber (ed). The Political Economy of Development and Underdevelopment, (New York, Random House).

Joel Samoff, "Underdevelopment and its Grass Roots in Africa," Paper presented at the Annual Conference of the African Studies Association, Baltimore, 1978.

Sagay, E.I. and Onwuka R.: "Attempts at Regional Economic Integration: An Examination" paper presented at the International Conference on Law and Economy in Africa, 15-20th February 1982, University of Ife, Nigeria.

Marasignle, P.L." "A Review of Regional Economic Integration in Africa, with particular reference to Equatorial Africa, West Africa, the Magreb and East Africa," paper presented at the International Conference on Law and Economy in Africa, 15-20th February 1982, University of Ife, Nigeria.

Kalonji Ntalaja: "L'impact de l'Association au marche Common sur l'integration Africaine" in W.A. Ndongko (ed.) Economic Cooperation and Integration in Africa, CODESRA Book Series, Dakar (forthcoming).

IRES, Kinshasa (Zaire), "Cooperation economique et financiere en Afrique. Etat de question," in W.A. Ndongko (ed.) Economic Cooperation and Integration in Africa, CODESRA Book Series, Dakar (forthcoming).

Etienne Bariqume, "Systeme economique et Cooperation Regionale en Afrique" in W.A. Ndongko (ed.) Economic Cooperation and Integration in Africa, CODESRA Book Series, Dakar (forthcoming).

Makhtar Diouf: "Le Problem du developpement inegal dans les experiences Africaines d'integration Economique," in W.A. Ndongko, (ed.) Economic Cooperation and Integration in Africa, CODESRA Book Series, Dakar (forthcoming).

Ndongko, W.A., "Trade Liberalization within the setting of multimembership in African Regional Groupings: Problems and

Prospects in W.A. Ndongko (ed.) Economic Cooperation and Integration in Africa. CODESRA Book Series, Dakar (forthcoming).

________, "The Future of Regional Economic Cooperation in Africa: A Critical Analysis" in W.A. Ndongko, (ed.) Economic Cooperation and Integration in Africa, CODESRA Book Series Dakar, (forthcoming).

Okwudiba Nnoli: "External Constraints on PanAfrican Economic Integration" in W.A. Ndongko (ed.) Economic Cooperation and Integration in Africa, CODESRA Book Series, Dakar (forthcoming).

Mestre T.: "Balance de las Relaciones Interafricanas del Africa Independendiente, Revista de Politica Internacional, 100, November - December 1968.

Mutharika, B.W.T.: Toward Multinational Economic Cooperation in Africa, (New York: Praeger, 1972).

Mytelka, L.K.: "A Genealogy of Francophone West and Equatorial African Regional Organization," Journal of Modern African Studies 12, 2, 1974.

Nkrumah, Kwame, Africa Must Unite. (New York, Praeger, 1963).

Ramoleje, A.M.R. and Sanders, A.J.G.M.: "The Structural Pattern of African Regionalism," Comparative and International Law Journal of Southern Africa, 4,2 July 1971, 155-192; 4,3 November 1971, 293-323, 5, 1 March 1972, 35-55; 5,2 July 1972, 181-188, 5,3, November 1972, 299-388 and 6, 1 March 1973, 82-105.

Premises and Process of Maldevelopment, Franklin Vivekananda (edt) Bethany Books, P.O. Box 7444, 103 91 Stockholm, Sweden 1986.

II. West Africa
Economic Cooperation and Integration

Abangwu, G.G.: "Systems Approach to Regional Integration in West Africa," Journal of Common Market Studies, Vol. XIII, No. 1 and 2.

Aluko, S.A.: "Problems of Financial and Monetary Integration in West Africa," The Nigerian Journal of Economic and Social Studies, Vol. 5, No. 1, 1963.

Adams, John: "External Linkages of National Economies in West Africa," African Urban Notes, Fall 1972.

Adedeji, A.: "Economic Community of West Africa States: Ideals and Realities" The Nigerian Trade Journal, Vol. 22, April/June 1975.

_______, "Prospects of Regional Economic Cooperation in West Africa," Journal of Modern African Studies, 8, 2 July 1970.

Barbour, Kenneth M., "Industrialization in West Africa: The Need for Sub-Regional Groupings with an Integrated Economic Community, Journal of Modern African Studies, October 1972.

Berg, E.J.: "The Economic Basis of Political Choice in French West Africa," American Political Science Review, 54, 2 June, 1960.

Bank of Sierra Leone, West African Economic Cooperation: Problems and Possibilities, Occasional Paper No. 1, April, 1972.

Central Bank of Nigeria, "Trade and Monetary Relations in West African Sub-Region: 1966-1970," Economic and Financial Review, Vol. 10, No. 1, June 1972.

Deschamps, Hubert: "Les Frontiers de la Senegambie," Revue Franciase d'Etudes Politiques Africanies, 80, August 1972.

Delancey, Mark. W.: "Early Attempts at West African Unity: Ghana, Guinea and Mah," Indian Journal of Politics, 7, 1 June 1973.

Doboslewies, S.: "Traditional Trade and Population Migration as Integrating Factors in West Africa," Africana Bulletin, 14, 1971.

"ECOWAS, on the Move," West Africa, 29 August, 1977.

"ECOWAS, on the Road," West Africa, 28 November 1977.

Food and Agricultural Organization: Integrated Agricultural Development in Gambia River Basin, Rome 1962.

Helliener, G.K.: "Nigeria and the African Common Market, The Nigerian Journal of Economic and Social Studies, Vol. 4, No. 3, 1962.

"Independence Within ECOWAS: I," West Africa, 10 October 1977.

Kumar, A. and Osagie, E.: "Problems of ECOWAS," Paper presented at the Conference on Nigeria and the World, Lagos, January, 1976.

Kurtz, D.M.: "Political Integration in Africa: The Mali Federation," Journal of Modern African Studies, 8, 3 October 1970.

Udokang, O.: "Nigeria and ECOWAS: Economic and Political Implications of Regional Integration. Paper presented at the Conference on Nigeria and the World (NIIA) Lagos, January 1976.

Ogundana, Babafam: "Seaport Development-Multi-National Cooperation in West Africa," Journal of Modern African Studies, 12, 3, 1974, 395-407, Map.

Onitiri, H.M.A.: "Towards a West African Economic community," in (Eicher and Liedbdin, (ed.) Growth and Development of the Nigerian Economy. (Michigan State University Press, 1970).

Osagie, Egbora: "Monetary Disintegration and Integration in West Africa," Nigerian Journal of International Studies, Vol. 1 No. 1, June 1975.

Plessz, Nicolas G.: Problems and Prospects of Economic Integration in West Africa, Center for Developing Area Studies, McGill University 1968.

Ramanmurthi, J.G.: "The Dynamics of Regional Integration in West Africa," India Quarterly, 26, 3 July - September 1970.

Robson, Peter: "The Problem of Senegambia," Journal of Modern African Studies, 111, 3, 1965.

Simmons, A.: "Economic Cooperation in West Africa," Western Political Quarterly, 25, 2 June 1972.

Thompson, Virgina M.: West Africa's Council of the Entente (Ithaca, New York Cornell University Press, 1972).

Treaty of the Economic Community of West African States (ECOWAS) Lagos, Federal Government Printers, 1975.

UNECA: Iron and Steel in West Africa, E/CN/IV/STC/24, 1963.

UNECA: Report on the Conference on Industrial Coordination in West Africa, E/CN.14/324,1965.

Welch, Claude: Dream of Unity: PanAfricanism and Political Unification in West Africa, Ithaca Cornell University Press, 1966.

"What ECOWAS Offers," West Africa, 22 November 1976.

Yansane, A.Y. "Experience in Monetary Independence and Transition to Socialism in West Africa: Case Study of Guinea," Paper presented at the 8th African Heritage Studies Association Conference, Atlanta, 22-25 April 1976.

________"Some Problems of Monetary Dependency in West African States of French Colonial Legacy." The Review of Black Political Economy 7, 1: (Fall) 1976.

Yoloye, E.A.: "Educational Exchange Between Western African Countries." West African Journal of Education 14, 3, 1970.

Nowzad B. "Economic Integration in Central and West Africa," Staff Papers, March 1969,.International Monetary Fund, Washington D.C.

"Etats Africains et Malagache Associes: Les Possibilites d'Industrialisation," Industries et Travaux d'outreler, Vol. 20, No. 219.

Kame, F.: "L'Aide au Developpement dans le Systeme de la Banque Mondiale et de la Communaute," Nations Nouvelles No. 20 June 1969 (Abidjan).

"Loncho's Coup in the Ivory Coast Ominois for OCAM Sugar Agreement," African Development, February 1971, pp. 8-9.

"OCAM, Regional Industrialization Programme Given" Translations on Africa, No. 1180, July 6, 1972.

"La participation populaire au developpement dans les pays de l'OCAM, Conference de l'OCAM." Developpement et Civilisation, No. 41-42, September - December 1970, pp. 21-82.

"Le retrait du Zaire de l'OCAM n'affecte pas l'avenir d'une organisation regionale." Marches Tropicaux, No. 1381, April 28, 1971, p. 1071.

"Sixieme Conference des Chefs d'Etat de l'OCAM," Bulletin de l'Afrique Noire, No. 631, February 1971, pp. 12754-12757.

Church, R.J. Harrison: "Some problems of Regional Economic Development in West Africa," Economic Geography, Vol. 45, No. 1 1969, pp. 53-62.

Curry, Robert L.: "A Note on West African Economic Cooperation" Journal of Modern African Studies, Vol. II, No. 1, pp. 136-140.

Daniel Cisse, "Problems de la Formation de l'epargne interne en Afrique occidentale," Presence Africaine (Paris), 1969.

"Development Trends in Inter Governmental Economic Cooperation in West Africa Since 1 July 1970," Presence African, Vol. 4, No. 2, June 1971, pp. 12-14.

Diagne, Pathe, Pour l'unite ouest Afriaine = Micro Etats et Integration Economique. Paris, Edition Anthropos, 1972.

Kodwo, Ewusi, West African Economies: Some Basic Economic Problems, Legon, University of Ghana, Institute of Social Statistical and Economic Research, 1971.

Ofoeegbu, Mazi Ray, "Functional Cooperation in West Africa: Ghana and its Neighbors," Insight and Opinion, Vol. 6, No. 1 1971, pp. 22-36.

"Perspectives des Marches des principales exportation ouest Africaines," Banque Centrale des Etates de l'Afrique de l'Ouest, Notes d'Information et Statistiques, (Paris), August - September 1969, pp. 1 - 36.

Delorme, Nicole: L'Association des Etats Africains et Malagache a la Communate Economique Europeanne, Paris: Librarie Generale de Droit et de Jurisprudence, 1972.

Vignes, D.: L'Association des Etats Africains et Malagache a la C.E.E. Paris, Armand Colin, 1970.

"Accords Commerciaux, douaniers et de paiement entre etats de l'Afrique de l'Ouest," Banque Centrale des Etats de l'Afrique de l'Ouest, Notes d'Information et Statistiques (Paris) No. 197, July.

"Towards Promotion of Intra-West African Trade," African Targets/Objectives, Vol. 4, No. 1, March 1971, pp. 14-17.

Trois nouveaux accords entre le Mali et le Senegal," Industries et Travaux d'Outremer, No. 218, January 1972.

"The West African Rice Development Association," African Targets/Objectifs Africains, Vol. 3, No. 7, December 1970.

"West African States," Establishment of West African Rice Development Association," International Legal Materials, Current Documents, Vol. 10, No. 3, May 1971, pp. 648-668.

Badel Gerard "L'entente Senghor-Houphet permettra la realisation de la Communaute de l'Afrique de l'Ouest," France Eurafrique Vol. 24, No. 232, February 1972, pp. 5-7.

"CEAO de quatre a huit partenaires" Revue Francaise d'Etudes Politique Africains, No. 79, July 1972, pp. 3-12.

"Effect of New Economic Community Questioned" Translations on Africa, No. 1023, April 20, 1971, pp. 1-6.

"Foreign Trade Regulations of the West African Customs Union (Dahomey, Ivory Coast, Mali, Mauritania, Niger, Senegal, Upper Volta, and Togo)" Overseas Business Reports, May 1970, pp. 1-11.

UDEAO, La Conference des Chefs d'Etat decide la creation d'une Communaute de l'Afrique de l'Ouest (Banako 23 Mai 1970), Afrique Contemporaine, No. 50. July-August, 1970 pp. 17-18.

"Apercus sur l'evolution des operation de la Banque Centrale des Etates de l'Afrique de l'Ouest, 1962-1969," Banque Centrale des Etats de l'Afrique de l'Ouest, Notes d'Information et Statistiques (Paris) No. 164, July 1969, pp. 1-16.

Banque Centrales des Etats de l'Afrique de l'Ouest, Paris, BCEAO, 1970.

Banque Central des Etats de l'Afrique de l'Ouest, Bilan des Banques et Etablissement Financiers de l'Union Monetaire Ouest-Africaine, 1968/70, Paris, BCEAO, 1972.

Banque Centrale des Etats de l'Afrique de l'Ouest, Rapport d'Activitie, 1968.

Bhaffia, Ratfan J.: "Factors Influencing Changes in Money Supply in ECEAO Countries," IMF Staff Papers (Washington, D.C.) Vol. 18, No. 2, July 1971, pp. 389-398.

"Le Commerce Exterieur Ouest Africain des Etats de l'Union Monetaire Ouest Africaine," Banque Centrale des Etats de l'Afrique de l'Ouest, Notes d'Information et Statistiques, Paris, No. 195, May 1972, pp. 1-16.

"Les etablissement financiers de ventes a credit de l'union monetaire ouest africaine," Sec 70, No. 197, July 1972, pp. 1 - 9.

Evolution generale et Orientation des exchanges exterieurs de l'Union Monetaire (see 70).

Perspectives de Production et d'Exportation en 1969-1970 de l'Union Monetaire Ouest Africaine, (see 70), December 1979, pp.1-4.

Sordiet, Monique: "Aucune date n'est encore fixee pour le retourn du Mali au Sein de l'Union Monetaire Ouest Africaine," Europe France Outremer, No. 506, May 1972, pp. 21-22.

"L'union Monetaire Ouest Africaine," Banque Centrale des Etats d'l'Afrique de l'Ouest, Notes d'Information et Statistique, No. 186, July 1971, pp. 1-16.

Born Stein, Ronald: "The Organization of Senegal River States" Journal of Modern African Studies, Vol. 10, No. 2, July 1972 pp. 267-283.

"Many Development Projects Studied," Translation on Africa, No. 1031, May, 5, 1971, pp. 1-5.

Mendy, Justin, "OERS (Organisation des Etats Riverains du Fleuve Senegal): A Real Chance for Development," Africa Quarterly, Vol. 10, No. 3, October-December 1970.

"New Three-State Organization Formed," West Africa (London), No. 2860, April 7, 1972, p. 425.

Organisation des Etats Reverains du Senegal. Note sur l'Organisation de la Structure de l'Enseignement dans les Etats de l'O.E.R.S. Dakar, OERS, 1970.

"Organisation des Etats Reverains du Senegal. 2e Conference au Summet (3 Fevrier 1970)," Revolution Democratique Africaine, (Conakry), No. 36, 1970.

"Table Rond de l'OERS sur les Perspective de developpement integre du bassin du fleuve Senegal," Bulletin de l'Afrique Noire, No. 639, March 1971, pp. 12924-12926,

"Drought in West Africa: Background, Impact and Implications for Seven Affected Nations," IMF Survey, Vol. 2; No. 8, September 1973, pp. 280-282.

UBA, SAM, "The Search for a West African Economic Union," Africa Development, Vol, 7, No. 9, September 1973, pp. 9-10.

Van Chein Nguyen: "L'Afique et le Marche Commun," Cahiers Zairois d'Etude Politique et Sociales, No. 1, April 1973.

Foltz, W.J.: From Frency West Africa to the Mali Federation, New Haven, 1965, Gonidec, P.F.

Dahomey, Journal Official, 1st September 1966, pp. 773-775.

Ivory Coast, Journal Official, 15th September 1966, pp. 1170-72.

Mauritania, Journal Official, 20th July, 1966, pp. 184-186.

Upper Volta, Journal Official, 13 October 1966, pp. 486-88 and 20 October 1966, pp. 498-500, 626-628.

Agreement to create an "Interim Organisation" with a view to The Establishment of a Permanent Organization for West African Economic Cooperation, signed at Freetown, Sierra Leone, 28 May, 1965, Society of International Law, (1965), International Legal Materials, pp. 916-920.

Articles of Association for the Establishment of an Economic Community of West Africa, Signed at Accra, Ghana, 4 May 1967, B/CN 14/399 (24 May 1967), Annex IV.

United Nations Economic Commission for Africa, Preliminary Draft of a Treaty for the Economic Community of West Africa and Explanatory Notes. (E/CN.14/INA/EC/5, 27 October 1967).

Senegal, Journal Official, 20 February 1965, pp. 171-172.

Nigerian's Treaties in Force, 1960-1968, Lagos, 1969, pp. 209-11.

Zartman, I.W.: "The Sahara: Bridge or Barrier?" 541 International Conciliation (January 1963), pp. 34-41.

Plessz. G. Nicholas: Problems and Prospects of Economic Integration in West Africa, Montreal; McGill University Press 1968.

Treaty of the Economic Community of West African States (ECOWAS) 1975, Lagos: Federal Government Printer.

"Senegal - Ivory Coast Friendship and Cooperation Treaty," Translation on Africa, No. 1103, January 14, 1972.

Claude M. "L'Esclavage en Afrique Precoloniale. Paris: Francois Maspero, 1975.

Arthur Abraham: Topics in Sierra Leone History: A Counter-Colonial Interpretation, Freetown, Leone Press.

Jerker Carlson: Transnational Companies in Liberia: The Role of Transnational Companies in the Economic Development of Liberia, Uppsala: the Scandinavian Institute of African Studies, 1977.

Michael Growder, Colonial West Africa: Collected Essays London: Frank Case, 1978.

V.P. Diejomaoh and M.A. Iyoha (eds) Industrialization in the Economic Community of West African States (ECOWAS) Heinemann Educational Books (Nig), Ltd., Ibadan, 1980.

J.P. Rennings, Multinational Cooperation for Development in West Africa, (New York: Pergamon Press, 1979), p. 112.

P.T. Onwuka, Integration and Development in West Africa: The Case of ECOWAS, Ilf Ile-Ife, University of Ife Press, 1982.

L. Adegbite, "Needs for Integration of Legal Systems Among ECOWAS States," presented at the International Conference on ECOWAS, NIIA, 23-27 August 1978.

Ndongko, W.A.: "Regional Economic Integration for French-speaking countries in Africa: The Case of the West African Economic Community," paper presented at the International Conference on Law and Economy in Africa, 15-20 February 1982, University of Ife, Nigeria.

Hassane Senyi Ganda, "Le Liptako-Gourma: Example d'une Integration economique totale et base d'une cooperation internationale vertibale, in: W.A. Ndongko (ed) Economic Cooperation and Integration in Africa, CODESRA Book Series Dakar, (forthcoming).

Akinola Owosekun: "Some Thorny Issues in the Economic Community of West African States" in W.A. Ndongko (ed) Economic Cooperation and Integration in Africa (CODESRA Book Series Dakar) (forthcoming).

W.A. Ndongko: "Regional Economic Cooperation in West Africa: The Case of CEAO" in W.A. Ndongko (ed), Economic Cooperation and Integration in Africa, CODESRA Book Series Dakar (forthcoming).

Second Edition Under Print.

Development Alternative

by

Amalendu Guha and Franklin Vivekananda

This book is a challenge to the ongoing structural thoughts and actions as well as the ideological and processes of vertically growth-oriented development. It put forward the premises and process for an alternative theory and action of development.

This is the alternative to the contemporary maldevelopment which consists the evil troika of underdevelopment and dependent development. The applicability of such a development alternative has been demonstrated through case studies. It is must for the new generation development thinkers.